MY HINDU FAITH
&
PERISCOPE

VOLUME I

SATISH C. BHATNAGAR

Books by the same Author

Scattered Matherticles: Mathematical Reflections, Volume I (Nov, 2010)
Vectors in History: Main Foci—India and USA, Volume 1 (Jan, 2012)
Epsilons of Deltas of Life: Everyday Stories, volume I (June, 2012)

Order this book online at www.trafford.com
or email orders@trafford.com

Most Trafford titles are also available at major online book retailers.

Printed in the United States of America.

ISBN: 978-1-4669-6097-8 (sc)
ISBN: 978-1-4669-6096-1 (e)

Trafford rev. 11/09/2012

 www.trafford.com

North America & international
toll-free: 1 888 232 4444 (USA & Canada)
phone: 250 383 6864 ♦ fax: 812 355 4082

COMMENTS FROM SOME READERS

Excellent article, I love history and India is emerging as such and economic and intellectual power that it is great to learn the background to it. **Steve Wunderink** (Pastor)

I am reading your e-mails. They really contain interesting topics. That way you are really a versatile writer with marvelous writing skills. **Sushil K. Bhatnagar**/Retired SSP/CBI

You seem to find so much at fault with Hinduism and so much to praise for Muslimism, may be you should convert to Muslimism! AR Bhatia, Emeritus Professor of Business, CSU, San Bernardino

Exceedingly well thought of! Wonderful thinking of a Great Thinker—like you only. Satish Gupta, Businessman and Hindu community leader in Mumbai, India.

I can see a strong Sikh influence on you in this article. Rahul Bhatnagar, MBBS (India)

Please let me know which article should I publish in September Navrang Times. Your articles are well read by our readers. Girish Khosla, Editor and Publisher, Detroit

Thank you so much for the *Reflections*—thy really make my day!! I enjoy them very much . . . . We forget that holidays are here to rejuvenate ourselves, to find love and care for others and to stop and think. It is time to bring joy to others. Prafulla Raval, Biochemistry Research Professor, Creighton University

Thanks for some insight into what you think about what concerns all of us—Hindus and like people. Keep me posted. N K Khetarpaul MBBS, Hissar

It was pleasure to read your article about Hinduism and how it is that secularism is imbedded in it. This should be read and understood by more and more people in India and abroad. How political ambition of Congress is distorting this years old pure Hindu philosophy needs to be spread. Ranjana Kumar from Charlotte, NC.

Very well written. I am going to use your couple of articles on my website. Ted/Sibia

No doubt, I see the 'writer' in you and suggest you should start collecting them to make a full book and publish it . . . . I value and relish your friendship very much. PVN Murthy

Many thanks for all your writings which are very interesting. While working on the computer for most of the time, I find your *Reflections* thought provoking, and informative intrusions into the mailbox—quite soothing. Raman Mittal, Associate Professor of Law, Delhi University, India

MY HINDU FAITH & PERISCOPE
VOLUME I

DEDICATED TO

THE ANCIENT *RISHIS*

CONTENTS

FINALLY, MY 'RELIGIOUS' PREFACE!

My first book contains *Mathematical Reflections*; the second one is a compilation of *Reflections* that are historical in nature; the third one has *Reflections* that are of philosophical types. Finally, in this fourth book, they are all topped by religious *Reflections*. At places, it may read like a personal manifesto, rather than Preface. It happens when you pour into an activity every ounce of your energy.

First—the Title of the Book

The titles of my books are very important to me. It takes me weeks and months to settle down on one. It goes back to my teen years in the college (1955-59) in Bathinda, when we were all crazy about reading mystery novels. Whereas the stories were all isomorphic, but the titles felt fresh and enticing. Of course, the black and white cover pictures were no less catchy. We used to have hearty laughs at the titles and would merrily spin out our own! Those laughters and guffaws over the titles still reverberate my mind. During the 1980s, thoughtful titles of Osho/Rajneesh's books (1931-90) impressed me. Incidentally, Rajneesh never wrote a single book; instead, he lectured all his life. A smart 'cut-copy-paste' approach generated a number of titles out of his lectures.

After having written nearly one thousand *Reflections*, during the last ten years, I have taken the whole gamut of choosing titles to a new height, as each *Reflection* has a title. A funny side of some titles is that after a few years, I can rarely recall what was written in those *Reflections*. A title captures the very essence of a *Reflection*, not its topical key. Nevertheless, a bigger challenge comes when a title is to be given to a book compiled out of a specific collection of *Reflections*.

After several trials—like in a beauty pageant—hit and runs and tinkering with word(s), I have settled on this title, *MY HINDU FAITH & PERISCOPE*. It crystallized only a week ago. Here is a bit of its end story. It was very important to include a word, 'Hindu' or 'Hinduism' in the title in order for the book to stand out with me. 'MY' is a very deliberative qualifier. 'MY' really took me back, perhaps, to my infancy, when the religious layers were beginning to form on my mind—consciously and subconsciously.

Before India's independence in 1947, there was literally no Hindu community temple in Bathinda, a city of 65,000 inhabitants. As compared with 2-3 gurdwaras, two *eidgah*/mosques and one stately church, there were only a couple of Hindu temples, which were tiny and located in dilapidated surroundings. One was in a private home and the other in a room of a *dharamshala* (free guesthouse) run by a few individuals. In daily public life, the collective pride in Hindu religion was absent, except for the sort of gaiety one observes during yearly festive celebrations of *Dewali, Dussehra and Janamashtami*. It was more fun and business rather than time and place to instill Hindu faith.

For example, on a personal note, when I was required to fill in my religion in the college admission form, I did not write Hindu religion, Hinduism, Arya Samaj, or *Sanatan Dharma*. I wrote something like, Humanism! I vividly remember that day in June, 1955. Simple reason: I did not have pride in Hinduism, as it was neither fully planted nor cultivated. It subconsciously gnawed at me for decades. But, in a reactionary mode, a foundation of a new pride was laid in and the construction work subconsciously went on. That is the rationale behind 'My'—in order to exorcise this complex and eliminate this guilt embedded for nearly six decades.

It explains a part, *MY HINDU FAITH* in the title, *MY HINDU FAITH & PERISCOPE*. The next question is: what is this *'PERISCOPE'*? Periscope is an instrument, involving various prisms, that enables a person, sitting inside a submarine under the ocean, to see the world above it. It is a powerful application of simple principles of light and positioning of perfect prisms.

Let me emphatically state that for me the terms—Hindu faith, Hindu religion, Hinduism, *Sanatan Dharma*, or Vedic religion, are all one and the same. No longer, do I like to quibble or argue about linguistic differences. The reason is simple: the non-Hindus do not care about these differences! Actually, 'MY' applies to HINDU FAITH and PERISCOPE both. In other words, 'PERISCOPE' is 'MY HINDU PERISCOPE'. The articles, essays, or *Reflections* that are included in this book would be different, if a non-Hindu would ever strive to write them.

Thus, MY HINDU FAITH & PERISCOPE is a distinct combination of MY HINDU FAITH AND MY HINDU PERISCOPE. It aptly describes the contents, captures the flavors and stresses the points. However, you will have to read them before judging this choice! Some of you may recall that the titles of my previous three books have subtitles too. This one does not need a subtitle.

What is Religion?

It really depends upon who asks this question and who replies it. As a part this Preface, I do pose it to myself too. After all, I must have understood some things about religions after 70+ years. That is one reason for bringing this book out. Generally, the Hindus evade an answer to this question by saying there is nothing equivalent to 'religion' in their lexicon. Or, they would say—that Hindi/Sanskrit term **dharma** is not semantically the same as 'religion' in English.

I say, so what? We must participate and debate within commonly accepted rules. So many times, I have heard Hindu lecturers, invited to speak on the Hindu religion, steer their talks into the sort of ethics and morality which are integral and common in every culture. Recently, I was disappointed to read this slant in a popular book, *The Hindu View of Life* by S. Radhakrishnan, a well-known philosopher. In every US college and university, courses on ethics are a part of the curriculum, though the courses on religious theology and divinity may not be offered.

On the other hand, the Buddhists, Christians, Muslims, and Sikhs are very clear about the basic tenets of their religion in terms of their respective founders, scriptures, obligations on their adherents regarding prayers, places of worship, taboos etc, etc. Hindus have them too, though there is a lot of diversity and flexibility in each aspect—partly due to some historical reasons.

It so happened that on Oct 02, I will be one of the seven weekly speakers in Dixie Forum, a semi public lecture series organized by Dixie State College, St George, Utah—located 120 miles north of Las Vegas. Along with other information, there came the following general guidelines on the lectures:

1) A very brief description of the history/basic teachings of your faith.
2) What are the very basic tenants of your faith that you feel are most strongly reflected in your own practice?
3) How does your faith perceive other religions? Do you feel accepted in American society?
4) What are the biggest misconceptions/stereotypes people have about your faith?
5) What is the importance of inter-faith dialogue in a democratic society? In particular, how do you personally feel about some of the acts of violence/persecution that have taken place in the USA towards non-Christian denominations during the previous decade?

It is a remarkable coincidence that the preparation for this hour-long lecture and writing of the Preface of this book are taking at the same time.

One unique feature of every religion is that it begins to make impressions on the minds of the young and adults very early on in life, while one has to wait for 10-20 years to be proficient in math, history and sciences etc. Throughout life, religious rituals, festivals, gatherings continue to mold the individuals and societies. **My point is that one does not have to have any degree in divinity or priesthood license to understand the mechanics of religions.**

In fairness, my 'authority' on religions grew out in the complement of my life where I was not actively engaged in Hinduism during early adulthood. It made me academically open and receptive to other religions. Christian thoughts were splashed all over in my college curriculum. My maternal uncle, Swami Deekshanand Saraswati (1920-2003), an Arya Samaj preacher and scholar, often engaged us in discussions on religious issues—both internal and cross religions. During my visits to India, I always spent a week with him. In Malaysia, I read through the Quran one and a half times during Ramadan fasting in Jan 1993. Also, I have gone through many portions of the Bible. Likewise, significant tracts on Sikhism and other religions have been studied. It does not make me an expert on religions, but I am genuinely open and receptive towards religions.

Personally, I have never been inclined to study Hindu mythology in depth, as Hindu scriptures are in Sanskrit language that I missed learning it formally. Also, having been raised in Arya Samaj culture with dominant emphasis on the formlessness of God and then mostly living off mathematical and scientific thinking in my profession, religious rituals have remained distant. But, I have no disrespect for those who observe religious rituals and worship deities through a medium of their idols. In fact, that is the strength of Hinduism. However, my independent studies of religions, interaction with people of different faiths, and my ability to observe and analyze an issue have given me confidence to penetrate into religious domains. My approach is neither scholarly nor full of abstraction. It is always story telling—starting around a point or two.

"It is a Way of life!"
During conversations and readings about religions, I often find the educated Hindus stating that Hinduism is not a religion in the sense Christianity and Islam are—but rather, it is a way of life. It puzzles me, irritates me and makes

me wonder, as to how come when the non-Hindus are clear about Hindu religion, the Hindus do not stand out on their beliefs which they generally practice in the recesses of their homes.

On examining this phrase amongst the followers of other religions, it becomes very clear that each religion does actually push specific ways for both public and private life. Look at the observance of the five Ks in Sikhism; the five pillars of Islam; the Holy Trinity of Christianity and various public practices in Buddhism, Judaism, and Jainism. As a sidebar, at UNLV, there is an academic policy for the students and faculty on the observance of religious days, except of Hinduism. For historical reasons, the present state of Hindu religion does not have any conforming or binding influence on the Hindus. Nevertheless, it is time to morally brave up and discard this copout attitude of not discussing Hindu faith in public forums. Every religion imposes a way of life and conversely. Period.

Religion measures Identity

I can't help describing a kind of corollary of this line of thinking in the reluctance of generations of Hindu students at UNLV in forming a Hindu Student Association. As a faculty member, I have been advocating and impressing upon individual students for the last 10 years. There are close to 100 Hindu students and most of them doing MS and PhD. I often sense a failure in convincing them on the importance of a faith based organization, especially considering how all major religions have their campus associations— something which UNLV encourages.

A religion gives identity to an individual and a society. In this respect, the Sikhism is at the top, as its one single follower in any scenario is described as *sava lakh*—meaning equal to 125,000 non-Sikhs! On a ten-point scale, if Sikhism gets 10 points, then Islam gets 9.7, Judaism 8.3, Christianity 7, Buddhism 5, and Hinduism 1.3. Obviously, the ranking is reversed, if a religion is measured by the freedom granted to an individual! A lesson of Indian history is that any two non-Hindus will take down any one strong and smart Hindu. The essential purpose of any religion is to organize its followers in the largest number. Often, I compare religions with soft drink companies. For example, look at the way—the giants like Coke and Pepsi affect the nations worldwide.

What about the Contents?

This volume has eighty-one distinct pieces—called *Reflections*—written through the year, 2008. The earliest one goes back to 1987 and two others belong to the years, 1996 and 1999. The original practice of noting the dates of the first draft of each *Reflection* is preserved. It reminds me as well as the readers about my general chronological state of mind. Personally, a reading is satisfying if the author's date line is known on it. Versions of some *Reflections* have appeared in Indian and US weeklies with and without my knowledge. However, each one is circulated to my worldwide readership. Their feedback has improved the final drafts for this volume.

After the first book, I realized that it is better to have a broad classification. These *Reflections* are divided into four sections. The *Reflections* in the first section are more directed towards Hinduism, the second one has socio-politico touches of Hinduism, the third one has topically educationals, and the fourth one has smorgasbord of *Reflections* transversal to Hinduism. It is to be understood that Hinduism as treated here includes Hindu mindset, Hindu men and women of significance, Hindu events and rituals. It would be interesting to notice that here are three *Reflections* where mathematical thinking gets closer to Hindu thinking without any bounds! At the end, a composite picture of Hinduism does emerge—both absolute and relative to other religions. Of course, it is an outcome of my approach and perspective.

Who will benefit from this book?
Every author believes that his/her book is meant for everyone. In this respect, however, I am the biggest beneficiary. In the process of writing these *Reflections* for over ten years, and lately compiling and editing them, I have finally understood my faith deeply. Consequently, confidence that I lacked about Hinduism during adult years has been replaced with pride in graying years!

At times, it has taken me to such a height that in a few *Reflections* I have propounded a thesis that India will be a true secular country only when it will be constitutionally a Hindu state. The practice of secularism in India since 1947 has been reduced to anti-Hinduism and Hindu bashing—paradoxically more so by Hindus than by non-Hindus. It is making India porous for attacks by the terrorists, who are both homegrown and foreign-based. History is repeating itself!

The Hindus remain totally divided in half a dozen political parties. A sterling lesson of India's history is that traders, preachers, and persecuted humanity of every foreign faith were permitted, sheltered, and welcomed by the Hindu kings whose kingdoms stretched from the coasts of Malabar in Kerala to Kuchh in Gujarat to Karachi in Sindh—starting more than 1000 years ago. Doesn't it make pristine Hinduism akin to Humanism? What an incredible journey of this realization to dawn after nearly six decades!

Some Features

Since all my ***Reflections*** cut across 2-3 themes, it is just not feasible to have any mutually disjoint classification. For the same reason, there is no Index at the end of my books, as any point is likely to appear in half a dozen places—defeating the purpose of a quick spot-checking. Lately, bibliographies have become anathema to me intellectually. However, the spaces are provided for adding personal comments after every six to eight ***Reflections***. Also, thumbnail sketches of select commentators are appended at the end of the book. Finally, each ***Reflection*** is fairly independent of the ones both preceding and proceeding it. Thus, one can browse the book from any ***Reflection*** and easily digest it.

Dedication: This book is dedicated to the nameless ***rishis***/sages whose wisdom has come down from ancient India. They are nameless for any combination of one of the three reasons—their names were erased in Hindu cultural holocausts during the last one millennium, or the present Hindus—including historians, have abandoned the efforts to trace them, or most likely, the ***rishi*** never wanted to leave their signatures on their profound thoughts, as seen in the creation of the Vedic ***mantras***.

Yes, there is no one person who has inspired me to write this book. At the same time, it is not all internally motivated. However, Hindu philosophical mind is religious and Hindu religious mind is philosophical. In eastern cultures, there are large intersections between philosophical and religious thoughts. The two are not as mutually exclusive, as they tend to be in western cultures.

Acknowledgements: I thank my numerous e-readers across the world, who, over the years, have provided occasional feedback. However, I must single out Francis A. Andrew, a science fiction writer and professor of English. In his latest book, he has marvelously blended IT, astronomy and Christian theology. We met three years ago during my assignment at the University of Nizwa, Oman. He has 'religiously' given syntactical and semantic improvements in each and every one of my ***Reflection***.

In closing, feedback on any aspect of the book, e-mailed at <u>bhatnaga@unlv.nevada.edu</u>, would be thankfully acknowledged. Also, post your comments on Amazon.com.

Satish C. Bhatnagar
Sep 12, 2012

I. ELEMENTS OF HINDUISM

A MATHEMATICAL LIMIT IS RELIGIOUS

I believe that the study of Calculus is as important for the total development of young minds, as the study of Shakespeare is in literature, Socrates and Plato in philosophy and critical thinking, and Aristotle in political science and history. Calculus sits on the concept of **Limit** that crystallized over a period of two thousand years. **In the entire gamut of human thought, there is no concept as profound, and yet as practical, as that of Limit in Calculus.**

Calculus is a defining moment in the history of Western Civilization. In the 11th century, Europe was in the dark ages and America undiscovered. Islamic empires were raging in the Middle East and North Africa. The Mongols formed the greatest empire in history. The travelogues, like that of Marco Polo, described the prosperity and glitter of Chinese royal courts. It inspired generations of Europeans to seek their fortunes in Indo-China. But mathematics and science did not make considerable headway despite the knowledge of Hindu Numerals and its decimal system. However, their power was released when the Hindu Numerals replaced the Roman Numerals in Italy, in the 14th century.

The discovery of Calculus was a quantum leap out of the union of deductive reasoning of mathematics and experimental demonstrability of modern science. It burst into the firmament when Newton came upon the scene in the 17th century. By this time, the European Civilization had caught up with others. Calculus is at the heart of progress in sciences. It eventually became a spark plug in the engine of industrialization in Europe.

Since the rest of the world had no clue of Calculus, it continued to lag behind Europe in mathematical discoveries and scientific inventions. Through the 17th to 19th centuries, it propelled Western Europe to explore the world. It resulted in the colonization of Asia, Africa, America, Middle East, and Far East. By the middle of the 20th century the colonization had ended, but the West still continues to forge ahead. The power unleashed by Calculus in 17th century transformed into nuclear power in the 20th century!

The magic of Calculus lies in the fact that it lets one have a glimpse of Infinity. The limiting processes are inherent in human experiences. For instance, it is in a 'limiting' process that average velocity becomes instantaneous, and a line joining two points on a curve turns into a tangent line at a point. Many ancient paradoxes, like that of **Zeno,** were laid to rest, once the concept of **Limit** was grasped. I characterize calculus as a story of Division by Zero, or a story of Infinity!

Calculus is the ultimate experience of a rational mind. A grasp of infinity through calculus brings one closer to an understanding of the Infinite Manifestation; call it God, the centerpiece of every religion! Calculus is a giant step of mankind in its intellectual evolution. Mathematics has been my window of life—to the extent becoming a religion.

June 09, 2003/Aug, 2012

INDIA'S NEW INTELLECTUAL TRADITIONS

(Dedicated to the 1st Memorial Anniversary of
Swami Deekshanand on May 15, 2004)

The year 1857 is a watershed mark in the history of modern India. The British chronicle 1857 as the year of Indian Soldiers' Mutiny, but the nationalist historians characterize it as India's First War of Independence from the British yoke. Irrespective of this debate whether it was well planned or not, the fact remains that it set off a period of 25 years (1858-1883) when a section of Indians masses was led by some thinkers! It gave birth to the first militant intellectual tradition in an impoverished country ridden with strife and superstitions. For the first time a wave of chivalry swept over India.

The regional ***Bhakti*** (devotional) trends are not intellectual traditions. **The *Bhakti* suspends the collective intellect of the people.** They are Bury-the-Head-in-Sand cults, or Hide-Under-Cover till the danger passes away. The ***Bhakti*** life style made the Hindus, by and large, very docile and obedience. For centuries, they did not even challenge their foreign subjugation. Swami Dayanand used ***HAVAN*** (fire oblations) to bring the Hindu together in a public place.

Dayanand (1824-1883) was 33 when the 1857 Mutiny set off. At that time he was very much near the hot fighting spots of Kanpur and Meerut. Surprisingly, no reliable record is known of his participation in the Mutiny. I have raised this question several times with Arya Samaj scholars—including eminent Swami Deekshanand, my mother's first cousin. After seeing how the Hindus in the British police and army were beating and killing the Hindu mutineers, the young Dayanand must have gone for the deeper reconstruction of the Hindu society. That is why the year 1858 is the beginning of the renaissance of modern India.

It is difficult to separate the life of Dayanand from his intellectual legacy. From the limited reliable sources on his early life that once he ran away from his parents' home in Gujarat, he spent most of his time in Banaras, Haridwar, and in the hinterland of UP—known as Uttaranchal today. His genius was in the realization that social re-construction of Hindu Society and new intellectual traditions must go hand in hand.

Intellectual traditions are often nurtured in prosperous societies. In this regard, in the impoverished India of the 19th century, Dayanand's emphasis on the full development of body, mind and spirit was an historic anomaly. Hailing from an insolvent state of Gujarat, but through the practice of *HATH YOGA* and dedicated scholarship, he transformed himself into an incredible champion of new traditions. There are well known legends of his physical prowess.

Swami Dayanand used *SHASTRARTHA* (public debates based on scriptures) on social issues and ills to his great advantage. They were no different from modern TV debates used in molding public opinions. Being an accomplished *HATHA YOGI* and erudite scholar topped with magnetic physique, he psychologically overwhelmed his adversaries. Consequently, for the next 100 years, most Hindu orators and freedom fighters came from Arya Samaj.

He popularized a headwear that continues to bear his trademark. Swami Vivekananda (1863-1902) popularized it in the west. When Gandhi took control of the freedom movement in the 1930s, his introducing a cap for the Congress Party workers may have been inspired by Swami Dayanand.

Shortly after his intellectual victory tours, several princes of Rajasthan became his devotees. The masses always follow their kings. This public relation recipe works all the time. If there was one place where he was quickly idolized in thoughts and actions, it was Lahore, the capital of united Punjab, and the nerve center of Northwest India during that period.

The great freedom fighter and scholar Lala Lajpat Rai (1865-1928) popularly known as the Lion of Punjab met Swami Dayanand while he was a student. Young Lajpat was active in a new Social Reform Movement in Punjab. This indicates that Swami Dayanand reached out the youth and intelligentsia of the states he visited. The founding leader of the Hindustan Gadar Party, Lala Hardayal (1884-1939) was also deeply influenced by the rationalism of Arya Samaj movement, when it reached Delhi.

Swami Dayanand was the first to awaken the intellect of the Hindu masses. His approach **Back to Basics** started with the declaration of the Vedas as the source of all knowledge. He boldly opened the gates of the Vedas to every section of Hindu society. He exhorted them to study the Vedas, if literate, or listen to its discourses, if not literate. It was his highest stroke of social engineering. For centuries, large sections of Hindus were forbidden from Vedic knowledge which gradually led to their total fragmentation.

Veda itself means knowledge. He realized that the Hindus too must have **one Book of Knowledge** for their unity. **It was an act of great moral courage on his part to tell the masses to seek the Vedas over a score of other Hindu scriptures**. Swami Dayanand was convinced that in order to bring unity amongst the Hindus, as he observed amongst the Muslims and Christians, one Hindu scripture must be singled out. The holy Gita carries the practical essence of the Vedas. It is always portable.

Because of the size of the Vedas, obscurity of Sanskrit language in which they are written, and lack of resources, the Vedas are still not publicly seen like the Bible and Quran. Swami Dayanand himself undertook the first authentic translation of the Rig-Veda. To the best of my knowledge, he was the one who said: ***WOH HINDU KAA GHAR NAHIN JIS GHAR MEIN VED NAHIN*** (It is not the home of a Hindu, if the Ved is not there). I was around 20, when I actually saw a copy of a Veda. In 1975, I bought the Arya Samaj centennial edition of all the four Vedas with Hindi translation.

It was for fostering unity amongst the Hindus that Dayanand stressed the worship of formless God in public. Dayanand never broke any idols of the deities. He was different from the Muslims, who driven by their religion, not only smashed the idols of Hindu gods and goddesses, but demolished millions of Hindu temples. Dayanand observed that Hindus had stopped at the idols, whereas, the search of the Supreme was beyond the idols.

Unfortunately, even his ardent followers did not grasp national unity behind his opposition to idol worship. Dayanand knew of terrible battles between the Hindu kingdoms of southern states—one worshipping God in Vishnu and the other in Shiva! That weakened every fabric of political life of the Hindus.

During discourses and debates, Dayanand always referred to the Vedas to validate his arguments, calls and appeals for the eradication of all social ills. He advocated universal education for the women and the remarriage of the widows. His advocacy for equal status to the Hindu women in the society was far ahead of time. In the UK, the women got **limited voting** rights in 1918, and in **USA in 1920 after the 19th Amendment of the US Constitution**. India was not free, but Dayanand was a free and fearless thinker. It is because of his groundwork for women's causes that women in free India got full voting privileges with men on the same day.

To unify the Hindus, his biggest and boldest attack was on the eradication of untouchability and caste system based on birth. Arya Samaj continues to lead in this direction even to the present. Again and again, his mastery of the Vedas brought resounding victories while advocating such combustible causes. Think of it for a moment that even in today's Tamilnad, Hindu untouchables in villages are treated the way it was 100 years ago all over India!

Dayanand is the first champion of the Dalits (depressed people) today. Dr Bhimrao Ambedkar (1891-1956) came upon the scene much later during the freedom movement. I vividly remember in late 1940's, Swami Deekshanand, then known as Acharya Krishna, used to visit the colonies of the schedule castes and untouchables in Bathinda (BTI). He eventually won their hearts to have their children come to his newly started *Gurukul* on the outskirts of the town. Arya Samaj remained in the forefront of caste eradication till the 1960's when Dalits adopted a militant stance and widened their political base.

Swami Dayanand's emphasis on the Vedas was never to stop at the Vedas! Unfortunately, his overzealous followers have taken it literally. Most Hindus erroneously believe that the Vedas contain the recipes of all ills, solutions of all problems, and even principles and formulas of all sciences and mathematics. **The Vedas only provide a template of a great mind rather than of unknown knowledge.**

Swami Dayanand sowed the seeds of several intellectual traditions both at individual and institutional levels. For instance, Dayanand Anglo Vedic (DAV) institutions have set high standards in all aspects of education in the country. However, the *Gurukuls* have taken a nosedive. Dayanand model of *Gurukul* was an amalgamation of *Shaastra* (The knowledge of Hindu heritage), *Shastra* (Weapon training to spread and defend Hindu beliefs and values) and *Shatru* (Identification and elimination of the enemy within and without).

Presently, the Gurukul curriculum has been reduced to the rote-study of *Shaastra* only. The *Gurukul* graduates lack self-confidence, skills and are generally misfits in modern life. Dayanand had envisioned a revival of *Gurukul* of *Ramayana* era, where Ram and his brothers went out to learn *Shaastra, Shastra and Shatru in the Gurukul of Rishi (Seer) Vishwamitra.*
At the first anniversary celebrations in Dec 2002 of a new *Gurukul* started near Jarora village, 50 KM from Nanded in Maharashtra, I reminded and exhorted the audience on this historic mission of the *Gurukuls*. Swami Deekshanand, being its Chancellor, was elated to hear my message. Later

on, he told me that from now on the graduates of *Gurukuls* will be called *SANSKRTI YODHA* [cultural warriors].

Chapter Three of the *SATYARTHPRAKASH* (means *Light of Truth's Meaning*), magnum opus of Swami Dayanand, delineates a timeline to finish the scriptural studies. To become a scholar of Hindu religion, one would take 15-20 years. That is what one takes to earn a doctorate in Divinity at Harvard University! Harvard University, started as Bible College in 1636, had only 9 students and one minister. The number grew to 1000 students in 1869. That was a kind of Dayanand's model of an educational institution/gurukul, where open researches on religion, arts and science would be carried on.

Dayanand was a prolific writer. His productivity is amazing when one finds him moving from one place to the other all the time. It was an era when India had no railroads or public transportation. He is the author of some ten books including *Satyarthaprakash*. According to legend, he dictated this book to a disciple in three months! He was unique combination of great intellect, social architect and nation builder

Dayanand's interaction with Europeans was very suave and political. He was fully aware of German support for the Indian nationalistic causes and took advantage of it. He communicated with a German professor of a technical school for providing training to Indians in watch making. Mind it—that was nearly 125 years ago, when he thought of **transfer of technology**! The correspondence is available in the archives of Arya Samaj. **It clearly proves that he would have never restricted the *Gurukul* curriculum to the memorization of the *Shaastra* only.**

His greatest intellectual coup was in using the word Arya in reference to India and in the naming of Arya Samaj, a rejuvenation movement of the Hindus. Arya Samaj founded in 1875 in Bombay, is neither a card membership party, nor another creed or sect of the Hindus. For over 125 years it has affected the lives of the Hindus of every stratum. It is a living tribute to the organizational acumen of Swami Dayanand.

Mid 19th century was a period when the colonization of Africa and Asia was at its zenith. The European scholars were hijacking the native cultures by denigrating and denouncing them. On realizing the wealth of knowledge in ancient Indian heritage, **the British intellectual conspiracy was to prove that the Aryans were not natives of India but were of European stock in**

central Asia etc. Dayanand single handedly outwitted them and popularized the word Arya in every social and political arena.

On a personal note, I vividly remember all the kids of 'untouchables' attending BTI *Gurukul* being given the last names Arya after their first names. My first cousin, Kusum Lata **Arya** (1947-1997), an acclaimed Vedic scholar of her times, preferred Arya over Bhatnagar. Interestingly, Arya is gender neutral, and applies to males and females equally.

It is not out of place to add an example of Dayanand's organizational acumen when he essentially refused to merge the Arya Samaj movement with the Theosophical Society, also started in 1875. There is an extensive correspondence between Swami Dayanand and Madam Blavatsky and Leadbeater, the two founders of Theosophical Society. The Theosophical society was more into occult, and Swami Dayanand knew that the Hindus were already steeped into social evils worse than occult. Without offending them, he kept Arya Samaj focused on the Hindus, and their societal regeneration.

Swami Dayanand was a multidimensional intellectual who rose from the ashes of the failed 1857 Mutiny like a phoenix. Quickly, he shot into the sky. As a meteor, he blazed many intellectual trails in the firmament that shall continue to inspire generations of Hindus.

Aug 06, 2004/June, 2012

PS: Some excerpts of this article were presented at the 5th biennial conference (July 9-11, 2004) of the World Association of Vedic Studies (WAVES), held in Washington DC. The theme of the conference was **India's Intellectual Traditions in Global Context**.

COMMENTS

1. Bhatnagar Sahib: Yours is a well-written brief commentary on the intellectual traditions of Arya Samaj. A number of reform movements started in the 19th century to reform the religion and society of India. Arya Samaj was the most successful of them all in bringing about a renaissance in Hindu society. The strength of this movement compared with others was also that its source of inspiration was indigenous rather than westward looking. The sheer force of reason and argument and intellect was used by Swami Dayanand and his followers to eradicate many ills to which the society had succumbed. At the same time Swami Dayanand made it clear that he was simply reviving the old traditions and not giving anything new. **V P Sharma** (Chair and Prof)

2. Excellent article. It contains not only message of Arya Samaj to Hindus and provide them food for thought in shedding the socio-cultural evils and lethargy, has given a picture of this movement for reformation of Hindu social structure and firm linkage with the political realities of colonialism and independence movement and sacrifices of the open minded intellectuals . . . . I thoroughly enjoyed this write up and suggest you mail it to the ORGANISER for publication.
   NIGAM (Retired, Director of Delhi School of Economics):

I wrote back: Thank You for your encouraging comments! This article also caught the attention of the organizers of the 15th annual Sammelan of North American Arya Samaj to be held in Toronto, Canada (Aug 20-22). They have invited me to be the keynote speaker on its 20th opening. The title is Arya Samaj in the Context of North America.
Swadeep, Gori and kids are in San Diego for the weekend. Yes, I shall be there for the Indore Conference. But I can't leave early enough for the Delhi Conference. I did send an e-mail to this effect. Regards.

3. Satish; Excellent article, I love history and India is emerging as such and economic and intellectual power that it is great to learn the background to it. Thx. **Steve Wunderink** (Pastor)

4. This is your best piece ever! Very very well written!!!!—**Vicky** (Sun Microsystems)

5. Dear BhatnagarJi Namaste. Thank you for your email. It was good to know some more facts about Arya Samaj, Maharishi Dayanand and

freedom fight of 1857. Although history of Maharishi Dayanand is not known between 1850 to 1857. As far as I remember one historian of India wrote something about that. One SANYASI was seen by many persons wandering between Satpura and Vindhyachal mountains inspiring people for freedom—battle riding on a horse. He was also seen by the people between Meerut and Kanpur. He was Maharishi Dayanand Saraswati. Maharani Lakshmi Bai lived with Maharishi for three days in Haridwar and gave him dakshina of 1000 rupees. At that time Lakshmi Bai was only seventeen year old. Unfortunately, I do not remember the name of that historian. In the struggle of freedom more than 75 percent were Arya Samajis, but this fact was ignored by the Government of India. **Subhash Vedalankar**

6. Namaste, Thanks for the article. I have a request, I am completing Vedic Satsang book. May I use this article in a slightly different version with full credit given to you as the primary author? I need your permission and blessings. Thanks. **Deen B Chandora**

IDENTITY AND ARYA SAMAJ

BACKGROUND
This article essentially forms the keynote address that I delivered at the 14th annual convention of the Arya Pratinidhi Sabha (the Apex body of Arya Samaj) of North America held in Toronto, Canada (August 20-22, 2004). It turns out to be a sequel to the paper, *The Intellectual Traditions in Arya Samaj* that was presented at the 5th biennial conference of the interdisciplinary organization, the World Association of Vedic Studies (WAVES) held on July 9-11, 2004 in Washington DC area. It was prompted by the conference theme, *India's Intellectual Traditions in Contemporary Global Context.*

In the choice of the title, there seems to be a divine hand. I did not choose or propose it. It was amazing to realize that this is what I often asked from the late Swami Deekshanand Saraswati during my annual visits to India: **What is the relevance of Arya Samaj today?** My brother-in-law Baba Anal, a social thinker, often told him: Arya Samaj has no mission in the present times. Swami MamaJi, as I always addressed him, smilingly avoided arguing over it. All his life, he breathed the message of the Vedas, spread the mission of Arya Samaj, and hailed the greatness of Swami Dayanand. Nevertheless, a good question eventually penetrates the consciousness at such a depth that the questioner alone has to dig out a satisfying answer.

OPENING
I put the following two questions to the audience and thematically came to them during the speech:

1. What was the mission of Arya Samaj when it started in 1875?
2. What is **your** identity? (*AAPAKI PEHCHAN KYA HAI?*)

I stressed upon the delegates to make mental notes of whatever the first answers pop up in the minds. Once their answers have registered, then my message won't be forgotten.

Knowing one's identity is self-realization, and establishing one's identity in a society is to raise its global consciousness. That defines a great life style. Elaborating it—there is an individual component of identity—at home, as a son, mother and grandfather etc. Also, individual identity is determined in an office, factory; or by profession, and so on. However, all these individual identities pale into insignificance when one digs deep into the psyche to search for what drives the moral conduct and ethical behavior. There is a definite identity that is capsulated by religious beliefs in God, values and rituals.

It was reminded that today we are nearly at the same crossroads at which Swami Dayanand stood in 1857. The Hindus were absolutely divided, emaciated and beaten up. By joining with the British in police and army, the Hindus were beating and killing their own brethren. The world knows 9/11, now called **The Attack on America**. But how many know 12/11 tragedy in the same year, 2001, when the Indian Parliament was attacked and its members escaped a massacre from the hands of all Muslim terrorists? It was followed by Hindu tragedies of untold proportions at the Godhara Railway Station and Alankeshwar Temple. To make it real worse, there is little reporting by Hindu journalists on these events!

The 9/11 Attack has united the Muslims more than ever before. The Christians are already organized. One or two instances of hate crimes against the Sikhs have forged a unity amongst them. Sadly, the question of unity amongst the Hindus does not even arise. The group identity is a function of individual identities in public. The sum total of infinite diversity at individual levels means that the collective Hindu identity is ZERO!

Does it amount to saying that there is no crystal clear identity of Hinduism? Paradoxically enough, the Christians, Muslims and Jews all know it well, who the Hindus are! There is no need to quibble about the terms—whether, it be called Hindu Dharma, Hinduism, or Hindu Religion. It is amorphous to the Hindus.

By and large, the Hindus publicly shirk in identifying themselves, in any manner, as Hindus. Often, they hide behind the national origin, Indians. No wonder a campaign was launched in the 1960s to awaken them up: 'Proudly say, that we are Hindus' (*GARVE SE KAHO HUM HINDU HAIN*). Thus, the question of individual identity is tied with the identity of Hindu religion. They are like two sides of the same coin.

Historic divisiveness of Hindus was/is entrenched in birth-based caste system, individual deities and their idols. Dayanand, supported by the Vedas, advocated work-based caste system. However, his biggest fight in life was against idol worship, as he understood the fall of the Hindus with the Muslim destruction Hindu temples and idols.

The mission of Arya Samaj was/is the awakening and unification of Hindus. It is paramount today. The Hindus continue to remain divided. They have no political and social identity in India, or in their adopted countries! The call of the hour is to define it—first and last. In the ultimate analysis, the unity of the Hindus brings out an identity of the individuals and Hindu religion. The two questions, thus raised, are reduced to one!

ARYA SAMAJ IN NORTH AMERICA

The one formless God, one Book (*VEDA*), and no birth-based castes are **three great pillars** of Arya Samaj. They are the beacons of the present times too. Every organization goes through a cycle of ups and downs. For a continual growth, an organization must have a nursery for replenishment and an infusion of new blood. Above all, it must have leaders and thinkers who can navigate with the changing lifestyles.

With the presence of only three kids in the audience it was obvious that the present activities of Arya Samaj were not in tune with the youth in North America. In contrast, next day being Sunday, I watched a couple of hundred Sikh teenagers resting in front of the Toronto City Hall after finishing a 125-mile relay race from Niagara Falls to Toronto. At least a thousand kids must have participated under the guidance of many adults. In the process, they raised $ 50,000 for the welfare of the overseas Sikh youth.

It is a myth, born out of long subjugation, that Hindus are the ones who are born only in Hindu families. Arya Samaj led in the re-conversion of erstwhile Hindus (Hindus to Muslims/Christians back to Hindus). However, in the open societies of North America, the non-Hindus should be invited and welcomed to the services and functions in Hindu places of worship. I tend to believe that proselytization is a free market of life styles and beliefs. It works on the principle of the survival of the fittest. Hindus have encountered it internally since the advent of Buddhism and Jainism in India—more than 2500 years ago.

The objectives of formless worship of the Supreme are to loosen the grip of idol worships on Hindu minds. Inertia of body and mind had set in amongst the Hindus since Muslim invasions started in the 10th century. However, the Arya Samajis have never gone on a rampage of smashing the idols. A few Arya Samajis have taken an extreme stance on it. I recalled an incident in which a renowned Arya Samaj scholar, when challenged by another scholar, publicly kicked a portrait of Swami Dayanand. Stupidity!

It is time to open dialogue with every group of Hindus. Arya Samaj can take a role of religious leadership in a federation of different Hindu creeds and sects. The Hindu youth in schools and colleges are not proud of their faith, when it comes to explaining and defending that every Hindu is free to worship his/her own god. I shared of my struggle in getting Hindu students form a Hindu Students Association on the UNLV campus. The US universities encourage student associations based on national origin as well as on religion. The students can publicly discuss formless god on scientific grounds.

The one great advantage that the Arya Samaj in North America has is of a common English language for communication. Swami Dayanand learnt Hindi and advocated Hindi for unification of the Hindus. During the convention, it would remain an unforgettable sight to see the Hindus from Fiji, Guyana, Holland, Kenya, and Surinam enthusiastic about Arya Samaj.

I also narrated the marriage of my younger daughter three months ago in a Hindu temple. It was performed in 45 minutes by a couple well versed in the Vedic marriage through scholarship rather than by birth. Recitation of the **Mantras** was in Sanskrit followed by English translation.

CONCLUSION

I said that neither we have assembled here to speak out our bits and leave, nor to out-speak others. Also, neither we are here to listen out any one, nor listen in everything. The purpose is to support and agree on a plan of action. That will be a measure of its success, when the convention meets next year. In 1986, while visiting a library of rare manuscripts in Tanjore/India, I read the following observation in the preface of a diary of a British officer who lived in India while serving the East India Company in early 18th century:

'The Muslims think and then act; Sikhs act and then think; Hindus think, and think.'

Aug 27, 2004/June, 2012

COMMENTS

1. Dear Dr. Bhatnagar: Thanks. I think you articulated the ideas well. Regards, **BhuDev Sharma**

2. My dear satish Ji, saprem Namaste; I am really thankful to you for coming to Toronto. It was a nice experience to meet you personally. My old days with swami Ji are assets to me. I remember in Feb 2000, after his recent bypass he was taking rest at Santosh Raheja's house in greater Kailash. In spite of doctor's order, he took me to Sahibabad. He was very affectionate. Several times, he asked me to be the trustee of the sansthaan, but I did not accept. I was telling every time may be next year. Now you are fully associated with Arya Pratinidhi Sabha. We need your guidance to run this organization. I will write you soon. Regards, **Girish**

3. Good speech for Arya Samaji audience. **Rahul**

4. Sh. Satish Ji Namaste . . . . Received your articles. They are really very nice. It's very nice to know that you are so devoted towards Arya Samaj . . . . I will read your articles thoroughly and write you again. Thanks. **DK Shastri**.

A TALE OF TWO TEMPLES

Some events do not fade away in their intensity, and they would remain unforgettable. This incidence happened five weeks ago during our brief stay in Houston, Texas. It was Sunday morning and we decided to visit a newly opened (BAPS) Swaminarayan Temple nearby. BAPS, standing for **Bochasanwasi Shri Akshar Purushottam Swaminarayan Sanstha** is a Hindu religious organization that has made international headlines by constructing scores of grandiose Hindu temples all over the world. I was taken in awe the moment I saw the Houston Temple from a distance. Its exterior is made of pure white Turkish limestone and interior of pure white Italian marble—reflecting pure white love of BAPS devotees.

Such temples are BAPS' dedication to Hindu heritage and tribute to the lineage of BAPS gurus. When I guessed its cost at $27 millions, the manager said it was only $7 million! The labor being voluntary, its cost is not included. On reading its literature, I learnt that the BAPS organization traces itself back to 1800. The present Shri Pramukh Swami is the fifth Guru in succession. The temple sits on the bank of an aqueduct in a 20-acre lot. Besides the best India gift shop that I have seen, the temple complex has a large community center and a small **gurukul**, school based on Vedic traditions.

The architecture of the temple simply takes the breath away. The carving on over 130 pillars and 70 sections of the ceiling is stunningly unique! Not even a square inch of pillar surface is left uncarved with a motif. There are high-tech illumination at night and other media projections.

Living in the post 9/11 period, I cautiously asked: Are there enough measures to protect this temple from defacing, vandalism and acts of terrorism? A BAPS temple in Gandhi Nagar was attacked by Muslim terrorists in Dec 2001. Beautiful objects attract extreme social elements. One group adores the beauty as divine, and the other abhors it out of sheer jealousy. I said it was time that the Hindu temples and **gurukuls** spread awareness and education **Shastra**, **Shaastra** and **Shatru**. If you cannot protect and fight for your beliefs, honor and treasures, then you, perhaps, do not deserve them.

After a couple of hours, we set out to visit the Houston Arya Samaj Mandir (temple) about 10 miles away. I was briefly acquainted with its founder and the resident priest. It was not easy to find the Mandir, though it was off a major street. Since I was still in the mental frame of Swaminarayan Temple, a comparison between the two was natural. The time being about 1 PM, the weekly Sunday *HAVAN* was over, but its organic fragrance was still in the air. The Mandir has a big hall for Sunday gatherings. It seems the building is minimally used during a week. In contrast, we were the only visitors in the Mandir.

The Mandir also has a place for outdoor *HAVAN* congregation and a Montessori school for kids. Besides a few pictures of the early leaders of Arya Samaj, there was nothing touristy about the Mandir. **To a large extent, the austerity of Arya Samaj mandirs is not very different from that of Muslin mosques**. There are no idols in the mandirs either, as Arya Samaj shifted the tilt away from idol worship. The Houston Mandir is located on a 5-acre parcel. It is the result of one Mahajan family's generosity and devotion to the ideals of Arya Samaj founded in 1875 to rejuvenate the Hindu religion and society.

A question arises; **where does Arya Samaj stand in its mission of cleansing the Hindu religion?** Today, the Arya Samajis are only exemplified by the ones who perform *Havan* everyday and recite *Sandhya* (a collection of Vedic Mantras) twice a day. At one time, Arya Samaj spearheaded against social evils—like, dowry and Hindu caste system. No identifiable agenda is seen today. Arya Samaj lays out ten cardinal principles on personal beliefs and social conducts. They are as solid as the Ten Commandments of the Bible. **Even great ideas need propagators**.

However, my thoughts were buffeted between these two temples. BAPS Temple is a Shiva dance in architecture. I share its heritage and its construction fills me with pride. The Arya Samaj Mandir is an integral part of my being as I grew up around Arya Samaj. Nonetheless, I didn't feel upbeat about Arya Samaj. No organization can sustain, flourish and expand without a clear mission consistent with the changing time. Most importantly, it needs periodic infusion of new members; men and women, young and old, and welcomed from other belief systems.

Such are my thoughts that seem to be clamoring for an outlet for a while. The websites www.baps.org and www.aryasamaj.com have more information on these temples and their organizations.

Nov 09, 2004/Mar, 2011

COMMENTS

1. Your ending was so abrupt after a beautiful picturing of the temples. I was surprised you did not include a vision or positive approach to remedy the situation, or at least propose an original idea. Are you sure you are complete with this writing? **Renee**

I wrote: My objective was only to bring a brief contrast. Its length had already exceeded my standard format. It is the last sentence that has obviously left this feeling of incompleteness. Thanks for your acute observation!

Renee: Yes . . . . last sentence. I scrolled down, and was disappointed there didn't seem to be closure. Contrast good and well described.

I wrote: With this minor revision, I complete the loop as it ties with the opening para too. Thanks.
Renee: Well done!

2. Dear Bhatnagar Sahib: I do not agree with you (as also on many other of your reflections) on the future of Hinduism which you say needs to be "protected" against terrorists and vandals, etc. since ". . . (If) you cannot protect and fight for your beliefs, honor and treasures, then you simply do not deserve to hold them." You also compare the ostentatious temple of the BAPS group and the abstentious Arya Samaj temples.-One of the secrets of the survival of Hinduism these last 5000+ years is its tolerance of the diversity of the way people are at liberty to practice this religion.

While the BAPS sect goes in for such grandiose and flamboyant displays of its devotion, it is these very practices that the Arya Samaj sect primarily was born against. And yet they are both as much a part of Hinduism as are the Ram Bhagats, the Shiv Bhagats, the Durga Bhagats, the Nagas, and the uncountable other sects that live and practice this religion in India and elsewhere. A religion that has survived the ravages of time and innumerable attempts to eradicate its very existence since times immemorial, I am sure, will survive into the future also. Sincerely, **Anand Bhatia**

3. Dear Bhai Sahib Ji! Namaskar. I am reading your e-mails. They really contain interesting topics. That way you are really a versatile writer with marvelous writing skills. Your affectionate brother, **Sushil**

HOW HINDUISM IS DIFFERENT

The **American Hindu Association** (AHA) has been meeting every third Wednesday of the month from 7:30 to 9 PM. for the last four months. In a nutshell, **its mission is to project a unified image of Hinduism (*Hindu Religion*)**. For historic reasons, the US society has either little idea, or has distorted images of Hinduism. This has been of concern to many of us, who have lived in the US for years. This forum has taken off with the initiative of Madhu and Anal. They are well known social and political activists in India, now settled in Las Vegas

A unique feature of its meetings is that not only one has to come to a consensus on a topic after discussion, but also be able to communicate it to the non-Hindus, in particular. Everyone is encouraged to speak for 2-3 minutes, preferably in English. Thus, this forum is also a communication (listening and speaking) 'training' arena. Knowing a topic is as important as being able to convey it to others. The meetings are moderated by Anal.

For November meeting, I was suggested to lead a discussion on a topic: *How Hinduism is different from other religions?* I would have 7-10 minutes to open this topic, and then to be followed by remarks from the rest. While pondering over, it occurred to me that why not to put my thoughts in black and white for my record as well as sharing it with others who are on my mailing list.

Since we live in a Judaic Christian society in the US, it is better to focus on differences with Christianity and Islam. Christians make at least 80% of the US population. Islam is the fastest growing religion in USA, and it is always in news after the **9/11 Attack on America**. I am more of an analytical thinker, than a scholar of religions.

The following fundamental contrasts between Hinduism and major western religions stand out in my mind:

1. **Scriptural Language**. Rarely, Hindu masses understand the Vedic Sanskrit in which Hindu scriptures are written and its rituals (*SANSKARS*) performed by the priests. On the contrary, Arabic, being simpler, is reasonably understood by the Muslims whose mother language in not Arabic. As far as Bible and Christian ceremonies are concerned, they are

translated and done in every language of the world. However, translation of Quran in other languages is restricted.

2. **Common Beliefs**. All Muslims believe in Five Pillars of Islam; Shahada (Faith), Saum (Fast), Zakat (Charity), Salat (Prayer), Hajj (Pilgrimage). On the other hand, the Hindus believe in the divinity of the Vedas, refrain from beef eating and perform some select pilgrimages in their lifetimes! Christians believe in Jesus Christ as the Son of God, and Bible a Word of God as common beliefs.

3. **Places of Worship**. Generally, the Hindus do not go to the temples regularly and have no stake in terms of membership, or financial obligation. Christians belong to a church as 'certified' members. Muslims can visit any mosque. Friday afternoon prayers are mandatory in masjids and mosques. In Islamic countries, there are state supported neighborhood mosques.

4. **Mindsets**. In Islam, the total emphasis is on getting organized, as stressed by its Five Pillars. Five prayers a day may be unrestricted in a sense, yet their timings are set for all. However, the Friday prayers in the mosques are binding on men. In churches, Sunday morning services are hallmarks of Christianity. By and large, the collective image of Hinduism has been shattered by numerous Muslim and Christian rulers of India. The present image of Hinduism promoting individualism is due to its scattered collective identity. Nevertheless, Christianity and Islam begin and flourish with a group.

5. **Religious Conversion.** Proselytization to Islam and Christianity is a part of a competition in life values and styles. Hinduism, presently focused on misplaced individuality, has no history for conversion as a strategy of welcoming new members. Thirty-five years ago, a Hindu math professor came up to me with a dilemma, when he asked, "If a Muslim/Christian decides to get converted to Hinduism, then in what caste that person shall be placed?" We, two mathematicians could not settle it!

6. **Caste System.** Hinduism is embedded in the caste system that sets it apart from other religions. Caste based divisions within subdivisions of a society based on birth or profession do not exist in Islam or Christianity. Muslims are often seen calling each other as brethren. No wonders, any attack on a Muslim community anywhere is responded by the Muslims from all over the world.

7. **State Religion** (*RAJ DHARMA*). Islam becomes a **state supported** religion, the moment a Muslim becomes a ruler of that country. **The politics and religion are one and the same in Islam**. Christianity has been state supported partly in practice and partly in beliefs. The US and West European countries have superficially tried to separate religion and government. Ironically, Hinduism, in India, has never been a state religion for well over the last 1000 years.

It is interesting to point out that at the time of India's partition in 1947, the new nation of Pakistan became immediately an Islamic theocratic state despite 40 % of its population being non-Muslim. However, the truncated India was neither renamed Hindustan, nor it became a Hindu theocratic state despite its 85% Hindu population.

There are other salient points, and a few corollaries of these seven points, but this write up is limited for the purpose of this meeting. Hopefully, the AHA shall continue to discuss these topics during the next meetings. For the time being, information on the AHA and its activities are communicated by several list servers of the members.

Nov 16, 2004/July, 2012

COMMENTS

Good effort. Keep it up and spread the WORD. Any ways, some comments as usual. Arabic is not understood by big majority of Muslims. Out of over 1 billion Muslims more than 50 million live in Indian Subcontinent and about 20 million in Indonesia. A big portion of them are illiterate.

And now about Hinduism. You have missed the most salient feature of Hinduism—**Reincarnation. Moksha and Karma being others.** It is also marked by an attitude which seems to accommodate religious and cultural perspectives other than one's own, and so is characterized by a rich variety of ideas and practices resulting in what appears as a **multiplicity of religions under one term 'Hinduism'.** Hinduism can never be neatly slotted into any particular belief system—monism, theism, monotheism, polytheism, pantheism,—for all these systems are reflected in its many facets.

Hinduism **does not have any one founder.** There is also no point in time when it could be said to have begun. It **does not require its adherents to accept any one idea,** and thus is cultural, not creedal, with a history contemporaneous with the peoples with which it is associated. **Rahul**

1. My Dear Bhai Sahib Ji! Namaskar! I have read your article on Hinduism. Hinduism is not a religion. It is in fact way of life consisting of traditions, rituals etc. Hindu is not bound to go to any temple or read any religious book or is not bound to offer prayers at any fixed time etc. I think this is the best religion in world, which does not bind any one. Hindu is free to worship any God which he likes viz. Brahma, Vishnu, Mahesh, Krishna, Rama, Ganesh, or any other deity. He can be follower of Arya Samaj sect or any other sect. He worships Tulsi plant because it is rich in many qualities. Hindu worships 'Peepal' tree because it is good for health and gives lot of oxygen. Similarly there are other useful plants/trees like Banana plant, 'Bel' tree etc. which are useful for the human beings.

Hindu civilization is the oldest civilization in the world at present. All old civilizations namely of Rome, Egypt, China etc. etc. have vanished long back but the Hindu civilization continues to exist with its head high. Hindus should feel proud of his civilization. So many invasions on Hindustan took place from various corners like Unan, Central Asia, Mongols, British etc. but u see the Indian culture continues to thrive despite so many barbarous attacks on Hindu culture.

In fact a Hindu is a person who belongs to Hindustan irrespective of his religion. When I was in Haiti I had gone to a school with my American Police colleague in connection with community policing. I was introduced by my American friend as 'Il est Hindu' i.e. he is Hindu. So it is clear that Hindu means a person coming from Hindustan, which used to be a large peninsula comprising of several countries. When I was in Haiti many people were not aware of the word 'India'. They knew Mahatma Gandhi so they used to say oh, you came from that country which belongs to Mahatma Gandhi.

As regards caste system in olden days a person used to be identified by his profession. If he was warrior he used be to Kshatri, if he was a learned man he used to be called Pandit, if he was doing business he used to be called Vaishya, if he was doing other menial jobs he used to be called Shudra so this was the system. Now if a Baniya is not doing business and suppose he is in Army then he should be called Kshatriya and if some Baniya is doing some service he should be graded as Shudra. So our caste system has been exploited by the certain group of people. Now for example again u r Pandit because of your teaching profession similarly Swami Mama was a Pandit and there may be so many such examples, Shashi and Lallu are now Baniyas because of their profession. I still repeat that the Hindu system is the best in the world.

India the name given by British but originally known as Hindustan will continue to rise and will be a super power one day soon or later whether we are there to see it. There was a time, which I vividly remember there, used to be hardly one Radio in the entire colony and that too a medium wave radio. That person used to be treated with respect. But now even a Jhuggi Wala is having colored TV besides having Fridge, Cooking Gas etc. in his small Jhuggi. Every Tom, Dick and Harry is flaunting a Mobile Phone in his hand whereas I m not having a functional Mobile. Is there not a sea change in Indian scenario?
Now there is a time to conclude though there is much to say. With all best wishes and regards to all including Anal Madhu, who are doing wonderful social work in USA. Your affectionate brother, **Sushil**

2. Dear Bhatnagar Sahib: You seem to find so much at fault with Hinduism and so much to praise for Muslimism, may be you should convert to Muslimism! Sincerely, A. **Bhatia**

SPOTLIGHT ON CHRISTIANITY AND HINDUISM

Yesterday, I lead a discussion in the monthly meeting of the American Hindu Association (AHA). The topic was '*How Hinduism is Different from Christianity*'. During initial remarks for 15 minutes, I briefly brought out seven points from my personal experiences. It was followed by comments from other members for another 40 minutes.

Understanding the differences bring closeness too. It is playing out the differences that widen a gulf. A religion is like a river whose source may be pinned down, but during its course, its takes the shapes and forms according to the terrain. Likewise, Christianity and Hinduism are interpreted, understood and practiced differently from country to country, and time to time. Here the focus is on the US. It may not be a Christian nation. Nevertheless, it is largely a nation of Christians and was founded on Christian ethos.

Christianity has one **founder**, Jesus Christ and one **book**, the Bible. In contrast, there is no single founder of Hinduism. There are many scriptures of Hinduism, but they are all derived from the Vedas. Yes, for the sake of religious affiliation, the Gita is publicly carried, and it aptly captures practical Hindu philosophy.

There are multitudes of denominational **churches**, but to the outsiders they project a unity in Christianity. Their differences seem academic to me. In the US, the churches play significant roles in social issues and political arenas. The Hindu temples, outside India, are beginning to incorporate adult and youth activities. However, closely related with churches, are institutions like YMCA that subtly promote Christian belief systems.

The image of **businessmen** or **business** varies with religious beliefs. Giving back to community is a buzzword in the US. The business houses work closely with churches in promoting religious values in the US and abroad. This component of Hindu religion is non-existent in the US. In India, it is subdued due to historical reasons.

Missionary spirit, a popular phrase, means selfless public service with love. It is the duo of Christian missionaries and trading companies in the 17th century that prepared the groundwork for political and military expansion by the Europeans. Currently, such a spirit is the call of the hour in Hinduism. The AHA is committed to bring awareness towards it.

Any organization, including religion, must have a door for new converts to join its nursery. It is commonly thought that Hinduism does not practice proselytization or **religious conversion**. However, the evidence of surviving rich and ancient Hindu heritage—from Bali in Southeast Asia to north in Cambodia, indicates that during the golden days (500-800 AD) of Hindu society, it sent preceptors, *sadhus*, and *sanyasis* in far off lands. Proselytization is no different from free market of ideas. In the US, there is no animosity between the Christians and Hindus.

Mar 17, 2005/Aug, 2012

COMMENTS

1. I am not clear on what are you trying to convey in this article. As for conversion, I think Hindu teachers in form of new age religion are doing it very effectively and aggressively. Also, I do not think differences between Christian churches are academic. The Mormon religion is not considered Christian by mainstream evangelical Christians. **Rahul**

I wrote: Expository differences too establish some spaces. The New age interest in Hindu culture is not what the classical conversion is. Yes, Mormons are aggressively establishing their identity different from the main stream—like the Sikhs did it.

Rahul: My feel is you intend in showing differences is to promote conversion. The classical conversion is not sexy enough to generate interest while new age is. I do not think Arya Samaj is attractive. Of all the philosophies coming out of India Arya Samaj has made least inroads in the West. The reason being very simple that it does not offer an Aradhya. It is too dry a philosophy. No instant gratification, as other philosophies do.
As for Mormons it is the other way around as they are considered outcasts or even non-Christians by the Evangelical Christians while Sikhs are not considered outcasts by Hindus.

I wrote: Yes, I am for opening the doors for the non-Hindus and welcome them into the folds of Hinduism. You have good points about the Arya Samaj in USA. Until recently Hindus did not accept the Sikhs distinct from them.

Rahul: Hindus still consider Sikhs to be Hindus but during the Khalistan movement this idea was propagated by pro-Khalistan and Sikhs started thinking them self as different . . . As about conversion, I think the door was opened by Vivekananda and the other saints/ religious heads who followed him. Why ask for a ritualistic conversion when the Hindu philosophy is spreading here. This is more effective way of spreading Hinduism. This way the spread is faster with less resistance and is more acceptable. Any ways ritual is not true religion but philosophy is.

2. The difference in Christianity and Hinduism are few. I would rather be Christian. Hinduism is a religion for which there is little to be proud of. When you talk of Hindu religion, it is hard for me to guess what actually you mean. **Subhash**

ARYA SAMAJ, *GURUKULS AND* DEEKSHANAND

BACKGROUND
This article essentially forms the address delivered at the 15th annual convention of Arya Pratinidhi Sabha of North America—held in Tampa, Florida during July 21-24, 2005. It is also a sequel to my keynote address at the 14th convention taken place in Toronto in Aug 2004. The focus of the address was **'What is your identity?'**

Three months ago, I had suggested to the President to adopt a theme for the convention since there was none for previous conventions. A theme generates synergy that eventually helps in identifying a plan of actions for future. Only a week before the convention, I learnt that *JAAGRAN* (means **Awakening**) was chosen as the theme. This theme needs to be continued for one more year till its outcomes become tangible.

JAAGRAN is very appropriate in the aftermath of 9/11, *Attack on America*. The Muslims, worldwide, are fiercely united now. The Christians in the US are organized enough that President Bush's re-election is attributed to the rightist Christians. After a few mistaken identity attacks on the Sikhs, their unified political action has stopped further racial crimes against them. The Hindus remain dis-united.

There are three components of awakening (*JAAGRAN*). 1. One who is totally awake, (*SAJAG*); mathematically speaking, 360-degree awake. 2. One who is sleepy, asleep *(MADHOSH or SUPTA)*. 3. The methods of awakening (*JAGAO*). Swami Dayanand was fully awake, (*TRIKAL DARSHI*). He knew the past, understood the present, and had a clear vision of the future of the Hindu Society.

Forget the masses, today, there are intellectuals who strongly believe that there is nothing wrong with the Hindu society since it had 'survived' 1000 years of various foreign rules! The Hindus, by and large, are impervious to portent events. The attack on the Indian Parliament on 12/11/01 was aimed to cripple a constitutional government. The brazen assault on the makeshift Hindu Temple in Ayodhya on 07/07/05 was to destroy symbols of the Hindu Heritage. The tragedies of Godhara train and Alankeshwar Temple were instigated by global Muslim resurgence.

The urgency to awaken the Hindu masses and intellectuals is called for more than ever before. It is pertinent to identify the ignorant and indulgent living in their false comfort zones. The methods of awakening may vary— nevertheless, courage is required for it. Swami Dayanand roared like a lion and walked like an elephant—unconcerned of the dogs barking around him. He prodigiously wrote and often risked his life. He debated (**SHASTRARATH**) on the interpretation of the scriptures in the dens of his adversaries. Above all, he founded Arya Samaj in 1875 for galvanizing pulverized Hindu Society.

HINDU LEADERSHIP

When the convention President asked for my input in the preparation of the program, I suggested a new session on the *Visionaries of Arya Samaj*. The references to its founder Swami Dayanand come in many contexts. Hindus either raise their leaders to a touch-me-not pedestal of divinity, or they tear them down with constant criticism and innuendos. The onslaughts on the person of BJP leader L. K. Advani is the latest example. That is why there is a vacuum in leadership in every aspect of Hindu life, though Hindus number up to nearly one billion. It is time to focus on systematic nurturing of leadership and give incentives to the US-born youth.

The Sikhs have plugged such holes by creating cadres in its socio political and temporal life. There is no trichotomy at individual, political and spiritual levels of the Sikhs. It is one seamless quilt! Celebrations of great lives in the past and honoring the living legends inspire younger generations. It provides benchmarks, educates and informs the general public. It pushes the rank and file to re-dedicate themselves to the ideals and goals of the organization. Overall, it serves as a compass.

PERSONAL CHALLENGE

The challenge before me was to choose a topic that fits into the theme, celebrates the life of a pillar of Arya Samaj, and tells about an institution that is also close to me. Someone recently asked me to describe Arya Samaj in one sentence. I said, "The genius of Swami Dayanand distillated the essence of Vedic heritage and codified it in the **Ten Principles of Arya Samaj** in the context of the 19th century Hindu Society." Arya Samaj, Swami Deekshanand and I are like three vertices of a triangle. The institution of Gurukul has affected each one of us. The present gurukuls are caricatures of places of higher learning of ancient India where students and teachers lived together in the premises.

While, starting on Swami Deekshanand, it reminded me of GandhiJi's personal secretary, Pyarelal's speech in 1966 at Kurukshetra University campus. It is still vivid in my memory. The light he shed on some intimate aspects on Gandhi's character had a unique impact on me, although I had studied Gandhi.

SWAMI DEEKSHANAND SARASWATI

In letters, I addressed him as Swami Mama Ji, but in person always, Mama Ji. The rest of his erstwhile (pre-Sanyas) family members—including his sisters, brothers, and scores of nephews and nieces, addressed him as Swami Ji. Towards the end, he had come to a realization of a special bonding with me that was not based upon any set of traditional Do's and Don'ts that some Arya Samajis are hung up on. During my annual visits, some of our dialogues used to take both of us to new intellectual heights and delights. Of course, in some instances, our positions were poles apart, since we intellectually matured up in very different modes and cultures.

Mama Ji was born in 1920 during the golden era of Arya Samaj in Punjab. He was fully awake at 16, as he refused to follow the profession of furniture designing for which he had completed a two-year course! He quietly protested and was essentially asked to seek his own livelihood. He did not run away from home as his mentor, Swami Dayanand did. But he received little family support in joining Dayanand Updeshak Vidyalaya (training school for the missionaries of Arya Samaj) in Lahore. This incident had cut such a deep groove into his psyche that the last time he recounted it in full detail was during our train journey from Nanded to Mumbai on Dec 29, 2002, hardly six months before his *NIRVANA DIVAS* (the day of his last breath) on May 15, 2003!

Throughout life, Mama Ji listened to his drummer inside. There are three segments of his life; Brahamchari Krishna (he never married) till 1956. He was known as Acharya Krishna, as popular preacher of Arya Samaj till 1976. After *Sanyas* (a renounced order in Hindu life), he was eminently known as Swami Deekshanand Saraswati.

An outstanding quality of his life was that he did everything to his best ability—whether it came to handwriting, cooking, peeling and dicing vegetables. He was never in a hurry and he never cut corners. There are interesting stories associated with each one of these ordinary chores. For instance, the jackets of dozens of books he published are small pieces of art!

Furthermore, he took interest in every aspect of the construction of his Vedic Research Institute in Sahibabad. He was a perfectionist of a high order.

PRESENT GURUKULS

Gurukul was a common thread in each phase of Mama Ji's life. Soon after Lahore training, he plunged into 1939—agitation launched by Arya Samaj against the atrocities of Nizam of Hyderabad. He was put behind bars for a year. After release, he opened his own gurukul on the outskirts of his hometown, Bathinda, and was also associated with another Bathinda gurukul started a few years earlier by Mahatma Hansraj. I have vivid memories of these gurukuls, as two of my cousins studied in one of them.

Pandit Buddha Dev (later known as Swami Samarpananad), a stalwart of Arya Samaj, persuaded MamaJi to move to Prabhat Ashram/Gurukul near Meerut, where he spent nearly 5-6 years. This gurukul was very dear to him, as he and its Acharya, Swami Vivekananda were friends since their Lahore days. Many a times, he wanted me to visit Prabhat Ashram, but I had little interest. Finally, he took me there in July 2000. The atmosphere of Gurukul always brought additional glow on his countenance. He showed me every place that had memories associated with him.

One *brahamchari*, as the male students of gurukuls are called, displayed his expertise in archery at the Olympic level. Mama Ji also introduced me to the others who had memorized one, two, three, or all the four Vedas and Panini's *Ashtadhayayi* (Sanskrit Grammar). At the end of the tour, he inquired about my impressions. I simply said, "In this age, what is the relevance of this curriculum? By memorization of the scriptures, they do not become Vedic scholars. A sharp knife is blunted, if its blade is mechanically grinded over a surface, so does the memorization to the sharpness of mind." He did not say anything.

SWAMI DAYANAND AND *GURUKUL*

A few scholars alone have read all the works of Swami Dayanand. However, on checking the 1975 centenary edition of ***SATYARTHPRAKASH*** (means **Light of the True Meaning**); his magnum opus, I was surprised to discover no mention of the word gurukul in it! Though, Chapter Three of ***SATYARTHPRAKASH*** delineates the course work and time taken to finish the scriptural studies.

On the other hand, Swami Dayanand had communicated with a German professor of a technical institute about providing training to Indian youth in watch making. That means nearly 125 years ago, he thought of transfer of technology! It is clear that Swami Dayanand would not have restricted the *Gurukul* curriculum to the memorization of the *Shaastra* only.

ARYA SAMAJ AND GURUKULS

The current state of Gurukul curricula is due to the historic efforts of Arya Samaj to eradicate Hindu caste system based on birth. Thus, its one corollary is to emancipate the scheduled castes by providing them the knowledge of the **Shaastra** that was forbidden to them for centuries. I vividly remember in late 1940s Mama Ji visiting the colonies of the schedule castes and untouchables in Bathinda. He ate their food and drank their water. Eventually, he won their hearts to have their children come to his **Gurukul.** Unfortunately, **Shaastra** became a norm in general, despite the fact that graduates of gurukuls neither have self-esteem nor job skills. Arya Samaj, understandably, has a monopoly over most of the gurukuls in India, but their number has been dwindling.

MODEL OF A GURUKUL

The ideal gurukul was that of Rishi Vishwamitra of Ramayana era. The goings of Raam and his brothers indicate the royal prestige of his Ashram (like that of Harvard University). The princes became adept in all three essential aspects of life viz., **Shaastra (scriptures)**, **Shastra (weaponry)** and **Shatru (enemy)**. The most important aspect was the identification of the enemies of the state. Raam and his brothers eliminated the enemies within the country and Ravana of Sri Lanka, outside.

I first promulgated this thesis of **Shaastra, Shastra** and **Shatru** at the anniversary celebrations of a new *Gurukul* near Jarora village, 50 KM from Nanded in Maharashtra during Dec 27-29, 2002. I reminded and exhorted the audience of the historic mission of the **gurukuls**. Swami Deekshanand, being its Chancellor, was elated to hear my clarion call. Later on, he declared that the **SANATAK** (graduates) of **GURUKULS** will be called **SANSKRTI YODHA** (cultural warriors)

The gurukul atmosphere used to transport MamaJi to Vedic times! The Gautam Nagar Gurukul in Delhi was like his place of rejuvenation. After a few weeks in Sahibabad, he would spend 4-5 days in this gurukul. During the late 1990s, he was actively associated with new gurukuls started with the support of leading industrialists Munjhals of Ludhiana and Delhi. Though his heart condition wasn't good during this period, still he gave a lot of time and energy. He was also actively involved in a girls gurukul near Bulandshahar, UP. Mama Ji was an eternal optimist in human nature. He often said, "**No one**

has ever placed an obstacle in my path." It speaks of his single-mindedness in his work.

TIME FOR ULTRA GURUKULS
The Islamic madrassas (religious schools) are prototypes of ancient Hindu gurukuls! The focus in Madrassa curriculum is on the memorization of 6666 verses of Quran. Simultaneously, the youths are trained in urban warfares with eyes on the enemy of Islam. Today, the madrassas are turning out the perfect fighting human machines. They are sought all over the world, but they are not mercenaries.

Most Arya Samaj gurukuls are ideally located—away from the population centers. In their large tracks of lands, the training can be imparted in all three aspects of life. It is time that Arya Samaj re-examine its commitment to the gurukuls. Certainly, the ongoing one-dimensional curriculum has no place in modern times.

CONCLUDING REMARK
The objective of such a convention is that we collectively redirect to the lofty ideals of the Hindu Religion as embodied in Arya Samaj. Redirecting means, to protect, preserve and preach it.

DHANYA HO (Hail thee) Rishi (refers to Swami Dayanand) and *DHANYA HO* Mama Ji! That is how I concluded my talk.

Aug, 2005/June, 2012

PERSONAL REMARKS

SANCTIFYING A HOUSE

"What did he (Anand Yogi) teach you?", inquired my brother-in-law last night. He meant some technique of meditation, a power *Mantra*, or a secret of life! Anand Yogi, an itinerant Hindu preacher stayed with us for 11 days. This inquiry compelled me to ponder over this question. Incidentally, several people had private consultations and public meetings with him, but no one invited him to be their houseguest.

During his stay, our house and phones were buzzing off. Anand Yogi was on his cell phone 90 % of his waking time. The calls came from all over the world, but mainly from India. He used to call several ministers, DGs Police, and artists—like, Anup Jalota and Anuradha Podwal for an April function on the Gita in his hometown, Ghazipur, UP.

I glimpsed the inside of his mind after listening to his several discourses in the Hindu temples and Sikh gurdwara. On my part, I impressed upon him the need for Hindu identity in the post **9/11 USA** and the role he can play. He is a polished speaker and can hold the audience in the palm of his hands. As a toastmaster, I scored him very high.

A general perception about Hindu *sadhus* (monks) is that they have spiritual powers to solve human problems of health and wealth. Partly, it has come due to century-old abject poverty of India. Many Hindus give up on their responsibilities of present life and start counting on the next birth! Yet, the same people bring delicacies for the *sadhus*. Anand Yogi is no exception. One health conscious lady brought a rare breakfast delicacy for him. She felt good in watching him eat it! Others brought *sarson ka saag, makki ki roti, halwa*, and one came up with *prathas* for his flight! He used to partake it all.

Naturally, Anand Yogi has gained weight, and he is aware of it. One day, he frankly told us that a reason for not shedding it off is that it makes him look less attractive to the US women! He is 38, well built, white attired, handsome, and draws anybody's attention. Point blank, I asked him how he controlled his sexual urges. Talking of his self-control, he said, "Even if a *MANEKA* (mythological seductress), comes along, he would not be swayed." "Your success is her failure since the entire purpose of her life is to bring you down to the ground," I remarked, "How can she be happy?" He had a broad smile.

His presence in our home was like an incense fragrance that is burnt once in a while. Also, the Las Vegas community benefiting is no less satisfying. Our daughter sought some advice and wanted him to tie **KALAWA** (a sacred thread) on her wrist. Individually, quite a few people seem to have felt spiritually elevated!

At the insistence of his admirers, call them 'spiritual investors', a non-profit organization has been set up in Washington, DC. I told Anand Yogi that the way his 'spiritual stock' has been rising, the future is certainly bright. Every modern guru aspires to become a million dollar man. **It is all one and the same-call it materialism or spiritualism!**

Feb 22, 2006/Aug, 2012

COMMENTS

1. Hi Satish: Evidently you were the spiritual conscience keeper of the community by hosting Anand Yogi for eleven days. I do admire what you have done it. We need Anand Yogis in the world to quell all the terrorism that is ravaging the world. **Moorty**

ENLIGHTENMENT WITH/OUT RELIGION

Last Sunday, two successive events took place. In the morning, my wife and I escorted Anand Yogi, an itinerant preacher from India, to the Hindu Temple. His morning discourse was set up there. I told her that afterwards, she and Anand Yogi would go back home with my brother-in-law, as I was to visit a former colleague admitted in a hospital.

Anand Yogi's discourse focused on the transient and evanescence nature of sensory pleasures. He talked of the infinite love of God for human beings to be mined by dedicating lives to Him. He assured the congregation that eventually this love will permeate to make life blissful. At the end, when he invited questions from the spellbound audience, he was urged to continue speaking for a few more minutes.

After the sermon, I straight away drove to the hospital. All the time I was thinking how I was going to see Michael in his eyes. I did not even call him about my coming to the hospital. Michael's physical conditions defy any description. Two weeks ago, both legs were marked for amputation, but the right leg is temporarily saved by a new procedure. The diabetes is slowly eating his body away. One eye is gone, and the other has minimal sight. He is on dialysis twice a week. A few years ago, he had a multiple cardiac surgery.

Despite these debilitating health problems, Michael has been thriving in mathematical researches! He took retirement for medical reasons 15 years ago, but he continues to engage the faculty in his research problems and that helps them in their promotion and tenure. When I entered the room, he was on the phone discussing a math problem. After 15 minutes, he engaged me into other math problems.

It was amazing to watch this man not complaining or seeking empathy for his plethora of ailments. He is both reconciled and not reconciled with the deterioration of his body in bits and pieces. However, his spirit has transcended his body! Michael told me that without these health problems, he would not have done a large body of math researches! I was aghast, as who in sane mind would invite a health problem to do intensive research?

Suddenly, I felt enlightened! It was in a hospital room—not in a temple, mosque, church, or gurdwara! Buddha was enlightened under a **Bodhi** tree, but nobody else got it from that tree. Newton was enlightened after observing an apple fall from a tree. Since then zillions of people have seen apples falling to the ground.

Enlightenment has no special place and time, but it strikes into the receptive and inquisitive minds. If nothing is permanent in the universe, then why not to accept it as God's plan, I posed it to Anand Yogi, one day. I don't remember what he said, but I am close to its resolution.

Feb, 15, 2006/Aug, 2012

COMMENTS

1. May be the enlightenment would not have come if you had not been to the temple and Anand Yogi's *pravachan* (discourse) before visiting the hospital. **Ved Sharma**

2. Hi Uncle, Sorry I have not responded of late. I just thought I would respond to this one as God is an interesting subject. To me God is not as important as the idea of God. Some would call it faith, but none of us know the truth about God and each culture has their own theories (because people have to be different). Inspiration, oddly enough, comes when we have a problem with life (physical ailment, mental ailment, losing your job, losing a loved one).

Michael feels he now has a finite amount of time left and bless him that he chose to do what he loves to do with more conviction. I don't see this as an inspiration of spirit or God, simply the man who had six months to live and chose to make the most of his life. It does sound extraordinary that a person has such spirit, but that is because all we are doing is comparing them to ourselves (who have health on our sides). I am sure that you too would be an inspiration in your last few months of ability (as long as you know ahead of time that you only have a few months).

I don't mean to downplay Michael's spirit as I am very impressed when people are inspired as opposed to falling apart because they think life is unfair. My point is that the inspiration was always there and it is ironic that it is realized only when we know death (or some other life changing situation) is not too far away . . . why not live with such inspiration all of the time . . . because we all take things for granted.

I don't believe enlightenment comes from a place or an ideology; it comes from within and very rarely before the glimpse of death (Mother Theresa being the only one. I consider as someone who had the inspiration throughout her life). I am an atheist at heart, but I do believe in Humanity. I feel that people are too self-absorbed to see the greater good in themselves unless forced to and when they finally do I don't feel surprised, I feel sad that it took so long. And trying to figure out where it came from (Church, Hospital or Tree) is futile . . . it always comes from within no matter the religion or belief.

I hope that you are feeling well and take the above as a hint that if you are, you should be enjoying and doing everything that you ever wanted to. I don't want to be surprised by the great inspiration that I already know exists in your heart. **Tarak**

I wrote: Just speak the following sentence loud a couple of times and notice the feeling it evokes: To me Tarak is not as important as the idea of Tarak. The next thing is to find out, why!

Hi Uncle, Actually, the words really don't mean anything to me. I can touch and feel Tarak. To me there is no such thing as the idea of Tarak, there is only Tarak. Only someone who knows of me but has never met or spoken to me could understand the idea of Tarak. A book or person that tells of God is still only an unverified description or idea. I cannot invoke a two-way communication with God or personally meet with him.

Ideas are converted to conviction and reality once they are universally verified. We can imagine God, but no one can say that they know God like they know a close friend. In a way you are helping me with my point. The idea of someone is less than knowing them. Why make assumptions and judgments when we cannot verify what a person is like? "Don't judge a book by its cover". Most people would say that this is a very admirable statement. And many of these same people would still hold true their ideas (or judgments) of God's true nature. Is it still admirable to judge what God is like without meeting him? Is this not what religion does . . . to spread the word of God and to have faith that they are the true words of God? Is there universal agreement of what these words are? The answer is no, but that is ok.

Psychologically, people have a need for immortality (life after death). Whether it is having a son to carry on the bloodline, the Hall of Fame, a building named after them, etc. God as an idea offers this. People live their lives and find strength in the idea of God and immortality when they are distressed and let their "faith" guide them through the tough times. If that is what it takes for some people to weather life, then I think it is a good thing. But it is still only an idea. If we could verify God, then there would be no more distress in life because we would know (and not hope) that things will be ok in the end.

For me the idea is to live. I am not worried about immortality or God, just what I can feel, see and hear now. I find peace in what is (Tarak), not what hopefully might be (idea of Tarak). Thanks for the reply. **Tarak**

I wrote: You are almost nailing the root of the metaphysical universe. Unless an experience is a gross or subtle extension of our sensory experiences, it is not acceptable to me either. Otherwise, God is not fair!! Stay on your right course.

3. What was your enlightenment? Actually seeing misery in hospital makes one a bigger philosopher than a whole day in place of worship. Watching cremation or burial gives one bigger lesson in spirituality than a day of meditation. I am still wondering what enlightenment you got in hospital? **Rahul**

4. Thanks for sharing this noble thing with me. I have additional ideas ALSO. I AGREE that BARRIERS are essential for progress and PROBLEM is the greatest STIMULUS. In that, I think same as Michael does. **Subhash**

ONLINE GAYATRI *YAJNA*

The Hindu religion is replete with inspiring stories about the power of **Gayatri Mantra (OM BHUR BHUVAH SVAH, TAT SAVITUR VARENYAM BHARGO DEVASYA DHIMAHI DHIYO YO NAH PRACHODAYAT)**, the Mother of all Vedic *mantras*. Since childhood, I have heard of its harmonious effects on a person, if recited individually, and on a community, if recited collectively. Mahesh Yogi (of TM fame) discovered a mathematical formula that if the square root of 1 % of citizens meditates in perfect consonance, then harmony prevails over them. In other words, for the world population, say, of 6.4 billions, only 8000 accomplished mediators (yogis) can transform it!

One may question, why the recitation of **Gayatri *Mantra*** works? My understanding of the rudiments of the yogic science is that the Vedic *Mantras* are potent enough to provide an external fuse for unleashing the neuronic power of the individual(s). Like an external nuclear fusion, it is an internal mental fusion. There is a resonant effect too. When two waves of the same frequencies coalesce, then the resultant can have infinite amplitude.

Recitation creates sound waves. The Ultimate Knowledge is called **SHABD**— derived from speech. The sound needs air to travel. But when the mind, through hours of daily meditation, reaches a super charged state, then it can send and receive even the subtlest electromagnetic signals from one point of the universe to the other!

The 'lost' yogic science of India is being re-discovered. It is like faded symbols on pieces of potteries and other artifacts that help in deciphering the level of sophistication of ancient civilizations. I am convinced that the yogic science in the Vedic period was, to a point, what the modern science is today. Finality to this claim lies in near future.

The whole idea is of total immersion in the sounds of **Gayatri *Mantra***. Its effectiveness lies in conscious repetition, not in mechanical reproduction! The power of internet has brought people together for intellectual activities. For instance, our neighbor plays Bridge with partners in different parts of the world. The online Gayatri *Yajna* is one of its kind.

No matter where you are, it only requires a right frame of mind. The speed of recitation should be uniform to realize its impact. With right pauses, four recitations in 60 seconds is a right pace. **It is a *Keertan*** (devotional singing).

The 24-hour Maa Gayatri *Maha Yajna* will begin at 11:00 AM on Sat, Aug 05 and end with *HAWAN & AARATI* at 11:00 AM on Aug 06. You can align your time with the US Pacific Standard Time.

Find a special place in your office, home, park, and just start reciting! Consider it a cosmic experiment—like science experiments done in school/ college labs. They have been performed millions of times, yet they are done again and again for the development of scientific minds. The Gayatri *Yajna,* in yogic sciences, develops holistic minds.

July 18, 2006/Sep 2011

COMMENTS

1. Hi Satish: Greetings! A thoughtful and meaningful reflection, it is! **Moorty**

2. Hello Uncle: By any chance do you have multiple email lists. I don't get all your reflections and I wonder whether I am not in the main mailing list that you have for people. Could you please add me to your reflection mailing list because I enjoy reading them very much? Regards. **Viji**

3. Dear Brother, Thank you for the immensely beneficial article. The equivalent mantra in our language is *OM SHIVAYANAMA*. My father—a mathematician—taught me when I was a boy. I used to recite whenever & wherever I can. I derived material as well as spiritual benefits. OM is a cosmic sound & it rejuvenates the mind & body. I am happy to find the resonance in your life also. Let the mantra lead us all to a glorious future!! Thank you for this great SERVICE.—**Soori**

4. The complete Gayatri Mantra is *OM BHUR BHUVAH SVAH, Maha, Jana, Tapa, satyam, TAT SAVITUR VARENYAM BHARGO DEVASYA DHIMAHI DHIYO YO NAH PRACHODAYAT. If you get a chance read about Gayatri Mantra in the book written by my father.* **Rahul**

GAYATRI-THON AND SOUND THERAPY

"Dutchie, I hear you are going to the Gayatri-thon, (24-hour non-stop recitation of the Gayatri *Mantra*)." "Yes, but I am not going for myself. Madhu explained it to me, and I am taking my blind friend over there." Today, my wife told me of her this dialog with our neighbor, Dutchie. Dutchie claims to be an atheist and is a member of an atheist club of Las Vegas. Once, I told her that she was a true believer in Super Power, may not be named God in English!

However, in the context of Gayatri-thon, I said, "**It is a session of sound therapy.**" A sightless person is able to tune with the sounds much quicker than a sightful one. In fact, it is common to see the eyes closing voluntarily during concentration, or meditation. The Gayatri-thon transcends the meaning of the Gayatri *Mantra*. It is fundamental to ask the question, how essential is it to know the meaning of the Gayatri words being enunciated?

My answer is Yes and No! Well, it is like a hit romantic song of a Hindi movie. Based on its lyrics and tunes, religious singers write several songs in the same melody. If a person is not aware of the wordings of other songs, then he/she will tune in accordingly. A person knowing more than one wording will have problem to focus the mind. If a person does not understand a song language, then what? It happens with me more often, since I enjoy the tunes without any filler words. One can buy music CDs of tunes alone.

The Hindu ethos of psychic energy is based on the trinity of *YANTRA, TANTRA AND MANTRA. Yantra* is the grossest form of energy transmission taking place at a physical level. A hammer and car are examples of *Yantra. Tantra* is less gross and works at the mental or psychic level. In India, *Tantra* is misunderstood to the extent that its masters, called *Tantriks,* are associated with black magic like the witchcraft of the 18th century Europe. A *Mantra* can transmit the highest form of syllabic energy, call it spiritual.

In the ultimate scientific analysis, the Gayatri-thon is about harnessing and releasing of the sound energy. During the WW II, German scientists had developed sound waves as weapons to paralyze the enemy within a few miles of the hilltops where the sound guns were positioned. Also, I have known newly born babies, in the region bordering Afghanistan and Pakistan, exposed to continuous metallic sounds for 40 days in order to strengthen their heart muscles. At the other extreme, persons are known to suffer heart attacks, if they are taken by surprise by deep thudding sound.

That is my approach to the Gayatri-thon to be held during Aug 5-6. If the atmosphere is conducive to the pure sound of the *Mantra*, then its reflection and refraction in the hall will let anyone experience a unique phenomenon. Indian controversial 'mystic' Rajneesh/Osho (1931-90) disallowed any perfumes in meditative gatherings, as that may cause sneeze or cough—thus adulterating the *Mantric* energy! It is a simple principle.

Aug 01, 2006/Sep, 2011

COMMENTS

1. Dear Satish, Thank you for this very understandable explanation. And I add, all things eventually die but music shall live forever. "Music" as a "sound" as in the Mantras. Anal explained his belief that nothing ever dies. I'm struggling with this concept and realize that there's a lot that is unknown to me about mysticism. Well, back to my thoughts. **Dutchie**

2. Thank you for the informative piece . . . it was indeed a "sound reflection". Thanks for the wonderful experience of Gayatri mantra. I too chanted the mantra for some minutes yesterday and today and saw some wonderful descriptions in Google, one sounds very scientific. Have you seen it? **Abraham**

3. Dear Shri Bhatnagar, It is a true observation. Many of Yogic principles are based on this. It is the sound of Mantra which matters which has no language, religion, caste, and creed. The old saints who achieved nearness to GOD followed sound of Mantra only. To the best of my information effect of Mantra does takes place even if one does not understand the meaning. Do you have more observation to add from your experience or knowledge? **Hardev Singh**

4. UncleJi, I have been reading these emails regarding Gayatri Mantra. It feels great to know that there are people who not only believe in the Power of Gayatri Mantra but at the same time they are creating awareness about it among other people too. I hope we would have been there and could have participated in such a noble idea. Regards. **Abnindra**

GAYATRI MEANS EMANCIPATOR

Faith is funny to observe in life. Sometimes, it sprouts after a series of consistent outcomes, and at times, remains elusive. Once in a while, a new project, begun with a leap of faith, takes one to new heights. The 24-hour Gayatri-thon has brought joy to nearly 200 people who participated in it—from a few minutes to a few hours. My sister and brother-in-law alone observed it for full 24 hours. On the top, they in-took nothing else, except water.

Whatever one understands of body, mind and soul, one yearns for heightened experiences in life. Some people may even be thriving in mundane routines, but stretching one's limits defines people in a society. Last month, Sri Chinmoy (1931-) organized the 3100-mile run in New York! Yes, 3100 miles of running in 51 consecutive days @ 61 miles a day. Its math is very simple, but running more than two marathons a day between 6 AM to midnight is only for a dozen people in the world! Every participant described it as unworldly experience. The 24-hour recitation of Gayatri Mantra is similar in total effect.

Last night, my second session started at 11 PM. It was not difficult to ward off sleep with some coffee and walking up and down. But around 2 PM, the focus just was gone, as I found myself checking time after every 5 minutes! I got up and drove home at 2:30 AM. While leaving a white person besides the two hosts, I felt as if I was deserting them.

Often, my sleep is for six hours uninterrupted. But last night it was just the opposite. Sleeping at 3:30 AM, I got up every hour and went to the restroom at 4:30, 5:30, and 6:30 AM. Finally, when I woke up 7:30, I left the bed. Gayatri Mantra was resonating my being. In the morning, I joined the recitation session in its last 24th hour. There is a renewed burst of energy when the goal line is inches away. One could see a collective fervor in recitation, glow on the faces, and bathed in a new spirit.

The ceremony was concluded with *Havan*, oblation, offerings, and *Aarti* to the Goddess Gayatri. The fire was openly lit in a special fire container. Gayatri Mantra begins with Aum, the Sanskrit name of God followed by the powers invoked into the Mantra. It ends with *SWAAHAA*. Those unfamiliar with Sanskrit only hear the two sounds of Aum and *SWAAHA*, partly due to their extreme positions and elongated enunciation.

With each utterance of *SWAAHA*, a very small quantity of special flammable material, *SAMAGRI* is ritually placed into the fire. As a matter of fact, the purifying effect on the environment of *SAMAGRI* ingredients with fire is thousand times greater than in their natural states. **Likewise, it means that by putting the self, the ego to the flames of hard work of sweat and blood, one's powers are multiplied thousand times to a divine level**. It is never meant to be interpreted, that after a 15-minute *Havan*, one waits for the superpowers just enter into the body!

Aug 06, 2006/Sep, 2011

COMMENTS

1. It's unfortunate that I couldn't have been there to participate in person, however, I was there in spirit as I took some time out on Saturday evening to chant the Gayatri Mantra. It was such a beautiful feeling. Namaste, **Shobha**

2. Thanks. I think spirituality cannot be explained. It has to be experienced and undoubtedly, faith can move mountains. **Abraham**

A LOOK-BACK AT GAYATRI-THON

"When I entered the *satsang* hall, almost everyone, chanting the Gayatri Mantra, was a white Caucasian," said a surprised Indian friend. The occasion was the second annual Gayatri-thon, a non-stop recitation of the Mahamantra for 24 hours. The place, being an 1800 sq-foot home, was overflowing with people. Fortunately, there are no capacity or fire regulations on private homes.

The event started on Friday at 5 PM with the ceremonial invocation of the deities, manifestations of the Universal Primordial Energy. The gods, in consciousness, are akin to super specializations in any field of knowledge whether in mathematics or medicine. Some of the recognizable deity names are—Lakshmi, Saraswati, Indra, Brahma, and Ganesh. The hosts, Anal and Madhu presided over the ceremonies with attention to meticulous details.

To satisfy the curiosity of the friend, I said, "These white Caucasians have been attending Anal's Saturday morning classes on *PRANAYAM* for the last 2-3 years in the Blue Yoga Center in downtown Las Vegas. Some of them have been so much influenced by the Vedic practices that they often wear Indian dresses, eat Indian foods, and have Vedic *Sanskars* (ceremonies) performed by Anal and Madhu. I have observed them doing naming and conception *Sanskars*!

Americans are fundamentally very curious people about life. It shows up in the incredible variety in entertainment, food and shopping, architecture, transportation etc. The youth, at 18, leaving for colleges, or thrown out of homes for 'troubling' the parents, are essentially ready for independent exploration of their life. In contrast, amongst Indians, blind 'obedience' to the parents, authorities, teachers, and elders, smothers experimentation in budding stages.

My physical participation was in two sittings. However, during the 24-hour period, either I was humming Gayatri, or my subconscious mind was doing it. Its realization was felt at the end of interludes. Since very few persons are able to attend midnight hours, I stayed on Friday from 11 PM-2 AM. When I left the premises, besides Anal and Madhu, the rest six were all Caucasians. With *Dholki* (drum) and improvised instrumentation, Madhu chanted different renderings of Gayatri. It felt good on ears, so I assume it must generate different Mantric powers too.

The Gayatri Deity was set up on a 2'x2'x2' box well decorated from every side. Seating for two was set on each side for non-stop ceremonial offerings of water. It was bottled water with a few green Tulsi leaves, a pinch of saffron, and drops of Holy Ganga brought water from India. After the ceremonial offerings, the holy water is poured back into the empty plastic bottles for the devotees to take them along. Well, I drank a bottle while outing for an hour yesterday.

There was an added fervor in the air, as the last hour started. No one wanted to be out of sight from the Center. The pitch, tone and volume in chants increased as the minutes were ticking away. It was quite a sight! Yes, I missed a deep personal experience by observing others! There is an unquantified law of spiritual forces, as one described for physical forces in physics. It was a huge come-and-go of admirers of Vedic values of life.

Aug 08, 2006/Sep, 2011

PERSONAL REMARKS

THE DAWN OF A NEW VEDA

It was dusky and quiet in the backyard, when I came out for bench press, a daily physio-meditative routine. My eyes close by themselves. A question surfaced up about the Vedas, the ancient scriptures of India. **How did this holy stream of Vedas stop at four**? Out of the four Vedas, RigVed is considered as the oldest and Atharva Ved, the youngest!

The essence of the Vedas lies in their meaning itself—stands for knowledge. Thus, the Vedas are akin with knowledge, but knowledge cannot be akin with the Vedas! The Vedas are not fixed and bounded! Knowledge is expanding with universe. **The Vedas were never supposed to stop at four.** It is the Hindus who have stopped in their tracks.

A pertinent question is: how and when did it happen? That is the saddest chapter of Hindu society! It marks a 1000-year subjugation of the most enlightened people in human history. When the very survival loses its zest, then who cares about the heritage? Sanskrit scholars admit that it is nearly impossible to construct a *mantra* like the ones in the Vedas. Vinoba, a great *rishi* (all round intellectual) of the 20th century composed a couple of *mantras* that are considered of the Vedic caliber. New knowledge and researches in every walk of life only flourish in a free and affluent society—like in the USA today.

Fifteen years ago, a friend launched a Hindi magazine in USA, and in its mission statement, he wrote: 'that any material against the lofty traditions of Hindu culture won't be published'. In a light and yet deeper vein, I wrote, "If persons like you and I can judge the lofty traditions of our heritage, then Hindus would not have suffered this fate for a thousand years. Also, it is terrible, if there are no persons left to re-kindle the torch!"

While India is heralded as software giant, the Hindus are becoming more superstitious. They consult priests for anything. Never in my memory, was astrology so much embedded in public life. My nephew, in the US, chose the time and date of his wife's C-delivery after consulting with a priest. He never thanked the modern neonatal technology that saved his first child. A friend credits the recovery his wife's illness to his 40 consecutive visits to a Sai temple rather than to the best medical treatment available in the US. In increasing numbers, the Hindus are seen wearing faded red-yellow thread (*Kalava*) tied around their wrists for 24-hour divine protection and blessings!

Swami Dayanand stressed upon the understanding of the Vedas, but never for their worship. Knowledge in the Vedas is in distilled form. During the dark period, intellect being less discriminating, the Hindus erroneously started believing that all past, present and future knowledge is locked up in the Vedas! Any time a great theory or principle is reported in the media, it is unabashedly 'linked' with the Vedas using a convoluted logic.

The Vedas only provide templates of developed minds! Fortunately, some Hindus are waking up out of this long slumber. If Tagore comes back to life today, then he would re-title his famous poem as, *Let My Hindu Brethren Awake*!

Sep 08, 2006/Aug, 2012

COMMENTS

1. Dear Shri Satish Ji, Saprem Namaste! GREAT! Exceedingly well thought of! Wonderful thinking of a Great Thinker—like you only. Innovation is the mother of all progress: with your such extra-ordinary, revolutionary explicit views even on our Vedas, we have to think afresh, do a lot of perpetual research & bring out some new things of our own, instead of confining ourselves to Just FOUR. Our four Vedas as you very rightly said, these could be templates for our guidance only; tremendous work has yet to be done on them, or on the basis of our guidelines . . . .

Yes, you are RIGHT that the superstitions have spread in every walks of our HINDU Life . . . . It is our luck that we are born in Arya Samaji Families, but others are NOT so lucky & hence they continue to believe what their parents, relatives believe or what they see in their own community. As an Arya Samaji, every day is a lucky & Good day, whether for a childbirth or for marriage or anything, even the day of death is equally lucky as on that day the soul, leaves this old & diseased body & travels to meet the Supreme Eternal Body. **Satish Gupta/Mumbai**.

2. Have you heard the subhashita: Bharat panchamo Veda . . . . jamata dashamo graha? There Mahabharata contains history of India and its Chandra vanshi rulers and also Shrimad Bhagavt Gita is considered 5th Veda. Incidentally, Mahabharata was written by the same person who wrote other 4 Vedas, namely Bhagavan Vedavyasa. **Bhanu Joshi**

LET THE HEART LEAD . . . .

The *Satya Narayan Katha* (SNK) is the briefest and the most popular scripture of the Hindus. Satya Narayan means a *Story of the God of Truth*. Gandhi lived life in his dictum: *Truth is God*. *Katha* does not mean story in the ordinary sense, but a tale in which deeper moral values are intricately wrapped in and around. The amazing thing about SNK is that it is told verbatim in every part of India, and in every common language. Interestingly, I have not known it being narrated in Sanskrit. The reason is simple; the great *Rishis* released it from the complexities of the Vedic Sanskrit accessible to countable scholars.

What I like about the SNK are its social locales. Once a king, while on a hunting expedition, loses his way in a forest. On noticing the poor woodcutters performing the SNK, he respectfully joins them. Imagine a king, with his large retinue, sitting amongst the lowliest in the caste hierarchy. The present Hindu priests, who continue to bar the non-Hindus or scheduled castes from entry into the Hindu temples, do not understand the practice of their own religion! At the conclusion of the SNK, the king partakes the *Prasad* with the woodcutters. **No-untouchability is the highest message of the SNK!**

A similar setting is described when a wealthy merchant joins the aborigines performing the SNK. Neither do they run helter-skelter searching for a high chair for him, nor did he expect it. No elaborate invitation for the SNK are extended, nor is any one excluded. One needs to have reverence for the Hindu heritage and the subliminal message of SNK. Wherever, a few devotees decide a place whether in homes or public parks, it is fine. It is unreal when we think of the cloistered life style in the US and urban India today.

This thought struck my mind today while chanting the Maha (great) *Gayatri Mantra* during a non-stop 8-hour recitation at the residence of a devotee. I overheard that some one did not come because he/she was not especially invited. Such a posture may have some merit, if the occasion is social or political. *Gayatri* recitation is purely a spiritual experience. Try it for 15 minutes, an hour, or for the entire duration. **The *Gayatri* recitation creates the mental Ganga of sound waves**. A short dip or long immersion into it has a cleansing and curative effect on the body, mind and soul.

The life style in the US society and in many industrialized places has come to a point that it is not easy to open the doors for the uninvited guests—forget strangers. Paradoxically, *Gayatri Mantra* is a perfect antidote for neutralizing this public fear. Besides, there is a will, there is a way.

We, in Las Vegas, are fortunate to have a core of individuals who are dedicated to the lofty public practices of Hinduism. I feel doubly blessed in communicating these experiences globally with the power of internet. Have the attitude of a scientist, artist, or faith of an ordinary person for trying an open forum next time. There is nothing to lose, except some ignorance. **Hail thee, Maa Gayatri!!**

May 12, 2007/Aug, 2012

PEEPAL CAPTURES HINDUISM

Hindu religion is like a *Peepal* tree when it comes to survivability. This observation struck me during travels in places particularly in north India. Taking pictures of social gatherings do not interest me any more, but I do take out my classic Olympus camera for the shots of natural and societal slices of life. A sight of a *Peepal* tree, in unusual places, often turns me on.

The *Peepal* saplings sprout in the most unusual places. With its invisible flying seeds, they grow out in inaccessible places—like rooftops, drain gutters, outside walls, and in crevices where the walls meet floors and roofs. Initially, they appear harmless little green growth. However, over a period of time, their growing roots cause cracks in structures. The scholars have commented on similar power of the Hindu religion in softening and eventually absorbing other religions.

Generally, the Hindus do not root out the *Peepal* saplings, as they are not considered as weeds. On the contrary, they revere *Peepal* trees even on the roadsides to the extent of worshipping them! A week ago, I witnessed an unforgettable sight in Nahan bus stand. A Hindu *mandir* (temple) and Muslim mosque have a common wall. Whereas, the back wall of the **mandir** had numerous *Peepal* saplings, there was none on the mosque wall, which was painted green!

Amongst all the trees, *Peeple* converts the carbon dioxide, in the atmosphere, into maximum amount of oxygen. It is one of the few large trees that ooze out milky sap when its leaf or twig is broken. An herbalist told me that if one regularly chews its twig in the morning, then one develops immunity from every fever. The public in India suffers from fevers due to unsanitary conditions. The *Peepal* sap is known to have natural quinine as one of its chemical compounds.

Nearly 80% of India's population has remained Hindus despite being ruled by numerous foreigners. The Muslims population, roughly zero before 1000 AD, jumped to over 10% by the end of the 17th century. The British could convert only 3% of the population to Christianity. To put the resilience of Hindu religion in perspective, one has to examine the history of other colonized countries ruled by the Muslims and Christians. In some cases, the old faiths disappeared with native populations.

Rarely, one sees a stately *Peepal* tree—like the pines, mango and poplar trees. Isn't the state of Hindu religion like this? When and where were its last golden days? Its present tragedy is twofold. The price of India's freedom in 1947 was that one third of India went to the Muslims for the creation of Pakistan, an Islamic theocratic state. Ironically, secularism, as practiced in the remaining India during the last 60 years, has turned out to be anti-Hindus!

Moreover, *Peepal* tree is not amenable to pruning. I enjoy pruning trees in order to fit them in the house landscape. Likewise, the Hindu religion defies any conformity! The ultimate freedom that present Hinduism enshrines upon its believers makes it a haven for free thinkers of the world.

During my two-year stay (1980-82) in India, I tried my hands in growing various Bonsai trees. The *Peepal* sapling is ideally suited for it. Its reason is simple; it survives under the harshest conditions of little water, soil, fertilizer, and care. **Isn't that the story of Hinduism?**

Oct 20, 2007 (India)/Sep, 2012

RAGE OF *KALAWA*: A CHEAPO AMULET

These days, the most visible symbol of Hindu identity is *kalava*. It is a reddish, white and yellow cotton braided thread wrapped around the wrists. Men wear it on the right hand, and women on the left. ***Kalava*** was rarely seen, when I was growing up in Punjab during the 1950s. It may be showing emerging Hindu unity that collectively is rarely seen. Nevertheless, it cuts across economic strata and caste barriers.

One may ask, if there is something else behind *kalava;* also, when it is tied and why? ***Kalava*** is often tied around by a temple priest, pooja (spiritual ceremony) host, or an assistant at the beginning of a ceremony. **The sole idea behind it is to bring the congregation in a common divine mood for which the pooja is being performed.**

Since *kalava* is noticeable, it may look as a part of dress to the non-Hindus. A pertinent question is when and how of its removal or disposal. Certainly, it can be taken off right after the pooja is over. Often, one removes the old *kalava* before getting the new one. But *kalava* is not a piece of trash, nor to be thrown into trash. *Kalava*, being a part of a divine exercise, may be consigned to fire, running water, or recycled with papers or clothes.

Over recent years, a weird connotation has been linked with *kalava*, that it protects the individuals from the enemies or natural disasters. Its wearing has gone to such an extreme that the wearers are scared to remove soiled and faded *kalavas* even after weeks and months for fear of incurring divine wrath. A perception is of a lightning strike, if it is un-naturally removed. This societal attitude of the Hindus has baffled me for years.

The Muslims or Christians don't wear such a charm. The Sikhs do wear a steel bangle on a right hand, but that is one of the five symbols of Sikh identity. This steel bangle protects the right hand during a combat. Militancy is integral in Sikhism. During the 26/11 Islamic terrorists attack on Mumbai landmarks, a couple of terrorists were shown wearing *kalavas*. They came to kill and be killed for their cause. *Kalava* was simply put on to dupe the Hindu public and various security checkpoints for not raising suspicion. They ridicule at any protective power of the *kalava*. Their reliance was on their years of combat training, marksmanship, latest weapons and communication technology.

Hindu history is replete with their enemies using Hindu symbols for sabotaging, and conspiring in warfare. After all, everything is fair in war. The most prominent instance in history is the battle for the protection of Dwarka and its holiest Somenath Temple. During the battle, the soldiers of Muhammed Ghazani hailed the names of Hindu deities when faced mortal strikes from Hindu warriors. The Hindu soldiers would stop, but they were summarily slain by Ghazni soldiers when unguarded. Their most sacred idol was smashed to the shock of high priests, as they continued to believe in protection from the idol. History repeats for those who refuse to learn from it. *Kalava* has gone too far.

Dec 16, 2008 (India)

PERSONAL REMARKS

II.   SOCIO—POLITICO OF HINDUISM

SATI, SAMADHI & SELF-REALIZATION

The term 'self-immolation' does not capture what *SATI* stands for—just as religion does not encompass the essence of *DHARMA*, or celibacy of *BRAHAMCHARYA*. Last October, there was hardly any coverage of Indian Prime Minister, Rajiv Gandhi's visit to the USA, but all the wire services and media have been covering *SATI* Roop Kunwar so extensively. *SATI* captivates Hindu imagination. Hitherto, 18-year old unknown girl has become an object of attention for the millions of people around the world. At the same time, this ritual has been condemned by the State and Central governments as well as by women organizations. Western press has found hot material from India which continues to baffle them ever since Rudyard Kipling (1865-1936) discovered some of its social fabrics.

The practice of *SATI* was declared illegal in 1829 in the British controlled East India. However, it made no impact on the Hindu masses, mainly because, women were not pushed into or going for *SATI* everywhere. It was a British ploy of telling the Hindus that the British were going to be their next rulers. Nowhere, in any Indian literature there is a social or religious dictate that a woman has to sit on the pyre of her dead husband.

Traditionally, only the ladies of warrior, *KSHATRIYA* clans have ever become *SATIS*. On the contrary, there are numerous instances when the *KSHATRIYA* women were stopped and dissuaded from becoming *SATIS*. For instance, in the *MAHABHARATA*, Subhadra was blocked from *SATI* after the treacherous death of her husband, Abhimanyu. According to the legends; *SATI HOTI HAI*: means that *SATI* just happens. Nobody forces a widow. Exceptions are there, of course. After the battle of *MAHABHARATA*, there were thousands of widows, but nowhere does it say that they burnt themselves on the pyres of their dead husbands.

A pertinent question is: why do some women become *SATI*? It is, perhaps, the ultimate union of two human souls on earth. There is so much love and devotion between husband and wife that death, instead of setting them apart, glues them forever. What a lofty ideal of death! The British were shocked in the 1780s, when the young prince, Nand Kumar put the death noose around his neck himself smilingly. What Nand Kumar could not do while he was alive, his manner of death achieved it. The impeachment trial of Warren Heisting, the Governor General of British India, reverberated the British Parliament and shook its moral values for a couple of decades.

The Hindus view death as the continuation of life in its cycle. Also, there is an element of purification associated with death. That is why capital punishment has been in vogue in India since the time immemorial. West views death as the terminal end of life. They like to prolong it which to an Indian is the prolongation of sufferings. Recently, West has started advocating euthanasia, mercy killing.

In the context of *SATI*, look at death in the form of the last *SAMADHI*. One wonders why the British did not ban *SAMADHI* too, as there are more last *SAMADHIS* than the SATIS. In the last *SAMADHI*, the person, generally—man, goes into a state of mind in which his soul relinquishes the body at his will—often, at an appointed time. The British did not ban it, because they could not argue that someone would force a man into doing it. Only few persons understand that *SAMADHI* is the result of years of training of the body and mind, when it achieves 360-degree vision of the life cycle itself. In the Oct issue of the *India Tribune*, there was coverage on a Jain *MUNI* who had taken up the last *SAMADHI* in Sonepat, India. It was reported that since then, nearly two thousand people have been going daily to that site for his last *DARSHAN*.

A related question is: Why people converge for the last *DARSHAN* of a *SATI* or *SAMADHI*? Ancient Indian ethos tells that in such states, individuals achieve self-realization, the ultimate goal of life and purpose of living. Those individuals have embarked on a new plane, and people come to witness this last act in order to seek inspiration in their own pursuits for truth. *DARSHAN* is another Hindu concept which has no counterpart in the West. *DARSHAN* is a totally sensory and transcendental experience. One day, a scientific experiment in a laboratory will establish that in such a state, powerful brain waves are succinctly transmitted by a High individual and duly received by the devotees around him.

The Hindus, living in the United States, react differently publicly and inwardly when such a religious episode is flashed in the media. One notion that stands out is that if a practice—like *SATI or SAMADHI*, has been around in India for thousands of years, it is arrogant on the part of petty politicians to legislate them. Incidentally, a section of American press had reported that Vinoba Bhave (1895-1982) committed suicide, when he refused all medications, food and drink before going into his last *SAMADHI*. Think of a scenario, if Indian government had prosecuted all Vinoba's devotees as accomplices!

Suicide is illegal in India; the British declared it, of course. I believe that prosecuting the relatives of Roop Kunwar that they were accomplices in that so-called illegal act of *SATI* is also out-rightly absurd, and political on the parts of the State and Central governments. Moreover, the state ordinance against any public adoration of *SATI* is an act of puerility. The Hindus psyche thrives on individual freedom. Any legislation is anathema to its flowering. The Hindus must guard it, particularly at a time when so much power is getting concentrated into the hands of opportunistic politicians.

Nov 14, 1987/July, 2012

CHANGED DEMOGRAPHY OF KASHMIR

August—1998 will remain unforgettable, because I fulfilled one of my long cherished desires of completing the Amarnath *yatra* (pilgrimage). In Hindu religious lores, it is ranked # 2 after the ultimate Kailash—Manasrover *yatra*. There are six major mountainous pilgrimages in the north of India. Each one of them tests a person's physical endurance, mental toughness, and above all, religious faith. My adventurous sister and brother-in-law gave me the company. After four days of grueling walk at an average altitude of 13,000', we decided to rest for four days in Srinagar.

It being my very first trip to Kashmir, I was naturally enthusiastic about seeing the proclaimed beauty of its flora, fauna; people, land and water. The depressing sights that were noticed during the bus ride from Jammu to Pahalgam and briefly in Pahalgam, I did not let them have any bearing on what lay ahead in the valley of Kashmir (Wadi-e-Kashmir).

We entered Srinagar at daytime by a bus boarded from Baltal via Sonemarg. Pahalgam and Sonemarg are most familiar names besides Srinagar. They were (**not now**) particularly known for their shooting locations for Indian film companies when they could not go abroad due to foreign exchange controls. By today's standards what I cursorily saw in these cities, did not hold my attention. The places appeared to have stunted in growth, and looked deserted. Relatively, there are a whole lot of military presence and defense installations.

During the bus ride, as I would notice the road markers—like, Srinagar 15 KM, 10 KM away, my eyes would start searching for something that I could say, aha. All along to the terminal point, where the bus driver suddenly asked us to get off (not a regular bus stand!) I only saw dust-laden trees and shrubberies, old and unfinished houses, and narrow roads. On the roadsides, the children were playing in filthy clothes, women toiling in house chores and men squatting on the ground in small groups. It painted a strange picture.

In the hotel, we found ourselves to be the sole occupants. It was an eerie feeling, but so was the case in a nearby hotel, where we were the only diners. The waiter was standing over our shoulders either to eavesdrop on us or to see us finish our meals quickly! We heard that 1998 has been the best tourist year since 1989, when the Muslim terrorists started taking control over the Valley. Like in Pakistan, they have successfully driven 95% of the Kashmiri

Hindus out of the state. It is the latest case of ethnic cleansing in the world. Yet, it is not reported in the media.

I must say that we went to Srinagar out of ignorance of the current state of Kashmir. The political conditions in Kashmir are very unstable. Abductions and ransoms are big time businesses. For the Amarnath *yatra*, the highest security measures were taken by Home and Defense ministries. Above all, Shiv Sena Supremo, Bal Thackeray had warned the Muslim secessionists and Pakistani infiltrators that Shiv Sena would retaliate against the Hajjis (Muslim pilgrims) going to Saudi Arabia for Hajj through Mumbai, if any Hindu *yatri* (pilgrim) to Amarnath was harmed. During the *yatra*, the security measures were excellent, and were abided by the parties till the last day of the *yatra*. However, such security measures could not be enforced in the Valley. It indicates that the Central Government has lost control of law and order in Kashmir.

On the first day, I decided to walk up to the top of the mountain, where Shankaracharya temple is situated. After a while, I sensed that I was the only person walking up the road. A few loaded three-wheelers did pass by me, but no one walked past me going up or down. Around midway, I nearly decided to turn back that a returning foreign couple encouraged me to continue going up. Heavy security posts were at the foot of the hill, at the entrance of the temple, and all around it! I tried to tune in with the vibrations of this holy place, but my mind seemed too concerned about going down—again a distance of 10 KM, and all alone! Somehow, I made it back without any untoward incident. May be, I was protected by the latent forces of the holy place.

The second day was on the Dal Lake—in the middle of the valley. We rented a **SHIKARA** (decorative boat) for an outing. A few boats were seen in the middle of the lake. However, once we were off the shore, we found out that those boats were floating shops! Thus, we found ourselves to be the only ones in a **Shikara**. On a landmark island of **Char Chinar**, a big security posse was posted. A part of the Dal lake where hotel **SHIKARAS** are permanently anchored, carried a deserted look. The area known for shopping in **SHIKARAS** was almost non-existent. When, we had an urge for tea/coffee, the boatman said there was no such place open anymore!

On the third day, we essentially went around the peripheral of Srinagar— starting from fabled Shalimar garden to Hazratbal, and on to Hari Parbat area, Maqbul Sahib Mosque, Jama Masjid, and Gurdwara. We lunched in Lal Chowk area, the heart of the city. That afternoon, most commercial establishments were suddenly 'ordered' closed in response to a protest call on the death of a terrorist leader. It happens very often. So, we rushed back to our hotel.

On the day of arrival in Srinagar we had stopped at the head office of the Dept. of Tourism. It was nearly impossible to enter the building due to heavy security. Essentially, we were told to go away. A few brochures that we saw were published in 1986! Being a compulsive reader, I went through them knowing the data and information were very old.

On the final day, we decided to take a boat tour of Jehlam River and visit a bazaar—accessible only by boats. That boat cruise remains as the most unforgettable visual experience of the Valley. First, ours was the only boat as far as we could see! The security forces could be seen in all strategic locations of buildings on either side of the river. But, the militants are indistinguishable from the civilians. We, like the sitting ducks, were the best targets for both!

Buildings on either side of the river were creaky old, burnt and shelled. It was clear that army and secessionists engaged in frequent skirmishes. There were some big houses and mansions, unoccupied, burnt out as if heavy bombardment had recently taken place. The banks had piles of garbage. The most shocking sights were of the destruction of nearly all Hindu temples— the major ones are derelict now. The Sikh gurdwaras are left unscathed in order to create a wedge between the Hindus and Sikhs. We saw flourishing auto parts and gold jewelry shops run by the Sikhs, but none by the Hindus. A couple of years later, there was a large-scale Sikh exodus from the Valley. We felt heaviness in our hearts while walking through.

At the end of the boat ride, we spent some time in the state museum by the river. In the visitors' book, I wrote: "Auction the remaining collection in an international market before they are gradually stolen away with the connivance of the museum employees or destroyed in crossfire between the insurgents and defense forces." They will be safe and useful for the posterity in foreign places—like private US museums. Being our last evening, I enjoyed the *ASWAN*, a full Kashmiri cuisine with seven non-vegetarian dishes, but no alcoholic drink was served for fear of retribution. Again, we were alone in a fancy restaurant in Lal Bagh area!

On my searching question about the beauty of Kashmir, I was disappointed. Shalimar Garden was all dug up for repairs. By modern standards, it has no appeal—unless one measures it by 400-year-old engineering standards. All

Mughal gardens in India have the same architecture, layout and locale. If greenery means beauty, then Kerala is far more beautiful round the year. The valleys and hills are beautiful in unraveled northeastern hill states of India.

Talk of beautiful women of Kashmir, forget ever seeing them! There are all kinds of horror stories. I did not see a single pretty face. No small disappointments were famous fruits. Not a single fruit orchard was seen, as one finds them for miles while driving in California and Florida. In the month of August, the pink and white streak apple varieties were tasteless, ugly looking and sourish. May be, these days, the growers, financiers, transporters, and connoisseurs, are all run out! The houses, buildings, roads and bazaars were all in the states of falling apart.

A saying goes—that from the ruins one can tell how lofty a structure must have been at its prime. Having seen a good part of the world by now, I could not imagine Kashmir ever being anything extraordinarily beautiful. So, I kept wondering at Firdose's famous description of Kashmir being a paradise on earth. Why did he call it a paradise? With a little research, I found a simple answer.

Firdose came from Iran, where he grew up in poverty in a region—mostly cold, barren, and rocky. For him, the valley of Kashmir has to be a paradise, particularly, when he rose up to become a court poet. During the reign of Shah Jahan, north India was prosperous. The Muslims streamed into India from countries as far as Turkey in the west and Tashkent in Central Asia. A popular social maxim, **DILLI CHALO** (Go to Delhi), was on the lips of people from Middle East. On nearly the same scale, India was a magnet then, as the USA is today for the people coming from the third world countries!

Sept. 25, 1998/July, 2012

ADVENT OF CHRISTIANITY IN INDIA

My mind stopped right away the moment I finished reading the following sentence in the leading editorial in the **India Post** of Jan 8—"Hindus and Christians have lived together in India for at least a millennium if not more." It is an historical milestone that Apostle Thomas came and settled in India in the 1st century AD, and was welcomed by the Hindu king of Malabar Coast. He had come with only a handful of his followers. This number did not mushroom into a thousand, even after a thousand year!

There is absolutely no record of any kind of conversion of the Hindus to Christianity, nor of mass migration of Christians from pre-Islamic Middle East, the land of Jesus and Judaism. In the 10th century, in order to escape the Islamic persecution, a lot more Parsis fled from Iran to India than Christians did in their early period. The first recorded visit of Christians from Europe was in the 16th century, when a physician employee of East India Company was presented in the Mughal court of Jalaluddin Akbar, for medical consultation. Subsequently, the East India Company was granted some trading privileges in the Gujarat coastal area.

The population of Christians remained in hundreds and confined in South until the East India Company established a foothold in India by the 17th century. It was after the disintegration of Mughal Empire in north India in the 18th century and after the East India Company established suzerainty over Bengal that hoards of missionaries started coming to India. It was then, that Indian masses and intellectuals—like Raja Ram Mohan Roy, came under the influence of Christianity.

Today, Christian population in India is more than 20 million! How did this number grow from a few hundred only 200 hundred years ago, is a story by itself. Look at a recent scenario. For example, the number of Christians in un-bifurcated Assam, at the time of India's partition in 1947, was hardly 1%, but today in some border Eastern states, it is 90%! The British never migrated to India. In fact, at no time in British India, their number was ever greater than 30,000, though they ruled over 300 million Indians!

Recent clashes with Christians are engineered to destabilize the present Govt. and malign the Hindus. However, it has to be stressed that as long as the Hindus were being converted to Christians or Muslims, it was fine with the world. When the Muslims and Christians decide to re-convert to Hindus, then it becomes a kind of crime against Islam and Christianity. That is what is giving an ugly image to the Hindus. It is not out of place to point out that the number of Christians in the neighboring country, Pakistan is fast diminishing to zero and their social status is deplorable.

Jan 01, 1999/June, 3-2012.

ON A HISTORIC GURDWARA

A week ago, the Canadian Prime Minister visited the 91-year old Abbottsford Gurdwara, BC, Canada, and declared it a national monument. This event is doubly historical, as it was the first gurdwara visit by any Canadian PM. The 170,000 strong Punjabi community of BC is politically strong enough to get a dignitary from anywhere in the world. It was built by the Punjabis who were shipped to Canada in the 1890s as indentured labor to work in the farms and factories of Canada, a new British Colony then. They were mostly uneducated. In a far-flung foreign soil this lack of colonial schooling kept them closer to each other as well as to their Sikh faith.

After the bond period of five years, the Punjabis established reputation as hard and honest workers. Eventually, they won over their fellow white workers and supervisors in the lumber factory they worked in Abbottsford. The factory donated free lumber for the construction and the white workers labored with the Punjabis in building up the first Gurdwara in North America. It happened in 1911, and is a proud monument of Sikh history.

The structures of temples, gurdwaras and cultural centers define an image of a community in terms of its unity and prosperity. The British have left a legacy of magnificent churches built in prime urban locations. Conversely, these churches make a statement of British superiority, power and wealth. On a recent India visit, I was amazed to read an inscription on a church in Missouri dating back to the 18th century! In my hometown Bathinda, a stately church in Railway Colony, where hardly a couple of English men lived at any given time, is older than any Hindu temple there! In fact, there is hardly a Hindu temple in any city of Punjab that is over 100 years old.

An important component of a temple or gurdwara is a 24-hour presence of a person(s) of spiritual attainments who could do community counseling besides taking care of daily *MARYADA/PARAMPARA* of Sikh religious traditions. The yogic or the meditative powers, progressively seen in the Gurus, culminated in Guru Gobind Singh. However, during the last few decades, this side of Sikh religion is not being highlighted.

Aug 05, 2002/July, 2012

RELIGION AND NATIONAL SECURITY

Tonight, I spoke on a historic perspective on homeland security and the US Bill of Rights. The occasion was a meeting of the *Las Vegas Provocateurs*, a toastmasters club. It started with the US Bill of Rights—the first ten Amendments to the US Constitution, enacted in 1791. There is very little that people do it today the way it was done 200 years ago. For instance, one may wonder at the present relevance of two specific Amendments: #7. Right of jury trial for an amount exceeding $20. #3. Not forcing a homeowner to house a soldier in it.

However, the most talked about is the First Amendment including religion. It says that the Congress shall not make laws to **establish** a religion nor **prohibit** people to freely exercise one. It must be noted since the 17th century, Christianity has been the backbone of all British colonial expansion and the US, being a British colony then, was no exception. The US started as a 'Christian' country and flourished on Judaic-Christian beliefs. The freedom that the Protestants and other church denominations did not have in England and Europe was now protected by the Constitution of a new nation.

Moreover, the early colonizers and missionaries forced and lured their black slaves and native Indians into Christian churches. At that time, the First Amendment was not addressed to the non-existent religions in the US—like Hinduism, Islam and Buddhism! **As a matter of fact and practice, all the rights in the Bill were not originally extended to the blacks and native Indians of the US**.

I recalled that India's prosperity through the 10th century attracted all foreigners—like the US is drawing today. Unfortunately, material prosperity eventually softens the later generations. **When the national issues are discussed from ethical, moral and universal grounds, then it tolls the decline of an affluent society.** They forget how their ancestors fought with their blood and sweat for it. The worst sign of chasmal weakness is when a later generation turns apologetic for any perceived act of injustice by their forefathers 100-200 years ago.

Historically, the Hindu populace of medieval India treated the Arab traders of the 10th century with generosity and warmth. Realizing the passivity in Hindu way of life, Mohamed Gori (1162-1206) invaded and took over northwest India. What they did to the temples, monuments, and women is so chilling that it dwarfs the 9/11 Attack on the US.

In particular, I described how in one raid on the Hindu holy city of Mathura, its magnificent temples were razed and set on fire. **Its huge gold idols took seven days to melt into ingots so that they could be carted away to Ghazni**. It changed the demographic landscape of India for the next 1000 years. Hindus started accepting holocausts as their fate! No one stood up to fight and protect. The Muslim atrocities destroyed the will of the Hindus in India to live in dignity for the next one thousand years.

I also asserted that 9/11 enemy is fully embedded in the US population. The Patriot Bills need full legislative and public support. The US borders are porous and internet and cellular technology have made the world virtually borderless. The Bill of Rights has to be interpreted in the context of modern times. Two hundred years ago, no one had thought that the US could ever be attacked.

After two major speeches, there was a very healthy discussion for 90 minutes in which opinions were freely expressed under a moderator. That also gave me an opportunity to add a few comments of clarification and elaboration. For instance, I reminded that India has miserably failed to protect its homeland since 1989, as it could not stop the 99.9 % ethnic cleansing of the Hindus from Kashmir.

The enemies of the Indian way of life and the American way of life are the same. In Dec 2001, the same Muslim terrorists attacked Indian Parliament. A massacre of 200 members of parliament was miraculously averted. India has not even taken one hundredth of the security and preventive measures what the USA has done for its homeland. Had India gone after the terrorists operating from Pakistan like the US did it in Afghanistan, then India and USA would have snuffed the terrorist networks—like Al Qaida, out of existence.

India has failed again, when a couple of days ago, it refused to send its troops to Iraq to help the USA. The Hindus, ethnically dominant in India and politically divided, have never learnt a lesson from their own history. That is why they are condemned to repeat it every fifty years. This is a lesson for the US public and the government. Only once this enemy has to win to change every landscape.

It was a great evening!

July 19, 2003/ July, 2012

POWER OF A RELIGION

It is amazing as well as appalling to read the reports of worldwide protests against the French legislation banning Muslim headscarves for women. Out of a population of 60 millions, 5 millions are Muslims! Not too long ago, Muslim population was hardly noticeable. The protests are being organized in all the major cities of France. The disturbing aspect of these protests is that they are simultaneously taking place in many European countries too. They are expected in predominantly Muslim countries in the Middle East, but the protest rallies are taking place in many cities of India. In Kashmir, the protesters are terrorizing the Hindus to leave Srinagar—act of open ethnic cleansing.

In the French context, two things are to be noted. One; the legislation has not become a law. Secondly, the proposed legislation also applies to the skullcaps of the Jews and Christian crosses. Historically, France was/is a Christian country and the government is banning the Christian crosses from any display! Can one think of any one thing that applies equally to all religious denomination in a Muslin country? They are all autocratic—none is democratic! For the last 20 years, the Muslim migration in European countries has been phenomenal. In Belgium and Germany, they make a bigger proportion of population.

The strategy of Muslim terrorists and their supporters is to take advantage of the democratic rules of law in European countries in order to gain political and social advantages. Once they are politically stronger, they can take over a country by force. The tolerant Hindus of Hindustan (India) of the 10th century were run over by many Muslim invaders. By 11th century, a few thousands took over western India, and gradually most of India. From zero Muslim population 1000 years ago, they are over 120 million Muslims in India even after carving away Pakistan and Bangladesh from India in 1947!

The laws of religious freedom in the US and Europe were enacted at a time when there were no non-Christian populations. It was never intended to give other religions the same rights and privilege. As a Hindu, I say it from a lesson that cost the Hindus their freedom in their own homeland—leading to their 1000 years of subjugation. This scenario is somewhat similar to poor relatives in India moving to the US. They cannot contain their jealousy on seeing the US life styles of their relatives. They want everything in a few days, not realizing that years of sweat and hard work had gone into building it up.

The non-Muslin nations of the world have to understand the latest techniques of Islamic expansionism. Instead banning headscarves, skullcaps, these countries should amend the laws to ensure that the laws of freedom do not equally apply. Otherwise, these countries will be taken over from within and without in a short time that happened to India.

Jan 19, 2004

COMMENTS

1. It is a very complex situation. Sleep on it for some days. Then work on a thing to do for non-Muslims that is statesman-like and possible to promote. **HSB**

2. Great article . . . you know more history so I cannot comment on that but it reads well and I certainly saw the Hindu cleansing in Srinagar. The people I met and stayed with had to flee the year after I was there . . . for their lives! **Rene'**

3. I am a broadminded person basically. I liked Muslims even in childhood. However this faith breeds contempt and fortifies hatred, violent streaks, and compulsive tendencies.
   You should send this article to President of France and USA and to Queen of England, and heads of States in Netherlands, Germany, Austria, Switzerland, Denmark, Sweden, Norway, Australia, and New Zealand. This faith has not produced any philosopher of any worth. Science itself does not progress on its people. **Subhash Sood**

4. Excellent article based on historical facts, rationality and reasoning. Indeed deserves a grade of "A". **Mr. "B"/Suresh**

5. Interesting article and views. Controversial to say the least. Proscribed Cure is worse than disease. **Rahul**

PS: You know Sikh's are also affected in France. Also India was among the first country to ban Satanic Verses.

PERSONAL REMARKS

MARRIAGES IN THE TEMPLES

In the USA, marriages of the celebrities often take place in fancy hotels or in exotic outdoors locales. On hearing similar planning for my daughter, Annie's wedding, I made it clear that it has to take place in a temple. After a prolonged thinking, the family agreed to hold it in a semi-covered pavilion of the Hindu Temple of Las Vegas.

Why did I insist upon a temple? My marriage, 40 years ago, was not solemnized in a temple. It was traditionally held in the premises of girl's home. There are a number of reasons for the temple. **The main reason is that Hindus will be seen coming together at a sacred place.** Otherwise, when and where do the Hindus gather at a place—once or twice month on a regular basis for displaying unity for their beliefs and life styles?

It is also an occasion for the non-Hindu friends to see the sanctity of a Hindu temple. For our family, it became all the more necessary, as Annie's in-laws are Christians. They had no idea of a Hindu temple and marriage ceremonies. Though a marriage is a union of two persons, yet it also brings the two families closer. It adds strength to the bonding, when a wedding is witnessed by a large number of people. Hindu temples are not closed out to any one at the time of any social ceremony.

A question may be posed why there is an immediate need for it? **After the 9/11 Attack on America, an identity of the Hindu community is called for.** Other ethnic groups are better organized. They quickly respond to any assault on individual members, or their life styles. Except in a temple, the Hindus are not routinely seen in public places.

The Hindu temples do not receive generous donations from its community. A time immemorial Rs 1.25 (*SAVA RUPAIYA*) offering has only moved up to $ 1.25, as if there is something auspicious about this unit. Other religions mandate certain percentages of income for religious missions. Hindu religion does not impose any monetary demand on its adherents. Consequently, the Hindu religious structures do not stand out in size and facilities. At the time of a marriage, there is a 'captive' gathering that are likely to put some money in the donation boxes (*HUNDIS*). Of course, nearly $1000 paid for the use of temple premises also goes to the temple treasury. But a lot more is needed.

Above all, when marriage ceremonies are losing solemnity, a spiritual atmosphere of a temple has a salubrious effect on the minds of everyone. Many cultures believe in the divine hand in the conjugal union of the two persons. If so, then why not to perform the weddings in a divine atmosphere of a temple? It does not guarantee any longevity or compatibility, yet the couple can always proudly tell that here was a place that we were married. Temple will most likely be there. The merits of my thoughts are more meaningful for the Hindus living out of India.

May 11, 2004/July, 2012

COMMENTS

1. I can see a strong Sikh influence on you in this article. If God is omnipresent then it does not matter where you get married. The social arguments carry some weight. **Rahul**

2. Yes, Hinduism is the most secular way of living and thought, by whatever definition, interpretation, angle, thinking one takes it. Temples of Hindus are no doubt fund starved but are open to everyone. Rituals are also self-explanatory and are of high moral, functional and practical order in every society and the fast changing socio-cultural environment. One should feel proud of being Hindu and as such, free from rigidities in thinking, believes and living. My favorite sentence 'BE HAPPY AND RADIATE HAPPINESS' can come only from my Hindu Sanskars which I embodied from my parents, teachers and other elders. Thanks for e-mailing your current reflections as and when they come into your thoughts and observations of the human beings and various facets of the society around us. **Nigam**

MASSACRE OF NEPALESE HINDUS

The gruesome worldwide TV beheading of one Nepalese Hindu and methodical executions of the remaining eleven Hindus in Iraq shook me for a moment this morning. If they weren't Hindus, then this orchestrated blood bath would not have taken place. Why was a recently abducted **American** reporter released, and negotiations for a **French** are still going on? In this case, neither the Nepalese government has any clout, nor collectively, the Hindus have any voice.

My thought went back to June 1993, when I spent a week in Nepal, the only Hindu nation in the world. My brother-in-law gave me company, as his sisters were married in Nepal. We crossed the border walking on a bridge over a river that separates India from Nepal. But the differences were noticeable right away in terms of business appearances, road signage, and Hindu temples and shrines at every kilometer.

During the stay, I vividly remember reading a news report on the Muslim influx in Nepal. They were not moving from the neighboring states of India, but from a far off state of Maharashtra that had earlier witnessed a wide spread Hindu Muslim communal riots. In a press interview, a leader of the Muslim community was asked: how come the Muslims are migrating to a Hindu nation after fleeing from India? The answer he gave stands out in my memory. "Muslims are safer in the Hindu Kingdom of Nepal than in secular India."

Did he not speak of a historical fact? Centuries ago, the Hindu kingdoms of southern and western states of India had generously welcomed the Jews, Muslims, Christians and Parsis. In that interview, the question of the Muslims going to any closer country, Islamic Pakistan or Bangladesh was not even raised!

But look at the historical return of such hospitality. Nepal has become a hot bed of international Islamic terrorists. Air India planes were hijacked from Nepal to the Taliban run Afghanistan. The passengers and planes were released only after the Islamic terrorists in Kashmir were freed from prisons. A peaceful Nepal has been destabilized forever.

To my dismay of public indifference, this news disappeared from the internet after a few hours—while the killing of 16 Israeli Jews in a bomb blast remains there. I know that after a couple of days, this tragedy will be forgotten even in Nepal. **Human beings are not equal in life and death**. It reminds me of a prevalent Muslim law on crimes in Saudi Arabia that apportions different punishment for the same crime. It essentially works like this: If crime is committed against a Muslim man, then it carries a fine of, **say** one million dollars; against Muslim woman, 500,000; against a European man, 100,000; against a European woman, 50,000; against a Hindu man, 1000, and against Hindu woman, 100. Such laws have existed for centuries, and still they do. It is time for the Hindus to examine and standup, as it is a question of survival with dignity.

Aug 31, 2004/July, 2012

COMMENTS

1. Maximum cruelty is shown to those who have already degraded themselves. (This could have exceptions. But exceptions do not prove the rule) **Subhash Sood**

I wrote: You are so right!

Subhash: Indians have been released because lot of money has exchanged hands secretly. Poor Nepalese neither had the financial support nor the negotiators.
Current form of Hinduism is an expendable commodity in terms of destiny or laws of survival.

2. Thanks for expressing what I have been feeling like ever since I got this news. What a savagery! **Harbans**

3. Did you know that Nepalese burnt mosques in Nepal in repercussion? This news was only on Al Jazeera. Any ways what is your action plan? **Rahul**

AYODHYA TEMPLE AND THE HINDUS

"We will build Ram Temple in Ayodhya," announced L K Advani this week at the 25th anniversary of the founding of the Bharatiya Janta Party (BJP). It has been nearly 15 years since a dilapidated structure, politicized as Babri Masjid (un-worshipped for years) was demolished by the Hindus out of decades of frustration and cultural stigma. Like numerous mosques, it was also built at the site of a very ancient Hindu Temple there.

Such frequent pronouncements have a diminishing effect on the Hindus community. My thoughts took a dive into my early days in Bathinda (BTI) of the 1950s. BTI is relatively a remote town in the hinterland of Punjab. Few people would move there from other states, or parts of Punjab. The local population of farmers and merchants was very rich. I vividly recall how any one visiting from UP or Bihar was made fun of for different language and life style. In a derogatory tone, they were referred as, *bhaiyas*.

For instance, as boys, while playing games some argument would erupt between a Punjabi and a *bhaiya*. The following sequence of events is imprinted on my mind for more than 50 years. The Punjabi would push the *bhaiya*, and *bhaiya* would say, "*ibke mar ke dikha*" (means, try pushing again!) Next time, the Punjabi would give him a slap on the face. *bhaiya* would simply growl, and repeat, *ibke mar ke dikha*. Punjabi would give a hard blow on the body and knock him down. *bhaiya* would be dusted and bleeding from the nose or mouth. Neither he would fight back nor stop saying: *ibke mar ke dikha*. Finally, a few of us would intervene and chide the poor *bhaiya* away.

In life, one who is physical strong always speaks with hands and the weak with mouth. It happens both at the individual and collective levels. This is a mindset of the Hindus regarding the Ayodhya Temple. Every couple of years, with all media attention, the RSS, VHP and BJP leaders announce a place, time and release an architect plan for the temple. They get a little political mileage out of it. But the Temple is getting farther away—far from its realization.

A temple, church, mosque is a symbol of power and strength of its adherers. Look at the modern palatial Sikh gurdwaras at all the four corners of Delhi—apart of from the historical ones. The fracturing of the Hindu society has to be stopped. The Hindu unity will emerge from constructive community service and causes. There is a dearth of Hindu leaders, and on the top there is a crisis in the present leadership!

All the politicians have been milking the Babri Masjid issue. The Hindus are getting turned off like the villagers in a folktale, who were periodically fooled by their own shepherd for raising false alarms of a lion marching down from a hilly forest. Eventually, the villagers stopped paying attention to him, and all know the rest.

April 07, 2005/Aug, 2012

COMMENTS

1. Much worse is the saying "Every Indian has a price" Have you thought about the reasons behind such state of affairs? Hindus are dead as a religion. I never had any doubts about it. Did you? The current Hinduism is not any worth. Hinduism in Vedas and Upanishads belongs to past only. Someone else will save them. **Subhash Sood**

I wrote: I am trying to do a little I can to better it. Your observations are right.

Subhash; It is my purpose too. You are welcome if you can do anything

2. Very well said. This has been the way of taking up with adversaries by the Hindu society for the last one thousand years. Unfortunately, even Hindu intellectuals and the entire media does not hesitate to denounce even the best of religious sentiments of Hindus. Hindutva has no more remained a vote catching devise. A host of Islamic/Urdu universities and minority (specially privileged and government financing) institutions are coming up as vote catching devices. Today Indore airport has been named as Ambedkar airport by the Union Cabinet. Since Muslims and upper class Dalits have come up as a well-organized vote bank, every party/group is wooing them without recourse to social and financing cost. A number of Haj terminals have come up in the last few years. Hindus and Sikhs seem to be discriminated. There is pilgrimage tax even for Vaishno Devi. For Kailash Yatra, which is organized by the Govt. of India, the recent advertisement requires a total cost of more than two lakhs of rupees and the intending pilgrims have to pay almost the entire amount to the central government. Even in Pakistan, there is no Haj subsidy; once it was announced by the Pakistan govt. but their high court turned it down. Indian minorities (and only Muslims) are the most privileged class in the world and that also at the cost of other sections of the population. **NIGAM**

3. Unfortunately this is how politics works. Empty promises. But BJP is not only the guilty party it is a universal truth for all political parties. The strength or even symbol of an adherer is not a building but ones conviction. **Rahul**

RELIGIOUS BIAS IN MEDIA

For the last couple of days, the media coverage of two political events has occupied a space in my mind. One is the 80th birth anniversary of the British Queen, Elizabeth. A reporter added that in 15 more years, she will break Queen Victoria's record of 64-year reign (1837-1901). It is a sign of total acceptance of monarchy in social, cultural and political aspects of British life. Historically, the monarchy has kept Britain dynamically unified, as do the Union Jack (flag) and God Save The Queen (national anthem).

The other event is the surge in violent protests against the Nepalese King, Gyanendra. Here, the worldwide media is projecting him and monarchy synonymously. If Gyanendra is incompetent and corrupt, then he must abdicate, or his excessive power curtained. But the abolition of the Nepalese Monarchy must be strongly opposed. I always foresee the ties between India and Nepal, as are between the USA and UK.

Varied forms of monarchy exist in several countries of Europe, Africa, and in almost every Muslim country. It is also prevalent in some Buddhist countries of South East Asia. The history of the Hindu kings of Nepal and India goes back to ancient times due to their common scriptures and heritage. The Nepalese monarchy preserved its identity during the 19th century when the bigger kingdoms in India fell before the Tsunami expansion of the British colonization. A political paradox is that whereas the Hindu kings of Nepal ruled with militancy, this edge was lost to the Hindu kings of India.

In recent times, the Nepalese monarchy did not champion the Hindu causes abroad. They project a subdued image of Hinduism. Some Muslims, fleeing Mumbai after the communal riots in 1993, felt safer in Hindu Nepal rather than in secular India. India's polices toward Nepal were exploited both by China and Pakistan. During the 1970s, Nepal was flooded with cheaper Chinese consumer goods. But along with them came the seeds of Mao ideology of anti-monarchy that are blooming in Nepal today!

Every folk tale of India begins with a king. For millennia, the Hindus have been inspired by great kings—Raam and Krishna. The present attitude of Indian masses against kings is a backlash against the licentious and treacherous princes who sided with the British.

However, at this juncture, the Hindus of India should stand by the Nepalese monarchy. There has been never been a move to abolish the British monarchy. Last week, the assets of Queen Elizabeth were ranked Number 192 amongst the richest persons in Britain. It does not upset the UK public.

In the new world countries, monarchy may be archaic, but in old countries, it nurtures institutions that ultimately make the backbone of a nation. A question in my mind: is there a monarchy in future for India, where people adore power figures along with their gods and goddesses?

April 23, 2006/Aug, 2012

COMMENTS

1. Respected Mausaji, Namaste, I don't agree at all with your views that India should have stood by King Gyanendra. There can be no comparison between the British Monarchy & the Nepalese. U.K. is run by Tony Blair, his elected government & hence by the people . . . . Comparing the historical rules of the Indian & Nepalese Kings won't be of much help in present times. Times have completely changed & world over, the people want democracy. The enormous public protests in Nepal were purely by the people who wanted their own government. A democratic Nepal is in India's favour too. People in England aren't protesting coz they know that the governance is not in the hands of the Royal British Family but in the hands of their elected government. **Anuj**

2. I tried reading your article twice but could not find a strong case to keep monarchy alive in Nepal. Do you know history of Nepal? Until early 1800's Nepal was composed of 50 states. Prithvi Narain Shah unified the country and started Shah Dynasty. During confrontation with British the Nepalese lost to British and per treaty they had to give up 1/3 of their territory, keep a British resident in Kathmandu and keep its borders closed to foreigners. **So much for the sovereignty**.

In mid 1850; Rana the prime minister took over the power and king became a puppet. In 1950 after public agitation and India's pressure King (Tribhuvan) who had fled to India got his powers back and Rana's were exiled in India. King Mahindra started Panchyat system with no real powers to Panchyat. Again in 1989 a mass movement occurred (mass movement was helped by India having a trade impasse and sealing entry points to Nepal) which led to formation of parliament. This was again dissolved by present King and you know rest of the story. **Rahul**

3. . . . . Nepalese Monarchy is puppet of Brahmanism or would it be better to describe that Brahmanism is puppet of Nepali Monarchy. But the British Monarchy was an instance of rebellion against Catholic Religion (Brahmanism in a certain sense. **Subhash**

A PAYBACK TIME

I just finished reading a recent write-up, ***HAVE PASSION!***, by Sudha Murthy, wife of Narayana Murthy, the founder and CEO of the Infosys, the iconic software company of India. On her personal note, the article is a nostalgic tribute to the late mega industrialist, JRD Tata. She must have told this encounter with JRD many a times, but the internet technology has spread her story to the nooks and corners of the world.

However, it evoked different thoughts in my mind. Sudha noted that presently 50% of the students in Indian engineering colleges are females, whereas, in 1975, she was the only one doing master's in engineering. During my recent visits to a college in Indore and a university in Baroda, it was amazing to note that 90% of the students doing MA in mathematics were females! On digging out their religious denominations, the statistics were astounding, as 99% were Hindus! There seems a statistical correlation between Hindu religion and higher education. It needs to be checked out.

Sudha iterated the contributions of the Tatas in the industrial development of India. But the Tatas have done nothing for the Hindu religion that gave the Parsees freedom to practice and preserve their religion, and pursue their trades in India. Let it be understood that in Iran, the home of the Parsees' (founder, Zoroaster), they were given a choice, either convert to Islam or put to sword. Some of them fled and escaped into India (from the 8th to 10th century). The Hindu kings of the region comprising present Gujarat and Maharashtra gave them the asylum. There in not even a single Parsee left in Iran today!

Since the 1947 partition of India/Hindustan into theocratic Pakistan and secular (now anti-Hinduism) India, a frequent question crops up about the allegiance of the Muslims towards India. Had the leadership of early generations of the Parsees come out in gratitude for Hindu religion, the communal climate in India would have been very different. It would have then put pressure on the Muslim leadership. **Historically, the Muslim population emerged in India after the settlement of Parsees.**

'**Giving back to the society**' is more than a cliché, a *Mantra* in the US public life. In modern India, it is a revolutionary thought, as giving seldom goes beyond one's immediate family. The infrastructures of a society are anchored in its religious beliefs. Unfortunately, the present Hindus distant themselves from their religion publicly, particularly after they have succeeded in business. I wonder if Infosys would trail blaze in building a Hindu temple in the premises of its world headquarters.

The Tatas are pioneers in the industrialization of India. However, their contributions are somewhat exaggerated. Some institutions that they started later on became the financial responsibility of the Government. Sudha's **Reflection** has prompted me to write this one. Whereas, her **Reflection** adds to the folklore of JRD, mine tries to balance the image of the Tatas.

Aug 20, 2006/Aug, 2012

COMMENTS

1. Hi, Uncle! Your reflection reflects the other problem in Indian society—
   where religion is never far away from any aspect of public life!
   Sangitha

I wrote: You mean all the major religions in India are equidistant from public life?! Think about it.

Sangitha: I wish we would disassociate all religions from corporate/sports/ other merit related achievements. We have a Wipro (Azim Premji) and an Infosys (majority Hindu founders), a Tata group (Parsi) and so many other behemoths that do not see beyond merit and achievement. If the Birlas build a temple at BITS Pilani, why did they not represent other religions as well? CMC Vellore (a Christian run medical institution) has a chapel and a temple. Love, **Sangitha**

2. Dear Bhatnagar Ji, please let me know which article should I publish in September Navrang Times. **Your articles are well read by our readers**. Regards. **Girish**

3. Dear Bhai Shri Satish Ji, Saprem Namaste ! **Allow me to state, Mrs. Sudha Murthy's as well as yours reflection, are simply Extra-ordinary; keep it up, sir!** My own comments: as Hindus have done to save the entire race of Parsees, there is No Doubt, Parsees have played a very positive & effective honest role in rebuilding modern India after the partition. Had there been No Parsees & JRD TATA in our country, Birlas would have swindled the country in their pocket & the entire nation would have gone to dogs under their MONOPOLISTIC Empire as we are being dragged into the DHIRU BHAI AMBANI Empire, who are fleecing the country in every possible manner. Sincerely yours, **Satish**.

A QUESTION BEGGING ANSWERS

"If a Hindu man marries a Christian girl in an Arya Samaj marriage rituals, would she have to compulsorily convert to Hinduism?" This morning, I received this question in a forwarded e-mail from a leader of the Arya Samaj of North America. I opined: ". . . . in my understanding any formal conversion to Hinduism is not necessary. Her agreeing to marry a Hindu in an Arya Samaj wedding is good enough. Let the Hindus practicing Arya Samaj show her the better sides of Hinduism after marriage." Nevertheless, this question and my answer continue to engage my mind.

The question has several variations. An answer also depends upon the place where the couple decides to live after marriage. My assumptions are that the two are living in a free country like the USA, are financially independent, and under no threat from the parents, or social boycott. Even with these boundary conditions, my answer may not be the best, but I did not want to duck it either.

A fundamental question is: **Does the present Hindu religion require a conversion?** Again, its answer may have all the shades depending upon one's Hindu roots. Currently, the Hindu religion has no central authority over the believers. The ancient Hindu seats (called *MUTHS*) of Shankaracharya, set up by the Adi Shankaracharya more than a thousand year ago, have played a unifying role amongst various believers of Hinduism. Even then, not all the four Shankaracharyas have been unanimous on most national issues affecting the Hindus.

It reminds me of an incident when the Late Prime Minister Indira Gandhi, married to a non-Hindu, Parsi, was not allowed entry in the famous Jagannath Temple in Puri. The Puri Shankaracharya was opposed, one favored, and others unequivocal. To the best of my memory, respecting the religious sentiments, she decided not to visit the Temple.

I know a Hindu who married a Muslim airhostess 30 years ago. What to talk of conversion, he never discouraged her from practicing Islamic beliefs she liked. In due course, they raised three daughters and enriched their lives with both religions. It was a joy to meet all of them last year in Jaipur.

The condition of Hinduism, as a punch bag for all religions for the last 1000 years, gives an impression that the Hindus can be converted to other religions, but not conversely. It is very wrong. The very fact of a large number of Hindu *Sanskars* (rituals) indicates that a non-Hindu can be initiated into the folds of Hinduism. The *SHUDHIKARAN* movement, first started by Arya Samaj, is pseudo conversion. It is welcoming back the misguided Hindus who had accepted Islam and Christianity for some pecuniary gains and survival.

The question assumes new dimensions after the **9/11 Attack on America** and continued ethnic cleansing of the Hindus from Bangladesh, and Kashmir in India.

Nov 14, 2006

COMMENTS

1. Dear Satish-Ji: A good question. My answer goes on following lines:
An oath of allegiance presupposes the adherence and acceptance of the system under which it is taken. If marriage is considered as a solemn oath of allegiance, a Hindu Marriage (Arya Samaj, which allows conversion), a conversion is needed/implied. By the way, Arya-Samaji marriage and Sanatani marriage procedures follow most of the common parts derived from Paraskar Grihya Sutra, with a minor difference of invoking of Devatas being substituted with Vedic mantras, in the beginning of the ceremony. So let us put some logic. Regards, **BhuDev Sharma**

2. Hi Satish, Great question and your reflections. I personally do not condone any conversion. Besides you are only converting the outer trappings not the person's inner believes or faith. Moreover Hindu faith respects all religions. How can we show this respect by insisting on conversion?

Here is another thought. Hindu is not a religion, it is a strictly a faith, a faith that one believes in, a faith that one willingly follows, a faith strictly of Dharma which is a code for all our life actions. Anyone who practices Dharma is by its very definition a Hindu. One does not need any other layer over it. Besides I do not believe that by chanting some mantra's and sprinkling "Holy water", etc. one really changes (converts) any one. The very practice of this, in my opinion, reflects shallow thinking and believing in sham rituals which I believe is against the very core of Hindu faith (Dharma). Once again thanks. I enjoyed your views. Love, **Gopal**

3. Hi Satish: An interesting piece! To my knowledge, Hinduism doesn't believe in proselytizing. According to Ronald Segal of "The Crisis of India," Hinduism is more a way of life. The Christian girl doesn't have to be converted to Hinduism, though I am unfamiliar with Arya Samaj traditions. Several years ago, one of my students, who took my Nonwestern literatures class, asked me in her note whether a Mormon could be converted to Hinduism. I told her that she can still follow Mormon religion and yet follow Hindu way of life and traditions. Your friend who married a Muslim woman, who keeps her religious beliefs, living happily together with children, is a prime example. Hinduism is not institutionalized; it doesn't have a founder; it has embraced several philosophical, social, and cultural traditions. It is not monolithic like Judaism, Christianity, and Islam. **Moorty**

A UNITY IN DIVERSITY SCENARIO

Never before had I spent 12 days with a group of total strangers, as just experienced during a *Vipashyanaa* training camp. It was held in a center located in a wooded area by the bank of a shallow Noon River; and on the outskirts of Dehradoon. I was amongst 55 persons including 18 females, who converged there from overseas and various places in India. Ten persons came from USA, Spain, France, Belgium, Korea and Israel. Age wise, the distribution ranged from one age 16 to two in their 80s. Nearing the **End** of their Journey, the geriatrics may be thinking of getting *Nirvana* after this course.

The uniqueness of the experience was the observance of **Noble Silence** defined by no speech, no body language or within mind. The posted signs constantly remind the meditators on the observance of Noble Silence and walking alone. It is practiced to an extent that the meditators and seekers would lower their eyes while passing each other.

The participants got to know each other only on the 10th day when the Nobel Silence was over. I shared a Spartan room with a 25-year old businessman and a 40-year old man coming out of drugs and alcohol addictions—both never married. A small-time painter came for the third time with his wife and two daughters. On being asked how he would relate meditation with his profession, he replied, that with *Vipashyanaa*, he can predict the sex of an unborn child! Due to female infanticide, sex determination tests are illegal in India.

The foreigners were mostly young spending their various sabbaticals in India like me! Two young men and a girl hailing from Israel indicate new cultural closeness between Hinduism and Judaism; both religions tracing their traditions to over 5000 years. It is unfortunate that Indian masses and the governments, since independence, have not woken up to the political, cultural and business realities in Middle East. Islam, being farthest from Hinduism, has no place for Yoga in general, and *Vipashyanaa*, in particular.

***Vipashyanaa* literally means observing life with the sharpness of mind**. The Hindu mind being inwardly, has given the world infinitely many meditation techniques over millennia. The ancient Hindu scripture, *Vigyan Bhairav Shastra*, known for 120 meditation techniques, hints that each human being can customize a technique according to his/her life style.

According to the stone edicts of Ashok, *Vipashyanaa* was first popularized by Gautam Buddha, nearly 2500 years ago. But its recent popularity is due to Satyanarain Goenka who was initiated into it by a monk in Burma (Myanmar).

The segregation of sexes was complete during dining hours, brief moments of relaxation, and in meditation sessions. Also, words with any sexual overtone were avoided in scores of Goenka's discourses. Unless sex is used for bringing mind into focus, it becomes its biggest obstacle. *Vipashyanaa*, being a common goal, it all made an unforgettable experience. Isn't that life all about?

Oct 14, 2007 (India)/Sep, 2012

SEX MEASURES HINDUISM

What a blessed day, it has been amidst the most beautiful and well-proportioned women in their attractive hairdos! Like the showgirls of Las Vegas, the jewelry is their only costume. It is not in a dream, not in the Islamic heaven of eternal virgins, and not in Hindu *Indralok* of *Apsaras* (fairies). As a matter of fact, they are chiseled out of the stones—decking the interiors and exteriors ancient Hindu temples of Khajuraho. These temples were built during the dynastic reign of Chandel kings of central India—from the 10th to 12th century.

It was in 1818 when Franklin, a British explorer, accidentally discovered these temples. It must be understood that the villagers around the temples fully knew of the existence of these temples. Here is a **social paradox**. A thousand Hindus knowing the ancient temples amounted to nothing to the world. But once a European explorer took notice of them, then it became a discovery! **It is the quality, not the quantity that often counts in life**

In search for sexual gratification, man is driven to extremes. Sex can become a paradigm of life. In the US, a sex jock, Howard K. Stern exemplifies a sexually pervasive and obsessive way of life. What happens to a nation, at large, when it is driven by sexual appetites? These temples combine the *Yoga*, a union of individual mind with the Supreme and the *Bhog*—a union of the soul with sensual pleasures. The synthesis is remarkable.

The present Hindu society is understandably prudish about display of sexual behaviors. In the US, on the other hand, sex, in the name of education, is being exposed too early. The temple statues depict sexual activities of every kind—like one man engaged with 3 to 4 women, 4 lesbian women in an act, couples in orgy, and in a few instances—men and women with animals too. They epitomize pervasive sexual culture of Hindu India. In the US, the only contemporary elite sensual atmosphere is seen high-class clubs of Playboy and Las Vegas casinos.

Khajuraho Museum of the Archaeological Survey of India houses a statue of an 'exposed' Lord Ganesh. I was confused whether it was His penis or a dangling ornament. But a museum curator explained that the huge penis was also decorated with jewelry! The Holy penis head was studded too. It reminded me of a US body artist who had his penis tattooed and pierced with studs making it look like a cobra. He splashed it on a website! It is seeking

Nirvana though sexual ecstasy, a *Tantrik* way of Hindu life. After the fall of Chandel Empire, Khajuraho turned into a Mecca of sexually liberated cults and individuals.

Thanks Khajuraho for the memories! There was a plenty of food for thought, and lot of thoughts on the ultimate sensual food.

Oct 28, 2007 (India)/Sep, 2012

MATHEMATICS, SCIENCE AND RELIGIONS

Lately, I have been getting wonderstruck by the impact of deeper religious beliefs on the mathematical achievements of individuals and societies at large. Often one probes into a mathematician's mind, as to how he/she came up with a breakthrough idea. However, it has not been investigated for any religious group. This area of ethno-mathematics lies in the domain common to meta mathematics and neurology of genius. French mathematician, J. Hadamard (1865-1963) did pioneering work (1954) in this direction.

This socio-psychological problem is an outcome of my mathematical experiences over the last 45+ years. It clicked during the academic year, 2006-07, while teaching graduate courses on history of mathematics and survey of mathematical problems. The correlation coefficient of mathematics with major religions of the world is not constant. It varies with each organized religion and its historical chronology. My students, fascinated with the question, researched a few solid facts and figures. This *Reflection* briefly touches the subject, but it does point out at various directions for further investigation.

Starting with Christianity, its major reformation was the emergence of Protestantism in the 16th century. It subsequently played a key role in the development of science and mathematics. It was a quantum leap in intellectual freedom. Briefly touching the religious depth of a few prominent mathematicians of modern era, Pascal (1623-1662) was converted into Jansenists, a fast growing sect within Catholic Church. His Provincial Letters, promoting Jansenists idea are considered classic in French literature. Newton's (1643-1727) interest in alchemy during his later years was driven by his religious beliefs. Euler (1707-1783) was the son of a Protestant minister and studied theology.

Giving an American touch to the subject, Harvard University, started in 1636, as a religious college, has its present Divinity School, which is as famous as its Law and Medical Schools. The University of California is named after Bishop Berkeley (1685-1753). The US has numerous colleges where science and mathematics are studied along with Christian theology. Mathematics and religion nurture each other subtly.

In India, the advent of Buddhism and Jainism over 2500 years ago are major milestones in the reformation cycles of Hinduism (synonymous with

Sanatan Dharma/Hindu Religion). The resultant emphasis on logic and experimentation generated new sciences and mathematics. Eventually, it dawned a golden period (400-700 AD) of unprecedented prosperity in every walk of life. As a matter of fact, India became a destination of fortunes seekers, scholars and adventurers. It was like the USA has been for the last 50 years.

However, the great Hindu mathematicians—like Aryabhatta (476-550), Bhaskara I (600-680 AD) and Brahmagupta (598-665) worshipped Brahma, Shiva, Vishnu, or Ganesh—the major deities in Hindu pantheon. The legendary Ramanujan (1887-1920) worshipped Namagiri, a family goddess. He credited his incredible theorems to her. He often said, "An equation for me has no meaning, unless it represents a thought of God." The seemingly unworldliness and complexities in Hindu religion and its mythology often run parallel to the rarified heights of abstraction and exotic symbols in mathematics.

It is simplistic to think that religion alone determines the development of mathematics. Stable political systems and general prosperity of a state play significant roles in the growth of science and mathematics. In the class, we examined these aspects under 'the necessary and sufficient conditions' for the flowering of mathematics at every level.

Two startling data emerged, when all the winners of Nobel Prizes, Field Medals, Abel and Nevanlinna Prizes in sciences and mathematics were examined. Let me add that the religious affiliation was derived from the names only. The number of Muslim winners was only two, Hindus five. However, the list of the Jew winners ran into two pages!

It is to be noted that amongst the Muslims, a vast majority of scientists and mathematicians are Shiias, an offshoot of Islam emerging during its infancy. It does not have any semblance with reformation in Islam. The branching of the Shiias came off due to the hereditary rights as the followers of Prophet Muhammad.

In the contemporary Muslim world, the Pakistani Imams of nearly 100,000 mosques, running madrassas (Islamic religion schools), overwhelmingly rejected the introduction of science and mathematics in their curricula. It happened 3-4 years ago, when the Bush administration offered nearly 50 million$$ for the curricular changes. The study of science and mathematics along with Quranic instructions may take the Muslim youths away from the path of terrorism. As it is, the madrassas are the Harvards for turning out fighting human machines.

After flourishing for six centuries in India, Buddhism, with royal patronage, spread in Afghanistan in the west, Sri Lanka in the south, China, Japan and other countries in north and Far East of present India. The 'reformation' and the spread of Mahayana Buddhism (Hinayana, later on, Theravada) catalyzed eventual development of science and mathematics during the Han Dynasty (3rd BC to 3rd AD) of China.

Interestingly enough, there was a transfer of mathematical applications in astrology from India to China. The knowledge of geometry, in the *yantra* in divination, was transformed into Chinese magical squares (cousins of Latin Squares). Similar influence on Far East countries is an open question. The whole subject is so fascinating!

Nov 18, 2007 (India)/Sep, 2012

RAJPUT FIRST—HINDU SECOND

During my 3-day stay in Udaipur, I was involuntarily soaked up with Maharana Pratap (1540-1597). His brave and defiant spirit pervades the air, and it is seen in his statues, and roads, businesses and institutions named after him, and his legendary horse, Chetak.

Had Pratap upgraded his army's artillery weapons, and hired the European mercenaries in contemporary warfare, history of India would have been different. Bhama Shah's wealth, as offered to Pratap, was enough to support 25,000 soldiers for 12 years! A war is fought with heart first, weapons second, and army's size third. All the Muslim invaders and Christian colonizers had the edge over the Hindus in the first two categories. However, Pratap's successful resistance to the Mughal rule in Rajasthan is the first example of guerilla warfare waged by a Hindu king. Fifty years later, it inspired Shivaji to engage in guerilla fight against Aurangzeb, a great grandson of Akbar.

In the present context, Al Qaeda, a global Islamic militant organization goes after the latest in strategies and weaponry. In stark contrast, a few days ago, it was funny to watch the members of Hindu RSS (75-year old National Volunteer Organization) marching the streets with *LATHIS* (sticks)! Historically, Hindus disarmed themselves before the Muslim and English rulers without any resistance. Consequently, they alone have been persecuted and plundered for centuries.

A visit to a newly built Museum and Hall of Heroism was worth it. Also, I went through *Maharana Pratap and his Times*, a publication of **Maharana Pratap *Smaarak Samiti***, Udaipur. The history of a family or nation is burdensome—no matter how glorious its past has been, unless it inspires the present for a greater future.

The leadership of Jalaluddin Muhammad (Akbar means great) (1542-1605) stands out in comparison with that of Pratap. With the support of his fiercely loyal generals and sterling advisors, Akbar convinced many Hindu kings of his vision of *sulh-i-kul*—a unified Hindustan under the Muslim rule.

On the other hand, Pratap never rose beyond being a Rajput. There is no evidence to show that Pratap tried to unify the Rajputs under the banner of

Hindutva for routing the Muslims from India. By the end of the 16th century, the Muslim population was hardly 400,000. Yet, the Hindus seem to have reconciled that the Muslims are there to stay in India forever. This national despondency enveloped them due to nearly 500 years of Muslim occupations of different parts of India.

Akbar fought with Pratap of Mewar and Chandra Sen of Marwar (1541-1581), the two rajputs coming from two proud dynasties. Together, Pratap and Chandra Sen could have vanquished unstable Akbar. Pratap fought without any unifying vision. Galvanization of present Hindu society needs generations of new leaders and first-rate institutions.

The Hindutva (essentially means reverence for Vedic heritage including epics, language and culture) alone can bring a Hindu renaissance in India. Moreover, it is under the Hindutva alone that India was and can be truly secular. The secularism, practiced during the last 60 years of independence, is reduced to anti-Hinduism.

In a short period of 20 discontinuous years of Mughal rule under Babar and Humanyu, Akbar won over key Hindu kings. His diplomacy along with ruthless stick and carrot approach was very effective. By encouraging matrimonial alliances with the Rajputs only, he broke a Mughal tradition of not marrying into the Hindus.

In contrast with the Mughals, the Rajputs miserably failed in maintaining peace in their forts. The most glaring scenario is of Pratap's three younger brothers fighting against him in several battles including the historic battle of Haldighati. It is a travesty of Hindu culture that a Muslim could win the loyalty of a Hindu to an extent that he would be willing to kill his real brother for his Muslim ruler. The British exploited this Hindu mindset to an extreme. They had the entire Hindu police and Hindu army fighting for them at home and abroad. In order to break this yoke of loyalty to the British that Gandhi had launched the Non-Cooperation Movement in 1920.

For the first time, I realized the merits in fratricidal wars for a crown. Whether it is modern democracy or monarchy, the political power comes from the blade of a sword or barrel of a gun, as Mao-Tse Tung put it. The Hindu succession principle of the eldest member has not brought out the best rulers. The ruler of a nation must embody the skills in administration, warfare and public welfare besides vision and leadership. The Hindu succession of the eldest is a derivative of the weakened Hindus who avoid any fighting.

It is scheming deception that India was not a nation before Akbar. Every colonizer perpetuates this myth in order to justify their rule! Since the time immemorial, India is clearly defined by its ancient culture, Sanskrit, the mother of all Indian languages, reverence for the Vedas, great epics of Ramayana and Mahabharata.

The locust like Muslim invasions and their sporadic rules during the previous 4-5 centuries had taken the fighting juices out of the ritualistic Hindus. They only wanted to fend and defend for themselves. In every chronicle—from the 11th to 20th century, the Muslims and later on the English branded the Hindus as ethnically inferior, not worthy of equal status. It is an irony that the Hindu subjects, out of their bizarre caste superiority, considered the Muslims and English as *Asurs and Maleeches* (lower beings)!

The only hallmark of Pratap's leadership was to get the non-Rajput Bhils to fight for him. For Bhil bravery, he broke the caste barriers by letting the Rajputs marry with Bhil women. The caste system had made the Hindus society very porous. This has not changed a bit to the present. It was the genius of Sikh Gurus to harness the fighting power of their Hindu followers by eliminating the castes amongst the Khalsas. That has made the Sikhs 100% fighters.

On the contrary, the glorification of defeat and not turning it around into victory are the weirdest features of Hindu life of the last millennium. One can even link it with historic battles; Pouroosh (not Porus!) lost to Alexander, Sanga lost to Babar, or the 1857 Mutiny. Alexander never fought the same enemy twice. The Muslims have the same strategy. Incidentally, the *Chanakya Doctrine*, espoused 2500 years ago, always advocated for the total annihilation of the enemy.

Pratap did not leave a flame of Hindu legacy burning for his successors to carry it forward. His son, Amar Singh resisted Akbar for a few years, but succumbed in 1615. There is no evidence that Pratap created any academic or political institutions for nationalism to sprout. Shivaji took the guerilla fighting with Aurangzeb to greater heights, but he too missed Hindu nationalism by a mile.

Nevertheless, Maharana Pratap is a benchmark of Hindu nationalism, but not the highest one in my opinion! Modi, in Gujarat, has already achieved no less in this direction. However, it will take several Modis to create a leader for the entire India.

Dec 04, 2007 (India)/Sep, 2012

COMMENTS

An article written with real passion. This article is a true reflection of your thoughts about Hinduism. Well written article. Enjoyed reading it. If you read history of all civilizations, then you will find parallels among them. All civilizations had rise and fall. Fall was a result of lack of vision, arrogance, lack of unity and recklessness. Unfortunately Bush is taking US on that route. Even mighty Mughals fell because of similar reasons. **Rahul**

NEW MONUMENTS OF HINDUISM

As soon as my travel plans included Vadodara, I decided to visit Godhara. "This is a pilgrimage for paying homage to 58 Hindu devotees who were toasted alive in a railway compartment on Feb 27, 2002," was my response for visiting the site. It was a preplanned attack by the local Muslims inspired by global Islamic terrorism. For the first time, the Hindus Gujaratis, particularly considered conflict-avoiding people, retaliated and communal riots started. "It seems you live in this railway colony?" I asked a lady on overhearing her conversation with a friend. At her affirmative response, I inquired of her knowledge of Godhara tragedy. This reference perked her up, and she pointed out at the location where the smoldered compartment was parked on a special rail track.

Before setting out, we were falsely told that the bogie had been removed from the site. It may be partly due to my persona and partly due to many investigators who had interrogated the railway staff, they all acted as if they had no knowledge of this holocaust. My thoughts were engaged in recreating this fireball. The objective was not to leave any spot untouched, as if the soil had become sacred with the lives of the innocence. Actually, they were holy martyrs since they were returning after visiting the controversial sites of Babri Masjid and Ram Mandir. The Hindus want to reclaim the site for the Ram Temple and the Muslims worldwide have challenged them about it

The sleeper compartment, S6 hidden in a grove of trees, is guarded by 24-hour security. Inside, there is no trace of any non-metallic material—including wood, plastic and foam. The fire must have been so quick and intense that it incinerated the passengers in no time. The outside paint on the lower half of the compartment was hardly affected. In some places, the steel frames of the upper berths were bent and twisted in the melee inside. All the four doors were jammed shut from outside. The compartment must have turned into an electric oven of the Nazis that killed the Jews @ thousands a day during the 1940s.

Right after the **9/11 Attack on America**, President Bush declared, that in this fight, either a country was with the US or against the US. The Pakistani President Mushrraff, supportive of Al Qaeda, publicly turned against it! Al Qaeda took this opportunity of scaring the Hindus with bolder terrorist attacks, which includes Indian Parliament (12/01), Godhara (02/02),

Akshardham (09/02). Consequently, the Indian Government, under the BJP coalition, did not join the US in squeezing Al Qaeda out of Kashmir!

A Hindu organization must purchase this compartment and place it in a Hindu Holocaust museum. Later in the day, on visiting Gandhinagar Akshardaham Temple, I inquired about the locations where 108 visitors were killed and wounded by only two Islamic terrorists. A volunteer simply waved his hand. **This disregard of Hindu lives by the Hindus is a national sickness**. Is it out of fear of another attack or belief in reincarnation? A society that forgets attacks on its sacred places and leaders lives in moral, social and political subjugation as second-rate nation.

Dec 07, 2007/Sep, 2012

COMMENTS

1. Dear Satish: You have justified the attack against Indian Men, Women and Children on the ground of burning of Hindus at Godhara in 2002. Any number of citizens inquiry commission and Banerjee commission has given ample proof that the fire in Sabarmati Express was lit from inside possibly accidentally.

No one not even Modi has claimed Al Qaida's involvement. Recent exposure by Tehelka gives clear-cut admission of murderers who committed the most heinous crimes and were garlanded by Modi. I am sorry, I do not see it the way you see it. Murder of innocent is not justified in any of Hindu Shastra. **Shrikumar Poddar**

2. You are mixing two things. Iraq war and Afghan war. India supported later. Pakistan did not support Iraq war either. As for Godhara tragedy Muslims (who were not involved in that carnage) paid by their blood. You have never alluded to what action Indian Government should have taken? I will like to listen to it.

3. It is eye opening. Probably due to our weakness. Doing great work. I am copying this to my friends. **Sham**

MUSINGS FROM MANDU

December 11 falling on Tuesday, my mind was looking for new angles in Mandu history. Tuesdays, being my days of total fasting, are helpful in bringing points in focus. For solid six hours, I walked up and down the ancient monuments. At times, I wondered and questioned my purpose of such close examinations. **New places generate newer ideas.**

During its heydays, Mandu had several huge security gates, but now only a few are standing in dilapidated conditions. The topography of rolling hills, deep gorges carved by Narmada River, lakes, valleys and plateaus are all compressed in a perimeter of 45 KM. It is beautiful! Mandu traces its history to 500 AD. The Archeological Survey of India (ASI) has a small museum of excavated artifacts. The legendary Hindu Raja Bhoj, known for his wisdom, was one of its rulers.

Seeking independence from the Sultanates was a remarkable feature of Muslim governors of the far-off provinces. As soon as political instability was rumored in Delhi or Agra, the local chiefs revolted for autonomy or tried to conquer the capital throne of Hindustan. Since the 18th century, the French, English and Portuguese also took advantage of unstable Mughal rulers. Amazingly, few Hindu kings ever tried to re-claim their own country! Raja Hem Chandra of the region around Delhi is the only exception. He challenged Akbar, and lost his head and kingdom in the second battle of Panipat.

A popular Mandu legend is of Hindu princess Rupmati made famous by a movie shot at her palace in Mandu. Her romantic associations with Baz Bahadur, Akbar and Jahangir speak of a sense of history of Indians! My curiosity was to know if a Hindu prince ever wooed her. **The empire builders go after the most beautiful women, and conversely.**

The monuments have undergone changes under different rulers; the Hindus, Muslims, and Europeans. The lotus motifs on the exterior walls indicate the influence of Hindu architecture. **However, my mind was revolting at this continued glorification of Afghani and Mughal rulers of Mandu.** What would the present Afghanis think of the Hindus after visiting Mandu? It reminded me of a Hollywood movie, set in a small US town, where a young man raped a girl. To add insult to this ghastly act, he often taunted and strutted in front of her house. One day, the girl picked up her father's gun and blasted him away. That is how my feelings were coiling up in my heart.

I wondered at the mission of the ASI. It is stupid to preserve the monuments that rub salt over the wounds of collective Hindu psyche. Everything ancient is not worth preserving. Though only one of the seven storeys is left of a tower symbolizing the victory of Mahmud Khilji over Rana Kumbha, but what is point of its glorification? Now I am beginning to see some merits in the implosion of the 2000-year Buddha statues by the Afghani Talibans (means pure Islamists) in March, 2001. **New national identity arises only over the ashes of the old eyesores**.

Dec 13, 2007 (India)/Sep, 2012

COMMENTS

It is simply elevating and inspiring. I am now saving these treasures. **Sham**

PERSONAL REMARKS

100 HOURS OF MEDITATION

It has been four months when I finished a 10-day course on *Vipashyanaa* (Vipassana in English) meditation. But every now and then, I am prompted to recall this experience. It is unforgettable. I would recommend it to any intellectually curious and open-minded person. After all, in life, we go after exotic experiences—whether they are visual, Audio; of palate, smell or touch. *Vipashyanaa* goes in opposite direction—minimizing all the sensory inputs. **It creates a sensory vacuum—thus enhancing the sensitivity of the body!** It only sounds extreme, but it is very rational.

The course is so well refined that when, at the end, I suggested some improvements, a course assistant firmly told, "Not even a single word can be changed." The course is 10+2 days long. The days of arrival and departure are important. After registration and orientation, the course is declared open by 8 PM with the first video discourse of S N Goenka, the founder and propouder of *Vipashyanaa*. However, he gives all the credits to his Burmese teacher, Sayagyi U Ba Khin.

A hallmark of the stay is the observance of *Arya Maun* (Golden Silence). It means no speaking, no communication with anyone in writing or through body/sign language. The emphasis is on immersion in yourself. What is this **self**? It is through gross body. *Vipashyanaa* starts from a specific miniscule part of the body and gradually envelops the entire body!

Vipashyanaa is a meditation technique going back to ancient India. It is Buddha (the Gautam) who dusted it off, polished it, and gave sermons on it. Emperor Ashok, after accepting Buddhism, spread it through thousands of stone edicts. Buddhist monks were sent to the neighboring countries. Due to India's dark period of the last millennium, *Vipashyanaa* was lost like many other treasures. But, it survived in its pristine form in neighboring Burma. Goenka, born and raised in Burma, came into contact with Sayagyi U Ba Khin under incredible circumstances.

A question is asked, "What did you get after 10 days?" I glimpsed at what Buddha laid it out as the mid path philosophy of life. **The core of *Vipashyanaa* lies in awakening every particle of the body inside and outside.** The meditation hours are from 4:30-6:30 AM, 8-11:00 AM, 1-4:30 PM and 6-9 PM. It goes on for solid 10 days, and parts of the arrival and departure days. Goenka gives 12 video discourses and explains *Vipashyanaa* in 11 steps. The amazing part of my experience was that while being unaware of technical details, I had been doing it in my own way!

The experience, of course, varies from person to person. My conflict with the course for a few reasons distracted me. Whether one is theist or not, believer in an organized religion or not, *Vipashyanaa* does not create any conflicts. As a matter of fact, it adds a new dimension of clarity. Personally, I got reaffirmation on my beliefs in god, soul, reincarnation, and salvation etc.

Was it easy to sit still for an hour? Yes, it is astonishing how the joints become nimble in a day or two. The simplicity of the center food, clean air and water helps too. I lost five pounds, as I sweated while trying to sit still! **Was it easy to observe this silence?** Yes, the environment helps a lot. One can get necessary information from the website: www.dhamma.org.

Jan 28, 2008/May 2010

COMMENTS

1. *Khamoshi be' jaa nahin Ghalib,*
   Koi to baat hai jiski parda poshi hai

How were the moments after you broke your *Maun*? **Rahul**

2. I might be going for a 1/2 day course this weekend. I have completed AOL after *Vipassana*.
   Interesting difference in the method +effects of the three techniques that I now know of (vip, AOL, kriya yoga). **Harpreet Singh**

PERSONAL REMARKS

III. HINDUISM—EDUCATIONALS

EDUCATION: DETERMINANT OF A RELIGION

This article is based on author's first-hand experience with Islamic countries—particularly with United Arab Emirates (UAE), which is west of India, and Malaysia, which is east of India. By and large, in Islamic countries, the educational institutions are guided by a pervasive Islamic ideology. The format of the article is non-traditional, in the form of pertinent questions and observations.

1. What is the Purpose of Education?

The purpose of education is the amelioration of the general lot of the people. There is no merit in institutional education for the sake of education. To provide and receive education is a function of many factors—from national priorities to individual mental capabilities to social and historical environments. Here, religion plays subtle, but very important role. Islam considers early Quranic education is paramount in the development of a person. In fact, the Talibans in Afghanistan have gone to a new extreme in implementing it at every level. Their entire purpose of education is to turn out young men into perfect fighting machines for Islam (*Mujahideen*). Historically, they have been very successful. These fighters are sought after in every Islamic movement and insurgency around the world. Whereas, India is number one in the world turning out 80% of world software engineers. This contrast is only explainable by Hinduism, the dominant religion of India.

2. Resource Priorities

In India, education is a rallying point at every level. Relatively, in Islamic countries, there is very little investment in modern education both from private and government sources. In the UAE, the oldest university is ten years old, and they do not have any medical or engineering college. In comparison, India, because of Hinduism, has the finest institutions of higher education in the world.

A singular data is that the literacy rate amongst the Muslims in India is highest amongst the Muslims in all other countries. Another scenario: Punjab University, Lahore, a premier university in Asia, went to Pakistan, when India was partitioned in 1947 at the time of independence. The Indian Panjab University, Chandigarh, started after 1947, has gone far ahead of its Pakistani counterpart.

3. College graduates—Demand and Supply

An economist has observed that institutions of higher education in India are brain factories set up for the West—a form of outsourcing. The human products of Indian educational institutions are greatly in demand and exported all over the world. The major consumers are USA, UK and Middle East, where multinationals are running gigantic global projects. Paradoxically, India does not have a local market for its own products.

During the 1970s and 80s, India had an unprecedented growth in the number of colleges and universities—only to be matched by the USA immediately after the WW II. Again, the propelling force in India is Hinduism. No Islamic country, including oil rich countries wealthier than India, can boast such a record of output on higher education.

4. Education in United Arab Emirates

UAE is a federation of **seven** emirates or sheikdoms around the Arabian Gulf, formed only 30 years ago. The well-known emirates are: Abu Dhabi, Dubai, Fujariah and Sharjah. In a nutshell, the UAE constitution allows absolute freedom for each Sheikh in his emirate. A few issues like defense are common. Just in 1998, two universities were started for women only with campuses in Dubai and Abu Dhabi. The MUCIA, a big consortium of US universities has been assisting the UAE in setting them up.

The vision of US educational enterprise is that once a US model of education is adopted abroad, then other US products or institutions can be easily pushed. In contrast, Indian education system is not 'export' oriented in the sense that its institutions are deemed as Indian products. However, they have started drawing international students.

5. Correlation between education prosperity

The prosperity of a nation is not always directly proportional to its educated elite. UAE is a perfect example. It is strikingly prosperous despite the fact it has little indigenous educational bases. The UAE imports human labor for construction projects, domestic help, and professionals in every field—including accountancy, engineering and medicine. In Dubai, there is no building that is more than 30 years old. Construction activities in Dubai are unprecedented in the world.

The oil wealth is pouring in. The infrastructure of highways, power, taxes and water through de-salination plants (turning seawater into drinking one) has made the UAE an attractive destination for varied investments. People have been getting uninterrupted water and power supply for the last 20 years. There is no comparison with India even after independence. Incidentally, Indians make a large percentage of expatriates in UAE and they are happy working there.

6. Why such a difference?

In the ultimate analysis, the dominant religions of the lands set India and UAE/MY apart. The government-funded mosques are prominent in every square mile of the developed land in UAE and Malaysia. These mosques provide the traditional Islamic education in **MADARSAS**. For years, only select few citizens went abroad to receive higher education.

There is a prevalent belief that education does not generate wealth; it drains away. Also, western educated citizenry may threaten autocratic political systems. The goal of these nations is generation of wealth. The per capita income of 500,000 Dubai citizens out of a population of 2 million (2,000,000) is more than US $50,000! Only 30 years ago, they were living in thatched dwellings. India's poverty is still proverbial in the world.

The sheikhs command a far greater awe and respect than any political leader in India. Display of full size pictures of the rulers in front offices and businesses is legally mandated for showing loyalty. A general sense of loyalty breeds national unity that is good for general public. Hinduism tolerating diversities means it promotes divisions.

7. What are the upshots on Education?

Education in India is being oversold. The urban areas are saturated with educationally constipated young men and women. Too much is expected out of college degrees based on stale education. Thus, it overwhelmingly discriminates against those who are not educationally inclined, or do not have opportunities to get education.

Earning power, not directly proportional to the number of years of education, is a consequence of the *Principle of Diminishing Return*. In India, the government resources in education reaching a saturation point, it is time to let the private organizations take a piece of primary and tertiary education. Government resources need to be largely allocated to fundamental interdisciplinary and applied research—far beyond traditional doctoral degrees. Despite the exponential growth in the number of universities, India is light years behind in quality research of the caliber needed for the Nobel Prizes.

Dec 2000/June, 2012

PS: This *Reflection* is modified from an article published in a 2001 issue of the *SAHI BUNIYAD*, a bimonthly educational magazine.

A SIGN OF CASTE RE-STRUCTURING

Recently, it was heartening to read a report on the admission of *Shudras* (untouchables) in the *Karmakand* (priestly rituals) courses run by the *Uttar Pradesh Sanskriti Sansthan*. First of all, it has to be understood that a person, who desires to learn Sanskrit and Hindu ritualistic system, is not, by any stretch, a *Shudra*. It is the pursuit of profession and potential that defines caste, and not birth in a family. The bane of birth caste was exploited by the British to further subdivide India.

The definition of caste system could have been changed after independence. But the collective vision of Gandhi, Nehru and Amebedkar failed the populace. India is paying a price for it today. By having constitutionally job reservations for the scheduled castes for decades, the divisions of Hindu society are far sharper today than they were ever before. India would be as strong, as its 80 % Hindu population is. But the Hindus are weak. Thus, India is weak politically, sociologically and economically.

Here is a typical post independence scenario. A scheduled caste person gets into the elite IAS, medical/engineering college, or a defense service academy. The person is now transformed into Brahmin, Kshatriya or Vaishya. Certainly, the person is not a *Shudra* anymore! He does not live in a segregated colony, does not clean toilets, and does not sweep the street, or any menial job. Instead, he lives in a sprawling government bungalow with house servants. But Indian Government continues to give the same person life-long benefits in promotion.

The worse is that the government continues the same benefits to his/her children. This is terrible! The net effect is the growing chasm between the upper and lower castes particularly, as witnessed in the states of Tamil Nadu and Bihar. I could never imagine Jagjeevan Ram being the leader of scheduled caste—till he died. He held every cabinet position including that of defense. He was an ultimate Kshatriya or a Kayastha!

I remember a story from the 1960s, when a friend told me that a guy with last name Malhotra was not a Khatri—but, a member of scheduled caste. I was puzzled and later on figured it out that who would bother to challenge him for this, when it does not harm anyone. The situation turned around in the 1980s, when the upper caste Hindus started getting fake certificates of backward regions and fringe castes in order to get the benefits of reservation policy for their children.

If one really thinks deep and closely watches at life, then within 24 hours everyone one of us is cast in all four-caste roles. Every time a person cleans his/her bottom after defecating, that person is a *Shudra.* Every mother is *Shudra,* as for years, she cleans the bottoms of her children. In the USA, like many, I have been cleaning my toilets, and sweeping the yards and patios. No matter what traditional caste one may claim to come from, every Hindu is a *Shudra* for a good part of the waking day. Interesting, during sleep hours, all are equal!

As the number of Hindu temples in North America increases, the need for qualified Hindu priests would be greater. Hopefully, this new class of priests will have broader vision of Hindu society that is increasingly threatened by Global Islamic and Christian forces within and without India.

June 1, 2002/July, 2012

NEW *KARVA CHOUTH* CELEBRATION

Hindu religion is unique in its lofty traditions. Every day of a Hindu calendar is a celebration of some relationship of man with his environment that includes family at its core. ***KARVA CHOUTH*** celebrates a bond between husband and wife. Though this day is more popular in Punjab, but its variations are known in other states of India too.

After the all day fasting, often a friendly group of 8-10 ladies assemble in one house for the main ceremony before the sunset. They wait for the moonrise to break the fast. Those of us who left India some 30-40 years ago feel a resurgent of obligations for the continuity of Indian traditions and customs. The challenge is not only to pass it to the next generation, but also to educate and inform the community at large about it.

Forty years ago, there were no Hindu temples in North America. **Generally, the Hindus feel that when there is a tiny temple in individual homes, then why to build a community temple, especially in grandeur.** The building of great temples in India was either expected from the rich—like the Birlas, or from kings. However, successful Hindus, particularly in the USA, have created a history of building magnificent temples. With the first generation of Indians phasing out in retirement and the next generations equally successful, temple building has been on the rise. The Hindu Temple of Las Vegas is an example of such a success story. A Sai Temple has been in existence in the backyard of private home for the last 18 years where Thursday Sai Pooja is regularly performed.

Every year, I insist my wife that why not group of ladies does the ***KARVA*** ceremony in a temple? My reason for it has been to generate a public pride and awareness in this husband and wife relationship that is so fragile in the US society at large.

The very sight of a bunch of Hindu ladies dressed in their finest saris, suits and jewelry makes an impact on the people. Besides, in a temple, the Hindus from one state can share their rituals and practices with the Hindus from other states of India. India is very vast and one really discovers it after leaving India! Well, that is what happened this year in a magnificent sanctorum of new Hindu Temple that opened up in April 2001. Some 25 ladies gathered there. Not all of them knew each other, but they had a common purpose.

The **PUJARI** (priest) though a Telugu was conversant with Punjabi rituals. He, with the assistance of a Punjabi lady, performed the main ceremony. Ladies arrived at 4 PM, mingled for a while before the ceremony began at 4:30 PM. It lasted for 30 minutes. For another 30 minutes **Prasad** and spiced milk were served. People started leaving at 5:30. It was a joyous and uplifting experience. I am sure it would be bigger next year. Afterwards, I suggested that before the inside ceremony, ladies, accompanied by their husbands, if free, also take 3-5 rounds (*PARIKRAMA)* of the temple from outside; signifying a parade of ancient culture!

Oct 25, 2002/Apr, 2011

HAVING SADHU AS HOUSEGUEST

Last year, my wife and her brother heard the *Gita* discourses of Anand Yogi at a friend's residence in Washington DC. She returned quite impressed with his knowledge and entertaining style delivery. He effectively weaves stories and jokes with the **SHOLAKAS** of the Gita and **MANTRAS** of the Vedas. They invited Anand Yogi to visit Las Vegas during his US trip. A month ago, one of his devotees called us from Atlanta, GA, "Swami Ji's program is to visit Las Vegas for a week on March 20."

That set in motion all kinds of conversational topics about his arrangements—from his diet to bedroom. First, my wife said let him stay in our son's room. Anand Yogi is of our son's age—both 1968 born. After a few days, she said that daughter's room would be better. About dietary restrictions and other requirements, she called friends in Washington DC.

However, I said, why not talk with Anand Yogi directly. He was very straightforward and summed it up by saying, "The way I live with my hosts is that they feel my absence, when I am gone after living with them for a month." Besides, being vegetarian, he had no special needs. A friend told my wife, "Your house would be blessed with such a spiritual person staying with you". That bolstered her mood. Traditionally, serving Hindu preachers is obligatory on the families.

I recall my young days in Bathinda where **SADHU** and **SANYASI** were a part of daily life. One met them in temples, in their tiny huts in **Sadhu Ashram**, usually on the outskirts of the city, or on religious festivals and functions. My college friend, Gulab Rai Mittal, used to joke, as to how at noontime the ladies of trading **BANIA** community would carry delicacies of foods and drinks for the **SADHUS,** while neglecting their husbands!

In India, there is another saying that having a **SANYASI** at home is like having 10 ordinary guests, as so much time and energy are spent in attending them. Swami Deekshanand Saraswati, my Mama Ji, used to stop at Bathinda at least once a year during his preaching circuits. His meals were cooked with **DESI GHEE** (refined butter), and served full cream milk and fruits. As kids, we really envied him!

My wife never had such an experience. Both of us being eldest in our families, our younger brothers and sisters have lived with us for months together. Now that we have crossed into the 60s and seen so much of life, I expect Anand Yogi's stay not affecting my routines. I clearly told my wife. We are the only two in the house. Certainly, I want Anand Yogi's stay in Las Vegas to be useful for Indian community. Free Yoga workshops at the university campus and *Gita* discourses in Hindu temples are planned.

Yet, I sensed some inner anxiety building up in the house for unseen reasons, as his arrival neared. One day, I noticed my wife concerned and curious how Anand Yogi would be dressed up while traveling in the plane! She could not imagine him in a *Sanyasi* garb. I said that I was not going to ask him about it, because I won't be embarrassed for him. Besides, I respect his individuality in this matter.

However, on the arrival day, she made sure that her brother and I both go to the airport to receive him, and not let him walk up to the passenger pick-up area. It was around 11 PM, when I saw Anand Yogi, a young man with trimmed beard, a big red mark (*BINDI*) on his *SANDALWOOD* painted forehead and upper arms. He had *RUDRAKSHA* strings around his wrists and neck, and wore high heel wooden toe sandals. Of course, one white sheet was wrapped around below his waist and the other thrown diagonally over a shoulder. He is well built and carries a persona of a *SADHU/SANYASI*. I felt like embracing him, but instead, greeted him with a pat on his bare shoulder!

April 03, 2003/July, 2012

COMMENTS

1. Bhai Sahib, I really enjoyed your graphic lucid narration of your account with a Sanyasi. You are indeed GREAT. I am still afraid hosting any Sadhu or Sanyasi in my home due to my bitter experience when I was deeply associated with the Washington, D.C. Hindu temple where so many Sadhus visited. But they left with no palatable memories. Greeting, hosting and feeding a sacred soul is indeed a holy task. But how to check his character and credentials? You did a good job! Your brother, **Suresh**

PERSONAL REMARKS

DEWALI OR *DEWALIA*

Today is Dewali, or Deepawali, the most joyous festival of the Hindus. Like Christmas in the US, Dewali is the name of a spirit that permeates the air for 3-4 weeks. One specific day is only a marker in a calendar. In India and the US, where Indians are now concentrated, business is feverish during a month preceding Dewali. Moreover, the houses are whitewashed, painted and decorated. Children and adults, with child at heart, go crazy with fireworks and sweets.

In the US, Dewali is celebrated, but its fragrance in the atmosphere is absent. Nevertheless, this cultural scene is far better than what it was 35 years ago when I came to the US. Mostly, Hindus perform *POOJA* (prayer) in their homes and gather in friends' homes. Temple celebrations are now gaining grounds. Yet, one who has lived in India for some years misses Dewali with a tinge. This morning, I decided to greet friends and relatives in India and the US. It gets you in a Dewali mood for a couple of hours.

First, I called my younger brother in Korea. It was 11:30 PM Korean time and 'technically' only 30 minute were left for Dewali. He was a little groggy, as he had just gone to bed. I do not have patience for a small talk since I started writing these reflections. I asked, **"Where is Dewali in your life this time**?" Not getting my point, he asked me instead, where I was going to be on a family Dewali gathering. Feeling a little out of tune, I said, **"It seems a Dewalia has set into your life!"**

Dewali symbolizes an illumination—it could be of heart, mind, and soul—including total environment. Because of its radiance, others notice it and feel joyous. On the other hand, **Dewalia means bankruptcy**. Again, bankruptcy could be one pertaining to heart, mind or soul too! Anything that is accumulated can be lost too.

Dewali is also a day of reckoning. Reflecting on this angle, I tangentially teased him, "Are you celebrating a Dewali or wallowing in a **Dewalia?** It is amazing how the two words when transliterated into English differ by only one letter 'a' at the end. However, their meanings are far apart. In fact, it takes a little effort to transform one mental state into the other! Happy Dewali to all of you!

Oct 25, 2003/July, 2012

COMMENTS

Thanks. In any language, there are words which change the meaning drastically by simply one letter or in Urdu by one dot (mehram vs. mujram written in Urdu language); God written by interchanging the word becomes dog, and so on.

These are two different words with different roots and Dewali is distortion of Deepawali. Having said that some people literally do become Diwalia on Diwali when they gamble and loose all. Gambling as you know is considered auspicious on this occasion

Thank you so much for the *Reflections* you have been sending me. It really makes my day!! I enjoy them very much. Yes, we forget the reason why we celebrate the holidays. We forget that holidays are here to rejuvenate ourselves, to find love and care for others and to stop and think. It is time to bring joy to others. Thank you!! Best wishes, **Prafulla**

SANSKRIT AND HINDU MARRIAGE

It has been a month since my younger daughter, Annie was married. People still ask me—how it all went? The one thing that stands out is her marriage ceremony. Annie and I were on the same page, though 41 years apart! It was 1963, when my marriage preparations were going on in Bathinda. Swami Deekshanand, then Acharya Krishna, was to perform the ceremony. I insisted that it be in Hindi, rather than in Sanskrit. I don't remember how he convinced me to stay with Sanskrit. But, a day before marriage, he spent two hours in explaining me the meanings of all the Sanskrit *mantras*. Without knowing Sanskrit, one cannot have any deep association with the rituals. Sanskrit, being an elitists' language, has hindered in forging national unity amongst the Hindus.

At the time of Annie's marriage, we also wanted that the ceremony be completed in 45 minutes with English translation of the Sanskrit *mantras*. My sister Madhu assisted by her husband Anal, did an outstanding job of performing the marriage ceremony. They laboriously scanned the entire *VEDIC VIVAH SANSKAR* (Vedic marriage manual), chose the right *mantras*, and translated them as close to the vernacular English as possible. A week before marriage, both of them went through a full rehearsal of marriage ceremony with Annie and her fiancé.

For the last twenty few years, I have been struck at the contrast of marriage ceremonies in Hindu religion with those in other religions. Sikh marriages, being in Punjabi, are understood by all gathered. A Muslim wedding is in a local language mixed with understandable Arabic words. Christian marriages are not in ancient Greek or Roman, but in national languages of the respective countries.

How does Sanskrit help in a marriage has been beyond me? It is a vestige of a Brahamnical caste hold on the Hindu society. For instance, in Punjab, there is a popular phrase—*EH KERE MANTAR PARNE HAIN. EH KAM TAN BARA ASAN HAI* (means: it is the recitation of the Sanskrit *mantras* that is difficult. This chore at hand is very easy). Recitation of Sanskrit mantras had become a benchmark of challenging task! A phrase captures the heart of social customs. **The more I ponder, the deeper I understand the abysmal state of Hindu society for centuries due to blind belief systems**. They nod and blindly do the rituals without any questioning on religious ceremonies.

Madhu and Anal have a computer file of the entire Hindu marriage ceremony in English. They are willing to share it with any interested party. A marriage ceremony is a social occasion that also brings a sense of unity in a community through common meaningful practices.

May 10, 2004/July, 2012

COMMENTS

1. The ceremony was beautiful . . . . whatever the language . . . . the people are beautiful . . . whatever the language . . . family love, support and involvement is necessary . . . . whatever the language! Blessings and have a wonderful day! Renee Riendeau

2. In principle I agree with your thoughts that wedding vows should be translated to the language of those being married. Rest of your conclusions is very much debatable. Rahul

3. Madhu and Anal have done a great job indeed. Entire Ceremony should be published in Hindi also. I would love to download it for someone's use. Brahmanism is the GREATEST CURSE. It might be next only to the CURSE of MYTHOLOGY inflicted upon the masses of this ancient land. Subhash

4. Well, I think that Sanskrit and Hindu marriage is something that have the relationship ever since we know religion have been originated. More than marriage it is related to our Hindu religion only. Sanskrit is the language in which all Vedas have been written, and if you believe in that, there were some era in which the gods Ram Bhagwan or Krishna used to live at that time.

5. It is indeed a tragedy that today's intellectuals pass their judgments on a subject of which they have little or no knowledge. One spends 20 years to get a Ph.D. degree in a discipline. How can one understand the esoteric and abstruse spiritual subjects by eating flesh and drinking liquor without observing any type of Sadhana which requires self-control, purity and austerity?

Vedic Mantras are potent with potency, efficacy and effectiveness. Their Correct pronunciation, comprehension of the correct meaning and their recitation with full faith will indeed charge the chanter and listeners with bubbling vibrations. Thanks. **Suresh**

ENCOUNTERS WITH RAMADAN & QURAN

After the **9/11 Attack on America**, each aspect of Islamic life style has drawn the attention of the US public at large. Ramadan is one of the hottest topics. Nearly 20 years ago, I started observing Tuesday fasts without any sip of water or bite of food till Wednesday morning. There has been a constant desire to experience an extended fasting including Ramadan month. However, my largely Hindu social circle in the US and India is not conducive to observe Ramadan fasting. A Hindu openly observing *ROZAS* (Ramadan fasts) means inviting too many questions and even criticism. In my opinion that defeats the purpose of any fasting.

However, during my two-year (1992-94) Indiana University assignment in Malaysia, an Islamic country, I decided to join my Muslim colleagues, students and neighbors in full spirit of the 1993 Ramadan (Feb 23-March 25). One visiting Professor Anwar Aziz from Delhi was very supportive in this experiment.

My desire was to experience Ramadan fasting at a deeper level. To make it complete in my way, I also decided to study Quran with an open mind throughout this month. It was a sheer coincidence, or call it providential, that a Malaysian neighbor presented an authentic English translation of the Holy Quran! Hajji Hanif, a Punjabi Malaysian lived in a house right across the one we had rented. I think if a scripture is presented by a believer, then its reading merits are enhanced. Talking of the Quran, I had one back in Las Vegas home—a beautiful two-volume set with calligraphic hardcover, in Arabic along with its English translation on the opposite pages. It had come to me as a gift from an Islamic Foundation 15 years ago.

In 1993, on the first day of Ramadan, I got up around 5 AM. After the usual preparation, I set the table for taking foods before dawn. Hardly had I taken a morsel or two that I felt like vomiting. I was told that it meant skip that fasting day, and make it up later. Being a little determined, I suppressed the vomit and went about the day without any solid food or drink. On sharing this dilemma with Professor Anwar, he told me that he never left the bed before 11 AM, and then he would go about the daily chores till sunset without eating and drinking. Since I had not taken a regular breakfast for years my digestive system was naturally thrown in a state of shock by the intake of solid food that early in the morning. Next day, I took nothing except my regular mug of tea. Two glasses of water are taken right after leaving the bed.

Doing any social thing together brings unity and power to a community. When you see the Muslim students and colleagues going without drinking water in over 90 degree Fahrenheit heat and high humidity, you are able to go through it too. **It is the thought of not eating that is problematic.** Any pangs of hunger or thirst are very short. The first week was rough with come and go pains in the back and stomach, and lightness in the head; all mainly due to no regular hydration. It takes at least one week for the body systems to adapt to sudden changes. Of course, I read the Quran every day. In one month, I gave it one full reading and went midway for the second! It has proved very informative and educative.

I am fully mindful of the act that the scriptures of any religion are not works of literature, history and science. What stands out is repetition of some lines and messages in several *SURAS* (Chapters of Quran). That is a feature of the Vedas too, where certain *MANTRAS* are repeated in different *SUKTAS* (Collection of *Mantras*) in different Vedas.

Also, there is a degree of esoteric nature and revelation about the scriptures in every religion. Otherwise, they would not have survived and been admired from centuries to a few millennia. Often the meanings are allegorical and metaphorical, rarely literal. For example, some British scholars of the 18th century have called the Vedic *MANTRAS*, as a collection of shepherd songs! Likewise are the ludicrous comments by non-believers on some stories and references in the Bible and Quran. I often explain this ignorance like this: Any ten-year-old kid can read the language in which a graduate level mathematics or physics textbook is written. But the kid understands little of mathematical ideas.

All the scriptures have a certain depth and breadth about them. I was cognizant of it while reading the Quran. Whenever, I ran into passages that defied my belief system, or found them non-rational, I would continue reading it after a long pause. I took copious notes, but decided not to discuss any point with a Muslim scholar for clarification, as I expected to reveal its meaning later on.

Recently, I wrote to a Muslim friend that Ramadan actually is a month of both fasting and feasting. Two hours before the sunset, the food stalls and eateries are decorated and stocked with exotic foods. Every one loads up with goodies while going back home. The entire family sits in front of the TV and waits for the daily announcement of fast break time. They literally pounce upon the food. Gandhi, a great exponent and experimenter with fasts had cautioned that keeping fast is easy, but breaking is difficult. I used to break my **ROZA** with a glass of juice and some fruit. After waiting for at least one hour would come full dinner followed by a glass of milk at bedtime.

I did not have any moment of divine understanding that Ramakrishna Paramhansa's disciple M (for Mahendra) wrote about Ramakrishna having it during Ramadan. Nor, I had an experience that prompted Vinoba to write a commentary after reading Quran. I for sure would have written several **Reflections**, but I was not in the writing mode then. I could not come close to Gandhi who was the most practical and pragmatic spiritualist ever to live. He eventually transcended all the scriptures! Personally, with my mathematical training and knowing its deductive power, the Ramadan fasting was all physiological, but certainly at a level never experienced before.

The main purpose of Ramadan fasting is to toughen the body and mind for battles and fights in the name of Islam. Prophet Mohammed was also a great army general and military strategist. A new testimony to the Muslim war preparedness is that amongst all ethnic groups serving the US forces, the Muslims have the best record in completing the grueling 8-10 weeks of basic training.

After 12-15 days of Ramadan fasting, the body goes into different gears. My case was unique since I continued to observe my Tuesday fasts on the top of it. Thus, I ate nothing on Tuesday nights. My body began to feel numb and started getting tingling sensations during waking hours. The major veins of the hands and legs almost vanished. They appeared wooden. But my ability to concentrate was increased. To feel a bit normal, I started light jogging in the morning and weight training for 25-30 minutes in the afternoon. That really energized me for the rest of the month, as exercise seemed to push blood circulation in the entire body.

As a part of the observance of fasting during Ramadan, one must avoid daytime sex besides food and drink. It is not weird; fasting instead of diminishing the carnal desire, gives it a boost! For men, it may have long-term unhealthy effect for not being able to replenish soon after a drop in physical agility. For me, it was made a little 'easier' in one sense and 'difficult' in the other, as my wife was gone to India for the first three weeks. Thus, Ramadan remains an unforgettable experience of our stay in Malaysia. I did not have any urge to observe it during 1994, nor ever again. My 52 Tuesday fasts in a year are enough, but I still wish to extend one to 5-7 days under some medical supervision.

On returning to Las Vegas in 1994, I did not find in the shipment the copy of Quran that I had studied in Malaysia. I felt sad and upset for a long time. However, 2-3 years later while passing through Malaysia, my landlord told me a story of its discovery since my name and notations were on it. I happily brought it to Las Vegas, and placed it amongst other scriptures. One day to my utter disbelief, I noticed that the Malaysian copy was gone from the bookshelf, and an entirely different copy was there! I checked it from all our acquaintances, but no logical explanation of the disappearance of the first and appearance of the second has ever been found to this day. The biggest surprise came two years ago, when the Malaysian copy reappeared again! This time, the other copy did not disappear.

This whole Quran phenomenon reminds me of the unscathed copy of the holy Quran belonging to President Mohammed Zia of Pakistan who died in a fiery plane crash in August 1988. The media covered his intact Quran no less than his tragic end. In fact, I also published a reflective piece then. In the absence of any rational explanation, I won't accept a non-rational one. Now with three copies of Quran on my shelf, a month ago, I presented the two-volume set to the permanent collection of Lied Library of UNLV. The Malaysian copy is still with me!

The 'mystery' copy of the Quran was passed on to my sister and brother-in-law (both devout Hindus) who have been observing Ramadan **Rozas** for the last 15 years. They are social activists and thinkers. A fundamental question arises: Does a Hindu observing *ROZAS* during *RAMADAN* become an instrument of weakening the Hindu society? Certainly, it does not promote unity amongst the Hindus. At the same time, nothing—like five pillars of Islam, rigidly conforms upon an individual in Hinduism.

Oct 20, 2004/July, 2012

COMMENTS

1. A Hindu cannot observe Rosas. That is a contradiction. Rosas is not merely fasting—as Westerners often think—but fasting in the name of Islam. A Hindu may fast in a manner similar to that performed by Muslims during Ramadan; but by definition, only Muslims may observe Rosas. Similarly, a non-Muslim may take a pilgrimage to Mecca (assuming they were allowed to); but only a Muslim takes the Hajj. Any non-Hindu can pray, but only Hindus perform Aarti. The differences in these terms are more than just semantic. So use them with care!—**Avnish**

2. Your reflections about fasting and Quran along with your personal experiments with fasting and mysterious disappearance and reappearance of the Malaysian copy of the Quran are informative and revealing. Mysteries are experienced by all of us once a few times in our life and we go on searching for rationale and explanation. Perhaps this is why all religious beliefs get sustained over centuries and followers are prepared to go through any amount of self-sacrifice. All religions owe their inception to the circumstance, environment and social value systems prevailing at the starting point of time at the particular geographical location. Although no religion preaches directly violence and intolerance; but in recent years these have got upper hand in some religions and even suicidal squads get into the organised and civilised society in the name of religion and getting every human being converted to the particular sect. THANKS. **NIGAM**

3. Rozas are not real fasting in real sense as one eats every 12 hours instead of 6-8 hours. In winters it is even less as the duration of day is shorter. You did not comment on contents of Koran. How similar or different did you find from other scriptures? As for your sister and brother in law keeping rozas, I say all power to them. Hinduism is a universal religion and keeping rozas does not weaken it but strengthens it. Having said that the way one practices religion should be the way one gets peace and bliss because religions are based on promise of eternal happiness. **Rahul**

ON COLLOQUIAL MECCA

This morning in an e-mail to a friend in Delhi, I wrote that during the 1960s through 80s, the Mathematics Department of Indiana University, Bloomington was the **Mecca of Operator Theory,** a sub-branch in higher mathematics. The students and experts from all over the world used to come there for study and research. Suddenly, my thoughts stopped in the tracks. In the aftermath of **9/11 Attack on America**, any Islamic reference strangely jolts the mind.

Substituting Mecca with a Hindu place of pilgrimage—like, Varanasi, Prayag, Puri, or Triputi, does not come close to the sense as conveyed by Mecca. Besides, the places in north India are not that well known in south, and vice versa. I settled on Haridwar. But does it convey the same spirit as Mecca does? Really not! Then I tried other religious places. Bodhgaya is holy to the Buddhists, but they don't flock over there. Jerusalem is sacred to the Christians and Jews, yet it is not a magnet for them, as Mecca is for the Muslims. For the Sikhs, all the five *TAKHATS* are holy. It is the proverbial use of Mecca by every denomination that really speaks of its global appeal and attraction.

The *Hajj* is one of the five pillars of Islam. During a certain lunar month, the Muslims converge to Mecca from all over the globe. It unifies them physically, mentally and spiritually. The *Aadi* Shankaracharya (788-820 AD) had grasped the urgency of the integration of the Hindus after the Buddhists and Jains had broken away from them. He simplified the number of Hindu temporal seats of authority to four *MUTHS* (Centers) headed by four Shankaracharyas (spiritual leaders)—one each in north, south, east and west. It was the first organized attempt to unify the Hindus in history.

Had this unification process continued in other aspects of Hindu life, some place of pilgrimage might have achieved a stature of Mecca. With all the freedom in picking a pilgrimage and prayer etc, the Hindus have remained divided and diluted in every walk of social and political life. Prophet Muhammad (570-632 AD) fully understood the causes that weakened a society. That is why each pillar of Islam lays emphasis on community. In Islam, individuality remains subservient to the Islamic society as a whole.

May 18, 2005/Apr, 2011

COMMENTS

1. Actually, Satish, you might know the concept of "dhams". Yamunotri, Gangotri, Kedarnath and Badrinath are the big ones. Some people count Puri as a dham, too. **Sandeep Krishnamurthy**

2. Satish: You have turned into a storyteller. I enjoyed reading it. Best wishes, **Alok**

3. I really am not clear on what points are you trying to make here. Is it Hinduism has no center hence are not united or Islam makes society subservient. Actually Varanasi is to Hindus what Mecca is to Muslim. In scriptures it is written that if one dies in Varanasi one goes to heaven. I do not know what makes you think that Hindus in South India are not aware of Varanasi or Prayag or vice versa. When a Hindu goes to pilgrimage he goes to all important temples including Haridwar, Varanasi, Allahabad, Triputi, Rameshwaram, Badri Nath, Kedar Nath to name a few. Have you heard about Kumbh Mela's they are as big as Hajj gatherings if not bigger?

If you think homogeneity (your so-called unity) leads to survival of a religion then you are dead wrong. Hindu heterogeneity survived the Muslims and Christians onslaught and will continue to do so. If Muslim religion was so strong they should never have been conquered. Right. But the history of Islamic nations proves this theory wrong. **Rahul**

4. Dear Bhatnagar Sahib, Thanks for your e-mail. It is a very nice thought you have expressed in your writing. The last line that you have mentioned, **"In Islam, individuality remains subservient to the society as a whole", is very thought provoking. Thanks for sharing your thoughts with me. Rajinder Singal**

FASTING BEYOND RELIGION

"Are you not having breakfast today?" asked my roommate in a Mexico hotel, where I was there to attend an archeological course on Mayan Mathematics and Astronomy. "I don't eat on Tuesdays, as a part of my fasting," said I simply. "Is it for any religious reasons?" followed its natural corollary. "Yes and no both. No, as it is not mandated by any authority, and yes, because anything that you do it for 15-20 years does become religious." He smiled and we quietly felt in agreement. Perhaps, two math professors having common interests tend to think alike!

It almost happens every week. A conversation on fasting takes different turns and twists amongst the Hindu acquaintances, as there is an infinite variety of fasting regimen in Hindu religion. Other religions have very specific fasting days. My reason has been very simple. Being indulgent in eating for six of the seven days in a week, one non-eating day provides a relief to my digestive system.

However, my line of thinking switched back to the notion of 'religious'. Is a mechanical reproduction or repetition of an activity truly religious? My answer is certainly, a no. Then I ask myself, why? A religious activity is an upward movement towards a goal whose shadow or edge is hardly visible. When Einstein while working on famous Unified Field Equations said, "God does not play dice," he was being religious in spirits, though he seldom went to a synagogue. Newton' name is also associated with a similar quote, as he was always at the frontiers of new knowledge.

The organized religions have a place in each section of a life span. Their very existence is a proof of some values. However, going to church, temple or mosque at age 5-10, tagged along with parents, is not the same as going at 25, or 65. The organized religions successfully organize masses for social and political ends. However, when it comes to individual consciousness, they definitely do lower its level, rather than raising it. It reminds me of a famous political quote: If you are not a socialist during your 20s, then you do not have a heart. But if you are a socialist after 40, then you don't have a head.

A religion is a sort of golden mean between aspirations of an individual and his/her community. It is bound to vary with each individual. After a certain period, if you do not cut the umbilical cord of your 'graduate' school, call it any organized religion, then the greater vistas of life are going to be missed. Such are my fasting thoughts today!

July 05, 2005/Aug, 2012
(Mexico)

COMMENTS

1. I fully agree with you and I have myself practiced fasting on Tuesdays for about twenty years. Now I have given up fasting as it put extra strain on heart, this is what I feel. As such I have reduced daily intake instead of fasting. Even on religious occasions my fasting is just symbolic as I take non-cereal food.
THANKS **NIGAM**

2. Hi Satish: I have just read this brief informative and witty piece. I like it. **Moorty**

3. This is true for all things including religion. One's views on all things keeps on changing and evolving as change is life. However your choice of Tuesday for fast does seem to have the subconscious Hindu effect. Any ways here is the gist of my comments on your reflection. (Again I choose Ghalib)
Hum ko maaloom hai jannat ki haqeeqat lekin dil ko khush rakhne ko, Ghalib' yeh khayaal achcha hai. **Rahul**

4. Hello Dr. Bhatnagar, Once again, a wonderfully insightful piece. Thanks. **Arti**

HINDUISM 101

"Chris, would you like to have a drink?" I asked my roommate in a Mexico Hotel where we, twenty-four US professors were attending a 6-day (June 30-July 5) archaeological course on *Mayan Astronomy and Mathematics*. "No, I don't drink." After a little pause, knowing that most Americans do drink socially, I said, "When did you stop drinking?" "Being born in a Mormon family, I never had a drink." Chris replied.

Amongst other things on my familiarity with Mormons in Las Vegas, I told Chris that I admire the Mormon practice in which 18-20 year old young boys leave their homes for 2-3 years on Church missions in foreign lands. My younger daughter has married a Mormon. Chris quietly listened, but it quieted me when suddenly he said, "I am no longer a Mormon! My elder brother and I have quit the Church." The Church of Jesus Christ of Latter-day Saints is commonly known as Mormon Church. It aroused my curiosity.

Chris, nearly age 50, is a family man and math professor in a Midwest college. After a day, he told me that over the years, he could not accept some religious tenets and practices of the Mormon Church. On the top, he was to continue to believe and not inquire and question. Feeling intellectually suffocated and against their conscience, both brothers (mathematicians) quit the Church. They have written a book on this aspect of their lives. One can read it online: www.suddenlystrangers.com.

"Have you now joined some other Judaic-Christian Church? I inquired. "No," he replied with conviction. "Now you are a Hindu!" I told him with firmness in my thoughts. Chris was startled and showed eagerness about Hinduism that he knew little about. **It is my firm belief that a scientist of a stature (like, Nobel laureates) and mathematician, in particular, cannot be a practitioner of any organized religion—whether of east or west**. He/she may have some dormant beliefs about an organized religion.

"Hinduism gives an individual ultimate freedom to seek his/her truths in life from any direction and angle. One can question any authority whether enshrined in a guru, prophet, avatar, institution, or scripture. Although there is no one scripture in Hinduism; yet there are at least 100 treatises each as profound as the Bible or Quran. Hinduism has no birth year, and has no one founder. But it has a galaxy of great minds, mostly nameless that have nourished it—from its roots to its flowers ever since man started thinking."

It was a sort of my short monologue. However, I cautioned, "Many sources of Hinduism—whether from internet, books or persons, are likely to confound you. Initially, stay focused on the inquiry of your thoughts." Finally, I broadly connected organized religions with mathematics. I said, "Practice of Islam is like getting the extent of knowledge of mathematics that comes after passing high school. Christianity and Buddhism are equivalent to acquiring mathematics with a bachelor's. It is Hinduism alone that takes one to a graduate/doctoral level and beyond to even lay claim of ownership on newly discovered mathematics!" Chris listened without saying a word.

Hinduism 101 was also the title of my toastmasters' speech delivered last Monday, July 25. It was a 12-minute speech with objectives for developing an entertaining dramatic talk about an experience including vivid imagery, characters and dialogues. This material has been hovering over my mind since the time spent in Mexico. It got a strange twist after attending a four-day (July 21-24) annual convention of Arya Samaj of North America in Tampa, Florida. Arya Samaj is a late 19th century reformist movement of Hinduism.

In the speech, I tempered my remarks by saying each religion has a place in a society. For example, Islam prepares its adherents as the best fighting human machines. On the other hand, I have not personally known any Muslim who has pursued PhD in an abstract area of pure mathematics. The reason is simple that its pillar of five prayers (**collective in Islam vs. individualistic in Hinduism**) a day does not leave long blocks of time needed to contemplate on research problems that may take several days! Of course, exceptions are always there in human situations.

I concluded my speech with a Lincolnian note—that Hinduism is a religion of the free, by the free, and for the eternal freedom of mind.

July 29, 2005/Apr, 2011

COMMENTS

1. . . . . Liked your Reflection on Hinduism. Hinduism is an open platform, like Linux. Participants are welcome to modify or improve the "code" (ideas or wisdom). If the improvement is "Good", i.e. adds value as perceived by the "community" of participants, it is accepted and others build on it. Its strength is that a large number of diverse participants contribute to its growth. Linux is always evolving & so is Hinduism. **Jyoti & Tushar**

2. Very well written article about Hinduism, It's really good to know that at least someone is taking efforts to educate others about Hinduism and that too without trying to convert them which are so common in other religions. **Nidhi**

3. Hi Satish: What an interesting piece—a piece that melds religion and mathematics. You are absolutely correct! Hinduism is liberating, inward looking, and satisfying without external restraints and constraints. In fact, all your life as a Hindu you don't have to go to a temple or attend an organized congregation. It enables you to attend any Christian church activity without feeling guilty. It is more a philosophy for the individual rather than a religion—it is a way of life. I like your articulation of thoughts on Hinduism. **Moorty**

4. This is one of your few Reflections where I agree with your thoughts. To quote "Hindu" Einstein: "I cannot imagine a god who rewards and punishes the object of his creation or who has a will of the kind we experience in ourselves. I am satisfied with the mystery of life's eternity and with the awareness of and glimpse into the marvelous construction of the existing world together with the steadfast determination to comprehend a portion, be it ever so tiny, of the reason that manifests itself in nature. This is the basis of cosmic religiosity and it appears to me that most important function of art and science is to awaken the feeling among the receptive and keep it alive". **Rahul**

5. Dear Dr. Bhatnagar: Yes this is really true and Hinduism is really very liberal and also no real authority or teachers at these temples. The priests are interested in making money just showing fire and giving water and chanting mantras no one understands. It is their job for the priests and they do not teach any religion and some do not even know what God is. It is interesting, now the Christians know that lots of things they do at

Churches are not real and that is the reason the membership is between 30 to 40%. I do scan the TV on Sundays and these evangelists just want to make money of the weak-minded people and some got their own jets and Rolls-Royces. **TV Rao**.

DISSEMINATION OF IDEAS & RELIGIONS

Every time, I come out of public lectures by renowned speakers in arts, sciences, or business, I am buffeted with a tide of thoughts. The main reaction is—how come such public dissemination of ideas is non-existent in independent India? Last December, I was in metropolitan Chandigarh of nearly 3 million people, only one or two educational functions were listed in the *Sunday Tribune*. It is the youngest modern city in India!

By way of contrast, yesterday, though a weekday, there were five major events on the UNLV campus alone—two of them were free to the public. One was a lecture by the Nobel Laureate (Literature, 1993), Toni Morrison, the first in a new Black Mountain Lecture Series. The other was by Michael S. Turner of University of Chicago cosmologist and a member of the National Academy of Sciences. His lecture was also the first in another new Arthur C. Clarke Lecture Series to encourage creativity in sciences.

Such lectures are a tip of an iceberg. The historic Chautauqua Courses and lecture circuits of scholars—like, Durant, define the unquenched thirst of the US public for new ideas. Will and Ariel Durant (1885-1981), the co-authors of the classic 11-volume, *The Story of (Western) Civilization*, were freelance speakers—became an institution in themselves!

UNLV provides a public setting and environment, but not the money. The financing comes from the endowments set up by visionary individuals and corporations who strongly believe that an enlightened public makes a stronger nation. Toni Morrison may have been paid $20,000 plus expenses, and Michael Turner around $15,000. It is not a small price tag, but the public is not charged! The cutting edges of science and mathematics belong to the societies that are organized, prosperous, and knowledge driven.

Where does this symphony of masses and intellectuals come from? In my opinion, it is basically embedded in the organized religion of the land! That is Christianity in the US and Western Europe. In the ultimate analysis, science becomes religious and religion scientific. In India, more than 80% of the population is of the Hindus. The Hinduism, giving absolute freedom to question and inquire, becomes inimical to its own organization. The challenge lies in balance.

However, until a current of ideas of the Ganga River breaks out of the boulders of the Himalaya, my reflective bits and pieces in this direction will continue. I am fully convinced of a strong correlation between the emanation of great ideas in arts, science and literature, and the organized religion. In the spirit of Tagore's famous poem, *Let My Country Awake*, I would say, **Let the Hindus of My Country Awake!** Then alone, Tagore's 75-year old dream in this poem will become a reality.

March 07, 2006/Aug, 2012

COMMENTS

1. . . . . I believe religion and science are same. Only misguided think that they are different. I also feel that it is not Hinduism which is required for growth of science. It is Humanism . . . . Hinduism existing in last two thousand years is not the same as that which was in days of Upanishads . . . . There is always a silver lining to the cloud. In Calcutta, New Delhi, Bombay, and Madras (Chennai. One can see Cultural activity. **Subhash Sood**

I wrote: It took a lot of my mental energy, and revised it even after clicking it away at 1 AM. Read Tagore's poem and then think of my twist on it. What you call Humanism at 70 I truly did it at 15; no offence!! Our time is running out.

Subhash: Thanks for a quick reply. It is 12 midnight and I am reading your letter. Our ideas are so close, it is so marvelous to behold . . . . You have not offended me. I consider that your intellect is indeed superior to mine. That of course has very little to do with one's ideas.

2. Hi Satish, Excellent observations but what is the solution? We Indians rarely consider anything outside of our work as worthwhile to pursue. Why this lack of vision? May be we all need to be awakened to realize that there is a world beyond our workplace that we are part of and must participate in. **Gopal Das**

A DILEMMA OF WOMEN AND HINDU MALES

".... What are the reasons behind such treacherous acts by our Hindu adult girls, whether it is Southall & Wembley of London or in India, USA/ Canada etc? Why we cannot educate them in the way Muslims infuse Islamic thoughts in their children from birth? . . ." This is an excerpt of a recent e-mail personally received from a widely traveled Hindu leader in India.

Sometimes, a *Reflection* needs a little external push to come out, as it has been incubating my mind for a while. I have asked my wife that how come the Hindu girls are attracted towards the Muslim youth in far greater proportion than the Muslim girls towards the Hindu men—apart from the Muslim laws restricting certain inter-religious marriages. The disproportionate dominance of Muslim actors in Hindi movies is a part of the same social tapestry.

Hindu society, in particular, the Hindu males suffer from the *LANGOT* (symbolized by an airtight three band 'brief' for males) syndrome. The *LANGOT* syndrome has many variations and offshoots in public life. The foremost effect is that it inhibits Hindu males looking at girls even with the mildest lust. On the top, the myths are perpetuated that the *LANGOTDHARIS* conserve their virility for later stages in life!

During my college days, the co-education was introduced in 1955. A pervert classmate used to declare every good-looking girl his sister to the extent that he would pick up fights with guys for making any enticing moves towards those girls. The Hindu males encounter sexual dilemmas in terms of their ties with females in close circles. For the Muslims, in particular, the only forbidden sexual relation is between real brother and sister.

For the Hindu males, since teen years, when the hormones start raging out of control, it is a daily battle to control passions towards sisters, female cousins, and even their female friends! The only release of sexual tension comes, perhaps, once a year, during the *Holi* festival when the two sexes have liberty to intimately play with colored water and dry colors! Another festival of *RAKHI (RAKSHA BANDHAN)* is precisely meant not only to publicly affirm the sanctity of bonds between real brothers and sisters, but also psychologically nip any mental weakness of brothers towards their real sisters. At times, it is extended to near and far off female cousins too.

Let me state it at the outset that I am not advocating for breaking, challenging, or abolishing the millennia old traditional bonds and barriers between the Hindu brothers and their biological sisters and female cousins. No other religion, except Hinduism, emphasizes that sex is not the only relationship between a man and woman. Nevertheless, there are two male scenarios in the society at large; one that has little sexual inhibition that includes religions of the east; the others are Hindus. The Sikhs can be grouped with the Hindus in this regard.

I have known two Hindu sisters, 20 and 22-year old, both having amorous relations with a Muslim man for a long time. Recently, an 18-year Sikh girl, studying in college away from her parents, has found her first love in a Muslim boy. The daughter of a Sharma friend, born and raised in London, started wearing **Burqua** the day after she married a Muslim lover! My small sample may not be statistically sound to draw definitive conclusions.

The Hindu society has to connect the dots. The time has been calling for years. The **LANGOT** on the loins suffocates the mind too. Often, it damages the phallus and libido of the males. To make it worse, the suppression legends are glorified by the myths of god **Hanuman** and the likes of Swami Dayanand, as **Brahamcharis** (celibates). The physical prowess has nothing to do with **LANGOT**, or not getting married!

When the **LANGOT** mentality and multiplicity of female ties are mixed, then Hindu males explode into confusion on confronting pretty females. The biggest insult of a charming woman is if she is repulsed by the males, or the males treat her as touch-me-not! So, when a woman is approached by two males—one wrestling with **LANGOT** syndrome and the other free from it, then it does not take Freudian analysis to tell who is going to win her favors.

There is a story about Chatrapati Shivaji (1630-1680), who was presented a beautiful Muslim woman of his enemy. Instead, he ordered his soldiers to safely escort her back home. The dream of every woman is to be closest to a man with the power of money, politics, status, or intellect. She would have gladly accepted to be a consort of Shivaji. In contrast, the legend of Alauddin Khilji's (ruled 1296-1316) infatuation with Queen Padmani of Chitor speaks of a different mindset towards women.

The Muslims marrying the Hindu girls has been a part of Muslim culture the way they convert Hindu temples into mosques. A few years after the

1947 partition of British India into India and Pakistan, a bilateral exchange of women took place. I vividly remember a Muslim girl in Bathinda happily married with a Hindu bearing three kids, was evicted. On the Indo—Pak border, she was quickly married with a Muslim man in waiting in line!

On the other hand, the Hindus disowned Hindu women from Pakistan and declared them impure for having lived with the Muslims. Most of them ended up as prostitutes on GB Road, Delhi, or committed suicides. Their lives fill the pages of contemporary novels and stories written by Jamanadas Akhtar, Amrita Preetam and Dutt Bharati. Being never empire builders in last 1000 years, the Hindus have not converted a mosque into a Temple.

Can the Hindu males win Muslim girls? By and large, after mixed marriages, the Hindu girls are more easily integrated with their Muslim in-laws than fewer Muslim girls with Hindu in-laws. Do I have a conclusion to draw? Yes, **liberate yourself from the mental *LANGOT***! Go a step further; do not put diapers on the male babies as long as possible! It is not funny; the results will show up. It is small step for a larger Hindu society!

Aug 11, 2006/Aug, 2012

COMMENTS

1. The reasoning why Hindu women marry Muslim men is hilarious and simplistic at best. **Rahul**

2. You're living in a time warp and you seem obsessed by *langots*. What world are you living in? I thought that the trips that you take to India every year would have shown you the changes that occurred from 1968, but it is true that we see what we want to see. According to you Hindu rulers like Shivaji were people whose low libido was responsible for their empathy. How weird is that?

For god's sake don't write these kinds of articles—they are completely irresponsible, not thought through and obsessed with LANGOTS. **Aniruddha**

3. Dear Dr. Bhatnagar, I could not agree with you more. The concern you have voiced in the first paragraph of your "reflection" is exactly what Pujya Pandurang Shastri Athavale's (**Pujya Dadaji**) Swadhyay work has been trying to do with good success. Historical characters like Hanumaan and Dayanand Saraswati exemplified certain virtues and qualities like devotion and dedication to culture. Not getting married was a life style they chose for their own reason/s. **Hasmukh Joshi**

4. I differ on this one, gone are the days when the Hindu men used to look at women like their sisters . . . .
   When it comes to lecherousness, **MEN** in general are very active participants it has got absolutely nothing to do with "*langots*" or religion. Men are men everywhere irrespective of their age, religion or relationships.

Regarding why Hindu girls fall for Muslim boys that's a different story all together you will always find a few cases everywhere, just like how Muslims don't appreciate getting their children married or rather all these marriages are "eloped" marriages or "love" marriages the same is found in Hindu households too. **Nidhi**

5. An astute observation and well-written commentary. I have to agree whole-heartedly with you.
   Also I have noticed over the years and commented informally about the following phenomenon. Undergraduate students from Pakistan land

here and within weeks find a white beautiful girl friend and go around with them. Some marry them, give them beautiful silk clothes and gold jewelry, take them for a visit to Pakistan, and the girls are soon speaking "insha Allah". The students get their green cards. Some of them try to go back to home country permanently after marriage, but the girls do not last there for more than a few months. The Indian (Hindu) students have done none of this and do not have the courage to ask the girls out. **Ved P. Sharma**

6. Excellent Factual observations, Sir! P.S.: I am taking the liberty to forward to other people for their possible benefit please. rgds/ **Satish Chandra Gupta**.
   (I am also enclosing a wonderful writings of our Shri Satish Chandra Bhatnagar, a highly learned Scholar in Nevada, USA, which is an eye opener please.)

7. Yes, I think there is a lot of truth in what you say especially in the Indian context. Thanks. **Abraham**

PERSONAL COMMENTS

A FOUNDATION OF HINDU VIEW OF SEX

"*GHAR MEIN TERI MAAN BEHAN NAHI HEH*? (means: don't you have mother, or sister at home?" is a very common retort from women accosted by boys in India. There are local variations. **It comes from a belief system that you look at every woman only as sister or mother**. The colloquial phrases capture deeper moral and ethical values of a society. The cumulative effect of such an atmosphere is repression of male libido.

A recorded incident in the life of Swami Dayanand is of a 7-year old naked beggar girl in Haridwar walking by him. Swami Dayanand, strolling on the bank of Ganga River, stopped and saluted her addressing as mother. Impact of this incident on the Hindu psyche is no less than that of his magnum opus, the *Satyartha Prakash* (Light of Truth).

The Hindu life overflows with psychological festivals. The first nine days of two lunar months, *Ashwani* and *Chetra,* six months apart, are considered very auspicious. On the 8th or 9th day, a bunch of 6-8 year-old neighbor girls are invited to the homes. They are treated as little goddesses (*Devis*), their feet washed by the hosts/hostesses and gifts given at the end of nice meals. The analysis of such a biannual event is that at the positive extreme, it sublimates male sexual energies. At the negative end is its repression that muffles individual creativity that often explodes in parallel with the sexual one.

In the Hindu kingdom of Nepal and adjoining regions of India, a girl of 4-5 year old is chosen according to astrological signs. The girl is elevated to the level of a living deity. She leads a protected life style and gives *DARSHAN* (appearance) to the masses, who seek her blessings. At the onset of puberty, she is retired and the search for a new Devi begins.

Hindu sex behavior is a reflection of multitudes of gods and goddesses in Hindu pantheon. Once my wife remarked, "I never heard of Santoshi Mata before leaving India." Last week, she innocently said, "Gayatri Ma resembles like Lakshmi." The images of all the gods and goddesses are only manifestations of humans. Their features, complexion, dresses are given according to local geography and prevalent customs.

The bombardment of female divine images has deeper effect on the Hindu mind. **The biggest is fear and the second is social ostracization,** if apprehended. In Punjab, the fiercest fights between two males take place when one swears the other invoking mother or sister. Honor killing is the other side of the same belief system.

An overtone of Hindu mythology is sexual suppression and inhibition. Sublimation of sexual energy is only for a few. The Hindu *Tantrics*, advocating free sex, remain underground. More Hindu masses worship various goddesses than the trinity of male gods—***Brahma, Vishnu and Mahesh*** combined. In contrast, the Muslims and Christians never face such situations. It is no brainer that sex wise they are relatively less inhibited.

Aug 14, 2006/Aug, 2012

COMMENTS

1. Dear Dr. Bhatnagar, I do not know from where or when outlook towards sex as a taboo got introduced to Hindu psyche. The idea that every woman is a mother or sister does not go with the purpose God created opposite sexes. This outlook towards other women is I think applicable to married men. For single young men and women it is natural to look upon a member of opposite sex as a potential like partner. In the 7th chapter Shloka 11 God himself says I am that desire that is righteous, *"Dharma Aviruddho Bhuteshu Kamosmi Bharatarshbha"*. Those who portray sex a taboo are mistaken as are those who profess free sex. **Hasmukh**

I wrote: A social practice is a recursive function of history and infusion of new ideas. A Book alone does not determine it.

Hasmukh: Unless the book is written with human psyche, needs and experiences in mind which the Bhagwat Geeta is. Human behavior is of course guided by a multitude of factors inclusive of what you have mentioned.

2. *How did u come to the conclusion that sex wise Muslims are at ease? I have never found such orthodox people in the world. Yes, they can marry 5, but nowadays, very few do that.* Abraham

3. Frankly I do not know where to begin. Your assumptions and conclusions are based on half-baked ideas. *Kamasutra* is very much Hindu. *Kamasutra* and Devi worship flourished together among Hindus. The stories in Mahabharata. Purans, Bhagwatam, plays by Kalidas and others are full of lust and sex. I will counter the argument that influence of Islam on Hinduism caused inhibition of sex. An example will be that *Pardha* (veil) was practiced among Hindus in Northern India where there was more Muslim influence. In South India it is not practiced. Islam on other hand is very controlling religion and controls interaction between sexes and sex. I am disappointed by your article.

USHA SHARMA: A HINDU PREACHER

The US is the biggest magnet in the world for a person of any vision, dream, and entrepreneurial spirit. It is safe to say that even if you have not succeeded anywhere else, you can still succeed in USA. Also, if you cannot succeed in USA, then you cannot succeed anywhere! That is why the USA is called a land of opportunities. More importantly, the US provides a level field for any enterprise one wants to engage in.

Two days ago, I spoke with Usha Sharma after many years. I have 'known' her for 40 years, but our paths never crossed more than a couple of times. It was a sequel of coincidences that I came to know of her visiting USA. Recently, Harish Chandra, a Hindu preacher of its own kind was introduced. During his 2-month USA-Canada visit, we had several communications. It was during our last exchange that he mentioned Mauritius and Arya Samaj. Usha Sharma was a natural corollary, as she is pretty well known in Mauritius for her Arya Samaj work in the community.

Jaidev Shastri, Usha Sharma's husband, is the first disciple of (Late) Swami Deekshanand Saraswati, my maternal uncle from his Bathinda *Gurukul* days. I met Jaidev each time I was with Swami MamaJi during my India visits. Both husband and wife have served the Hindu community in Greater Delhi for years. As a matter of fact, she comes from a family of dedicated Hindu leaders from Tamilnadu. After PhD in Sanskrit from Delhi University, she taught in Delhi, and later on in Mauritius. During her stay in Mauritius and Kenya for 6-7 years, she authored a number of books and booklets. Incidentally, both husband and wife have been leading a *Vanprastha* (dedicated to public service) life.

The strength of a community lies in its unity, and the unifying force of any community is also in the hands of its religious leaders. **They too have the ability of bringing the masses and intelligentsia of all rank and files together at one place**. Honoring them is our cultural obligation. While giving her an idea of **Post 9/11 Attack On USA**, I apprised her that whereas, the Christians and Muslims are far more than united, but the Hindus are further marginalized in the US. It is a challenge for any Hindu preacher to first bring the Hindus out in the open, and then convince them to drink water from the same fountain.

Arya Samaj, Oakland is the first to host Usha Sharma. Interested parties may contact her through Pandit Krishen Dev: (510)-654-3217. Besides Hindi and Sanskrit, she is fluent in several other Indian languages, and well versed in performing Vedic *Sanskars* (Hindu religious ceremonies). This being her first visit to USA, she is here through the end of March. Female preachers are very rare even in India. But they are not unexpected in the realm of Arya Samaj, as its founder, Swami Dayanand Saraswati (1824-1883) advocated for women's emancipation—including widow marriages, education and social equality far more than any other social reformer of India.

Jan 02, 2007/Aug, 2012

COMMENTS

1. It has been a challenge for any preacher (not just Hindu) to convince people to drink water from same fountain. Look at so many sects in all religions. Since time immemorial it has been a dream of all humans to make everyone else like what they are (because they think they are the most righteous) and it never happens. Diversity is the law of nature. Humans have independent thoughts and even these thoughts within one human being are never the same. **Rahul**

I wrote: Yes, if the focus remains on individual all the time. My observation is relative to other communities. Of course, that is where a challenge is.

2. Best Wishes to Usha Sharma, this is a lot from a hard-core scientologist. Subhash Sood (This is Subhash's last comment, as he died of a sudden stroke in April, 2007)

A *PEEPLE* STORY

During a smorgasbord of conversations in India, I told an uncle about my flair with *Peeple* trees. My eyes fall upon the *Peeple* sprouts in all weird places. A few days ago, I took an unusual picture of two *Peeple trees* growing 10 feet apart (uncommon). Strangeness about them was a wall built in a manner that half of the tree trunks were on one side and the rest on the other. The wall was not going through the trees as often seen in the US parks. The Hindu ethos is to keep boundary walls straight while not disturbing the trees.

The Hindus not only have reverence for *Peeple* trees, but they are also very superstitious, if a *Peeple* tree is accidentally uprooted. Anyway, I told my uncle about photographing two nearby *Peeple trees* in the same neighborhood he lives. The moment he heard of them, he was fired up! I could not believe his excitement at age 82.

Being the President of the housing society when the colony was under construction (25 years ago), he had the entire development landscaped. All the *Peeple trees* in this colony have a story about them. Years ago, uncle owned a rental house in another city. He had a problem selling it due to a humongous *Peeple* tree growing out on its own terms. The buyers were naturally reluctant to buy it because of this monstrous *Peeple* in the yard.

Despite high unemployment in India, even daily wage labor flatly refused to cut this *Peeple* down for fear of divine reprisals. The Hindus don't even prune a *Peeple*, so chopping it down is absolutely unthinkable. At that time, uncle was a top-notch government bureaucrat. He sought the assistance of relatively a junior officer heading the horticulture department that takes care of public parks and buildings in the capital.

The horticulturist staff removed the *Peeple* from the yard. Uncle avoided knowing its details. He knew no Hindus would swing an axe or run a chainsaw on a *Peeple* tree. While the chopping project going on, uncle was not really at inner peace with the whole scenario. Hindu reverence for *Peeple* is independent of their economic strata.

In the meanwhile, uncle read in a book of KM Munshi, a well-known Hindu thinker on atoning sins of cutting down a *Peeple* tree by planting 10 of them! The story really takes a twist here. Uncle went to a limit in this regard. He had ten offshoots of the *Peeple* in his yard transplanted in his colony. He gleefully explained that all the *Peeple* **trees** in this colony are the offsprings of that tree. Technically, that *Peeple* is living in its progeny!

Peeple is not a houseplant—for the front or backyard. In the *Geeta*, Lord Krishna, sermonizing Arjun, lauds *Peeple* to the extent that amongst the trees, He is *Ashwatha* (Sanskrit name for *Peeple)*. In Hindu mythology, people worship *Peeple* to exorcise demons and ghosts due to the curse of Planet Saturn in the Zodiac. Life thrives on bedrock of faith as long as there are no obvious contradictions. **However, faith is not a resort or refuge of irrational life styles**.

Nov 03, 2007 (India)

COMMENTS

You have very ably highlighted the religious diktat, among the Hindus, against the cutting of the *PEEPLE* tree and planting ten new ones if one has to be cut down out of dire necessity. The piece was highly informative and provided an interesting and enjoyable reading. What perhaps, you could add, for your readers, was its two qualities making it an ideal absorber of green house gases and thereby making a significant contribution to environment protection. It has a very long life. Secondly its leaves remain green all the year around and very few of them fall in autumn.

You could also mention the Hindu custom of watering the tree regularly to ensure its longevity. Its regular watering is believed to ensure for the believer a place in heaven. In my colony there are two Peeple trees; one falls on the way to the park where I in the morning for my Yoga. I had befriended an 80+ lady who would water the tree and apply vermin and tie the sacred red coloured thread-'Atta' to its trunk every day along with a few more old ladies. One day I found a signboard placed by the owner of the house in front of which stood this majestic tree stood—prohibiting persons from its worshiping. The old lady was crest fallen and complained to me about it. With great difficulty and with the intervention of the President of the Colony's Welfare Association, we could get the puja restored with the modification that instead of putting vermin and tying coloured thread around the trunk of the tree, the ladies could place some rice grains there. Of course the practice of daily watering was restored.

WHEEL BEARINGS OF HINDUISM

Being in a mood to see myself through different prisms, I decided to go for an organized weekend tour to the famous Hanuman temple in Salasar. My 2nd younger brother, recently retired, also came along. The group of nearly 50 persons was heterogeneous, as it included infants, teens, adults, and seniors at age 70+—but more males than females.

The bus started off at 7 AM for its 10-hour journey in Rajasthan. Hanuman is a major Hindu deity symbolizing service with humility despite being the ultimate embodiment of physical strength and courage. Instead of sweating for those qualities everyday, the Hindus believe in being blessed by recitation of *Hanuman Chalisa* and offerings at His temples. If physical courage and strength lacks in any religious group, then paradoxically it is amongst the Hindus. Unfortunately, the idols and deities have been in the general Hindu psyche for the last 1000 years. It thus makes them vulnerable to every invader.

During the ride, the mood was periodically revved up by the religious videos of various devotional songs and dances. Often someone would loudly hail Hanuman and then exhort the rest to hail back. It creates religious camaraderie. Eventually, I got to know a few passengers. Four of us shared a dormitory type accommodation and restrooms.

The window seat that I always prefer lets me contemplate as the landscape is constantly changing. I carried a copy of the *Noopur*, a Hindi publication focusing on the stories of Ramakrishna Paramhans and a diary for my notes. Thus during the 24-hour journey, my time was divided between four frames of thoughts.

It was obvious that this part of the country belonged to the Hanuman devotees. Apart from the names of cities like Hanumangarh, there were several Hanuman temples on the roadside and in places where we halted for breaks and meals. Preparation of some food items and drinks made it a religious picnic. That was a highlight of the trip too.

We visited four temples including three ancient ones. The temple in Sardar Shahar was clean and only three years old. It is a marvelous piece of temple architecture, made with red stone and marble. Yet, it attracted the least number of devotees! On the other hand, at the *Aarti* time, the crowds in

Salasar and Khatu Shyam were so tight that weak ones could get suffocated and trampled, if tripped and felled down. The filth and squalor inside and around the temples are signs of its ***Pracheenta*** (old age). It does not bother the Hindu devotees. Cleanliness is next to godliness—it rarely applies to the ancient Hindu temples.

The crowds were managed by police. But it is free for all, when Hanuman ***DARSHAN*** time clicks in. People are transported in different states and seem disconnected from life around them. For instance, no one is concerned about the bomb blasts by the Muslim terrorists in cities: Lucknow, Faizabad, and Banaras over the same weekend. However, a few fellows were keeping scores of a current cricket match between India and Pakistan!

Nov 27, 2007 (India)

IT HAPPENS IN AMBALA

There is no point in differentiating between a saint and saintly person, but Bhaisab (his only name), at 70, has arrived at *spiritude*, a state of 'certainty' in spirituality. He started on this journey 32 years ago after winding up his flourishing college, known as Sadashiv in Ambala Cantt. Bhaisab was born, raised, educated and employed as college lecturer in Ambala. Thus he has defied a popular saying: *GHAR KAA JOGI JOGNAA, BAAHAR KAA JOGI SIDDHA*. It means a local person, no matter how great are his achievements, is good-for-nothing, whereas, an outside achiever is deemed divine.

A secret of Bhaisab's recognition is that he not only completely withdrew from active public life, but also secluded himself indoors. That naturally adds to mystery and mystique to the persona. Recently, he started writing short pieces on the devotional aspects of Hinduism. A book, *GOD 'N US,* written in a question-answer format, contains his views on aspects of Hindu divine life. His discourses on the Bhagvad are telecast on local cable networks.

My Oct meeting with Bhaisab was brief, but it stands out in its own manner. It fits into the saga of a home search for Sadashiv, the congregation. Ever since the first location was dramatically vacated 20 years ago, they have moved 5-6 times. Bhaisab has his own mind. The main reason for selling the previous home was that he wanted the members to take their money out as it was needed during old age. Once the Center was sold, the dilemma was to find a new place for *Gambhira*, a new name of the congregation.

Well, here a divine drama unfolds. A retired couple moves from Delhi to Ambala—man served in the elite Indian Police Service. It is very uncommon for the Delhites to retire into a sleepy town like Ambala. Any ways, the couple with devotional bent of mind, got actively involved and figured Bhaisab's dilemma out. They sold their property in Delhi and bought an 'investment' property in Ambala that met Bhaisab's conditions. The financing is very creative. The monthly 'payments' come out of the members' capital gain placed in a fixed deposit. It is win-win situation for everyone!

On the one hand this home saga always has a divine twist in it, but on the other hand, I wondered at the making of Indian police or army, where the officers have such a devotional bent of mind. Belief in God is one thing, but being devoted to the Krishna and his Gopis does not send a right message to the criminals and the enemies of India.

The idol worshippers have weakened the Hindu army since the battle of Somenath Temple in the 11th century. It encouraged hoards of foreign invaders to attack India. Today, the Chinese, Pakistanis and Al Qaeda must be happy on finding such a devotional mindset taking hold of Indian Police and defense forces. They need not penetrate the rank and files. **A paradox of life is that the excessive love of God is not good for everyone!** It supports a popular saying that the excess of everything is bad.

Jan 12, 2008/Sep, 2012

COMMENTS

1. Some how your article does not jive. Har Har Mahadev, Jai Kali Ma, Jai Durga are some of the war cries of Shiv Bhakats and Devi Bhakats. I do not see how this will affect the mindset of defense forces. A retired police officer joining a group of Krishna devotees has no effect on security of country. Both Ram and Krishan were warrior kings and if anything their worship should install in a person to stand against evil. I do not see any weight in your arguments. Sorry. **Rahul**

2. Bhai Shri Satishji Sasneh Namaste! Your reflections of Ambala & "Bhai Sahib" are wonderful pieces of literature once again—besides giving us immense thoughts on the pseudo Hindus worship before the idols in the temples, doing Nothing to do anything neither for the Society nor for the country, & getting killed mercilessly by the Muslim Invaders like Mohd. Gauri in the 11th Century.

Initially, with the advent of Maharishi Dayanand Saraswati & awakening which were created by his followers, namely, Arya Samaj, things seemed to be improving earlier, but once again, all the MEDIA is taking back our Hindus, to 18th / 19th century, which is a pity. Best regards. **Satish Chandra Gupta.**

MUMMY JI: BUILDER OF HINDU COMMUNITY

The beauty of life is that it can shine on most uncommon places and persons. Yesterday, it struck me, when I attended a memorial *pooja* (prayer) for an unassuming, and yet a graceful lady, who was simply known as Mummy Ji in her small circle. A week ago, she took her Last Breath.

Every life is defined by its legacy. Mummy was instrumental in building the first Hindu Temple (Sai Baba) of Las Vegas (LV), in 1985. That earns her a rightful place in the history of Indians in LV. She and her husband moved here nearly 25 years ago after retiring from a successful business, perhaps, in Hong Kong. The first thing they did was to build a small temple in the backyard of their house. Soon after her husband's death, Mummy immersed herself in her Temple. Gradually, her large family of children, grandchildren, and great grandchildren cooperated with her in the upkeep, running, serving **Prasadm**, cleaning, and in the maintenance of the Temple. Thursday evening *satsang* quenches a thirst for Hindu spirituality in LV desert.

History of most Hindu temples is that an affluent devotee comes forward and builds a temple for the community. Temples built by communities are post-independence phenomena, particularly outside India. The Sai Temple may look small for a large Hindu community of LV. But it must be borne in mind that at construction time, the community was also very small.

During the **pooja**, I inquired, "Sushma, what was Mummy's name?" "Thakur Bai Asnani," responded Sushma, her youngest daughter-in-law. I could not believe my ears. **Thakur Bai** literally means a lady in the service of the Lord! All these years, none cared to know her name. Amongst the Hindus, the name is given according to horoscope charts during a specific naming ceremony. Mummy truly lived up to her name! What else is the purpose of life?

Mummy's wearing impeccable white saris added a glow to her fair complexion. Her sights often stirred memories of my own mother. The years of temple service in the name of Narain Baba, the family Guru—in line with Sai Baba (Shirarhi), eventually rubbed into her persona. At the conclusion of every service, when she invoked blessings for each devotee after gently touching a holy headwear on the forehead, her face glowed with divinity. My steps were irresistibly drawn towards her. What a sight and good feelings!

While sitting in the congregation, it bolted me, that here was a lady who did not even have a high school diploma. But look at her legacy of love, compassion and care for the people who came in her contact. The wisdom does not come from the college degrees alone! Lovingly, Mummy 'trained' the youngers in the chores of the temple. This continuity of temple care is remarkable.

The sacrifices of her next generation for the temple are already impressive. In order to expand the temple size by a small area, and meet the city building ordnances, two adjoining houses were demolished and re-built! Life of a temple is longer than the life of an individual, and of a family. In Mummy's name, the family may set up a Trust, if not already there, so that this tiny temple is remembered as one of the historic landmarks of Hindu community of LV.

Apr 11, 2008/Sep, 2012

COMMENTS

1. Great obituary. **Rahul**

2. Reflection on 'Mummy Ji' is touching and evocative. Good job. **Moorty**

SANATAN MEANS NOT-ETERNAL!

If the mind revolves around a certain question or problem—whether deep or mundane, then new insights do flash up. It does not mean right or wrong, but new perspectives are different from stereotypes. Such an experience bolted out last Saturday. I was at the Hindu Temple and listening to a group of devotional singers. The lead singer, referring to Hinduism (***Hindu Dharma***), stressed that it is more appropriately be called as, ***Sanatan Dharma*** (Eternal Religion).

I have heard it said since childhood. One gets conditioned by repetitions. Rejection of a thought requires courage; physical and intellectual. But it was a different moment at age nearing 70. My mind stopped there. While the singers continued to sing, I was probing on a parallel track the 'whyness' of eternity of Hinduism, or ***Sanatan Dharma*** (no quibbling over the terminologies).

Human beings are biologically prone to chronology. Their collective will makes traditions and histories. Thus, I scanned Hindu landscapes. Beginning with birth records—before independence, 90% of Indians lived in villages. Records or markers of births and deaths are in shreds. The British introduced it in city municipalities, but its registration was not mandatory. For the literates, birth dates entered in the 10th grade were official! Reincarnation, a pillar of Hinduism, makes dating unimportant. Cremation of the dead focuses on the insignificance of human life.

What about chronologies of Hindu educational, political and social institutions? Specifically, I tried to track institutions that could be dated as 100-1000 years old. While the devotees were swaying with devotional melodies, my mind was wrestling with this question. I could not find any solid national institution started by the Hindus. Exception; Dayanand founded Arya Samaj, a reformist social organization in 1875; still going robust. However, the big picture is depressing.

What about the dates of Hindu monuments—palaces, gardens, and temples etc? Yes, my hometown, Bathinda has the oldest fort in Punjab dated (by carbon or neutron?) more than 1200 years old. In 1965, I was awed even by total ruins of a palace of Emperor Harsh Vardhan in Thaneshwar, now a twin city of Kurukshetra. **The destruction and ruins of Hindu monuments across India politically symbolize the weakest state of Hindu Diaspora today**. In the caves of Ajanta/Ellora, or in ancient temples like Trichipallai,

Meenakshi, and Puri, their dating and naming seem sacrilegious. It is made secondary to divine! But that does not make them eternal!

Hindu mindset looks at finer pleasures of life obliquely. It only became a cornerstone of Hindu life after their subjugation by waves of foreign invaders (100s of them!), who plundered and massacred the populace countless times since 1000 AD. Disproportionate number of Hindus living in the villages is due to their escaping from humiliations in towns controlled by foreign rulers. **Chronology is an attribute of free and brave mind**—it defines every identity.

There is nothing eternal in the universe. Even the points on a circle, once you identify with one point, then circle becomes linear. Hinduism is not *Sanatan* or eternal in my mind! There is a starting point. It is lost, but can be found. That is how I walked out of the temple premises.

Sep 24, 2008

COMMENTS

1. Satish Ji, You are right that Hinduism is not **Sanatan**. Other than that I see a lot of confusion between the literal meaning of the word "**Sanatan**", its rough translation and its equivalency to Hinduism . . . .
Unfortunately, Hinduism cannot be claimed to be **Sanatan** (though we will all love to proclaim it). Our Vedas are the only scriptures that can truly be called **Sanatan**. However, after the introduction of **Puraan**, things changed. **Puraan**'s mixed myth with facts. One small bit of lie invalidates the whole statement. Today, we actually follow the teachings of **Puraans** instead of Vedas. Not only that, we claim everything to be Vedic (even though it is **Puraanic**). No distinction is made between Vedic and **Puraanic** literature. My apologies, but you have done the same thing in your open letters. But **Sanatan** does mean Eternal truth. It has nothing to do with the chronology of events that you have mentioned. Regards, **Arvind**

I wrote: This *Reflection* is written in the context of a popular observation, that there is a definite starting year of Buddhism, Jainism, Christianity, Islam, and Sikhism; but Hinduism is eternal/Sanatan. I have stayed away from any scriptures or any claims about them. A scholarly challenge is to agree on a time frame.

2. Shri Satish Ji, Saprem Namaste! Having gone thru your noted article, I admire yr deep Thinking & wonderful Analysis. Thanks & Congratulations! Warmest regards, Sincerely yrs, **Satish**/Mumbai

3. Thanks for some insight into what you think about what concerns all of us—Hindus and like people. Keep me posted. **Narinder**/Dr N K Khetarpaul MBBS, Hissar

4. Namaste: The present Hinduism is far away from the Vedic Dharma. However, the Vedas have their origin in God. Thus, Vedic Dharma is eternal, i.e. it doesn't change with time. It's common to hear 'Satya Sanatan Vedic Dharma'. Some people term Hinduism as equivalent of 'Satya Sanatan Dharma' though present Hinduism has many non-Vedic ideas such as idol worship, God reincarnating, etc. Sometimes I get to read your articles after a long period. I like to read them leisurely. Warm regards, = **Harish Chandra**

THEOLOGY AND MATHEMATICS

"In 1669, Isaac Barrow, the first occupier of the Lucasian Chair of Mathematics at Trinity College, Cambridge, resigned to devote himself to theology, and Isaac Newton was appointed to the chair on Barrow's recommendation." As I read this sentence in Stillwell's book, *Mathematics and its History* (2002), it unleashed a stream of thoughts.

My study of Newton's life and work is ongoing. Partly, it is due to the colonial connection between England and India, the land of my national origin. For that very reason, during India stay, my exposure to the European minds was limited. Before independence in 1947, the indigenous sprouts of modern science and mathematics were very rare in India. Despite having read numerous accounts of Newton's life and works, there is a definite time and space when the mind is more sensitive to the depth of a certain idea connected with the era.

A gamut of thoughts that ran through my mind is: 1. Did Barrow find mathematics intellectually less challenging than theology? 2. Did he go for more money, power or/ and prestige than the new Lucasian Chair offered him? 3. Certainly, Barrow's scholarship in theology and mathematics must have been close that he could easily jump from one area to the other. 4. Like—this closeness between Christian theology and mathematics, since the 16th century, is there a similar closeness between Islamic theology and mathematics, Hindu theology and mathematics, Buddhist, Jain and Sikh? However, the focus of my investigation is on Number 4.

As my mind was still engaged with these questions, a colleague remarked, "Fundamental research in mathematics gets more difficult past the youthful years, often mathematicians turn towards soft intellectual pursuits, in later years." Yes, that is a well established, since mathematician, GH Hardy laid it out, in his book, *A Mathematician's Apology (1940).*

However, Barrow turned only 36, when he resigned from the Lucasian Chair! During his Lucasian tenure, he had published two mathematical works of great learning and elegance, the first on Geometry and the second on Optics. Later, he composed his **Expositions of the Creed, the Lord's Prayer, Decalogue, and Sacraments**. Some of his works in theology, particularly on the power of papacy, are immortal. The Popes in Christianity are like the Ayatollahs and Muftis in Islam, Lamas in Buddhism, and Shankaracharyas in Hinduism. However, the authorities they wield over their followers are extremely different in respective societies.

Whereas, Newton's statues and portraits are displayed far beyond the corridors of Trinity College, Barrow's statue sits right inside the Trinity Chapel. Trinity became a leading confluence of theology, mathematics and sciences for the next 300 years. Incidentally, Astro-mathematical physicist, Stephen Hawking, the 16th holder of Lucasian Chair since 1980, has just stepped down in May 2009. It is worth noting that before Newton became the Master of Mint in 1696, his interest in science and mathematics were already weaned away by theology and esoteric pursuit of alchemy, 'the art or/ and science' of converting base metals into gold. Newton also wrote several tracts in theology during the 1690s.

In the backdrop of Newtonian era, the present off-and-on controversy between creationists and evolutionists are intellectually puerile. As compared with the 17th century Europeans minds, the intellectual making of a present person is lopsided. Generally, the study of science excludes religion, and conversely. In the US state universities, theology is completely out of the curriculum. To me, it is ridiculous, as during my student days in India, one was not allowed to study science and mathematics with philosophy and humanities. It took me years to fill these deficiencies in my intellectual development.

An offshoot of theology is the dual role Jesuits friars/fathers played in proselytizing and educating in European colonies during the 19th and 20th centuries. In India, these celibate friars taught in several Catholic colleges—like, St. Stephen and St. Xavier. Their high academic standards and professional devotion with deep religious values influenced generations of Indian leaders. In Europe, from the 16th to 19th century, many discoveries in sciences and mathematics came out of men steeped in Christian theology.

Islamic theology ever coming close to science and mathematics is an open question. And that was one of the reasons of my spending 2009 spring semester in the University of Nizwa, Oman, an Islamic Sultanate in Gulf region. Six years ago, the Islamic clerics in Pakistan rejected Bush Administration's offer of nearly 500 million dollars for introducing science and mathematics in over 50,000 *madrassas*, the Islamic religious schools. It was rejected in a referendum by a vote of 84:16. Without a good nursery, there is no plantation; without a lab there is no science.

The dominance of Jewish scholars in science and mathematics strongly suggest a correlation with Judaic theology. The Nazi Holocaust pushed the Jewish theology in every aspect of Jewish life. **The Jewish Nobel Laureates almost outnumber the rest from other religions combined!** These achievements are simply amazing for people with worldwide population of only 15 millions—spread in 50 countries!

I am a Hindu and born in a Hindu family, but it took me sixty years to realize the depth of my thinking process, and its connection with Hinduism. The question of Hindu theology and its interaction with science and mathematics is uniquely different. The religions of the west stress upon organization over individuals. For the last one millennium, Hindu religion has become essentially individualistic—letting individuals have absolute freedom of thought and inquiry. Consequently, the historic Christian crusades against the unbelievers, ongoing Islamic Jihads and Fatwas against the infidels, and Sikh Hukamanamas against the non-conformists, have no counterparts in Hinduism.

Conceptually, the abstract mathematical inquiries and Hindu theological thoughts appear to be the closest. Great Hindu mathematicians of the yore or the recent ones, like Ramanujan, attribute and dedicate their mathematical discoveries to their personal/family gods or goddesses. Ramanujan's famous line, **"An equation for me has no meaning, unless it represents a thought of God "**, is an ultimate synthesis of mathematical thinking and Hindu religious rituals.

However, the modern history of the Hindus in science and mathematics is relatively too short to make any viable connection with Hindus theology— lying buried for centuries due to foreign subjugations. It needs intellectual dusting and polishing by new generations of Hindu scholars. The only exception is Shankaracharya Bharathi Krishna Tirath whose groundbreaking book, *Vedic Mathematics* (1965), brought mathematics and Hindu theology closer in modern times.

In India, the Hindus got their political freedom in 1947, but the Hindu governance of India has a long way to go. Psychologically, the Hindus have yet to emerge from several forgotten holocausts suffered during the last 1000 years of political domination by foreign rulers—Muslims from all over and Christians from Portugal, France and England.

Buddhism, started as a 6th century BC reform movement of Hinduism, eventually crystallized its theology on a far greater analytical plane. It puts equal emphasis on organization and individuals. As its ethos spread over China and Japan between 3rd BC and 3rd AD, it transformed the intellectual culture of the new lands while enriching the native traditions. During Han Dynasty, for example, science and mathematics showed the first great signs of development.

In the study of mathematics or theology, one easily accepts the premises in one body of knowledge over the other. Without any common platform for the resolution of apparent differences, in a present US culture, one outrightly rejects the other. For instance, the current foundations of mathematics are no less questionable, and they will continue to remain in flux. Yet, the applications of mathematics are producing marvelous results.

On the 'non-mathematical' side, the lives of persons like Gandhi and Mother Teresa were grounded in their respective Hindu and Christian theologies. They have equally impacted mankind. Such men and women live in every age and place. On Gandhi's assassination, Albert Einstein had famously said, "Generations to come will scarcely believe that such a man, as this ever in flesh and blood, walked upon this earth." Einstein combined science with humanism at the highest levels.

In conclusion, theology, science, math, and all other intellectual ideas emanate from one human mind. After ricocheting and traversing, they bounce back onto the human mind. **It is a wonderful scenario of unity in diversity, and diversity in oneness**. The ultimate purpose of theology or of science and mathematics is to enhance our understanding of the universe, solve human problems, and leave the world a better place for the next generations. Any differences are superficial, indeed. Nevertheless, mathematics remains a 'sport' of the young, and the theology of the matured. The twains meet at a Golden Point in life—in me at 70!

Oct 15, 2008/Sep, 2012

PERSONAL REMARKS

IV.   HINDUISM—
   MISCELLANY

GRASSROOTS OF INDIA'S SECULARISM

A Muslim colleague, known for six years, expressed his relief and jubilation at the fall of the BJP Govt. He, like most Muslims, strongly believes that BJP is a party of Hindu fundamentalists, and Congress Party a bastion of secularism in India. This colleague comes from a well-connected family in Bangladesh. I explained that BJP's negative image is mainly a media creation—both in India and abroad, and orchestrated by power hungry Congress Party. Nevertheless, intellectuals are not easily swayed. However, it became a personal challenge to be clear in my own mind on the understanding of India's secularism vis-a-vis Hindu fundamentalism, if any.

Secularism in the Constitution of India: First, it is worth recalling, that the members of the Constitution Draft Committee and the Constituent Assembly which approved and adopted the Constitution represented all political parties. The concept of secularism was not much of a moot point as some Articles of the Constitution were. India was partitioned and the Muslim League, with British connivance, got new Islamic theoretic state of Pakistan, as a haven for only 60 % Muslims in the region. The remaining India was renamed Bharat—not Hindustan, the land of the Hindus, as the entire India was known to the world since the 10th century.

However, according to the founding fathers, Bharat, or newly divided India was to be a place for everyone who did not believe in the two-nation theory of the Muslim League. To the best of my knowledge, there were no walkouts, boycotts on the inclusion of 'secularism' in the Constitution of new India. Nor, was there a debate on a brand of secularism—like projected by the Congress Party, Communist, Akali Dal, or Hindu Mahasabha, etc.

In this context it is also to be pointed out that when India's independence was imminent, Gandhi wished that the Congress Party be dissolved, as it was much more than a political party under his leadership. It symbolized a huge national movement. Gandhi was not even a primary member of the Congress Party. But Nehru, Patel and Azad did not like this thought. They knew that dissolving the Congress would spell multi polarizations, and they may not get public mandate they enjoyed. Above all, they were impatient to get into the seats of new power.

Secularism is not Congress Hegemony: Secularism in Bharat/India, supposed to be more for religious tolerance in public life, has lead to communal vote banks during the Congress regime. It is astonishing to note that bigger and more communal riots have taken place during 25 years of continuous rule of Congress than during the British rule! The entire blame may not be attributed to Congress, as the then national leaders did not have any experience of governing a vast and diverse population. On the record, either Congress has failed, or has failed the current interpretation and practice of secularism. The time for a fundamental change is overdue.

The Fountainhead of Secularism: Secularism, as envisioned by the founding fathers and for which Gandhi gave his life, is embedded in the cherished ancient heritage of India. If we briefly look at the early leaders of freedom movement—from the end of the 19th century to the beginning of the 20th, then to name a few, one encounters great men like—Vidyasagar, Gokhley, Tilak, in political arena, and high souls like—Swami Vivekananda and Raam Tirath in Indian public consciousness.

They were all staunch Hindus, and they believed in the Hinduism of ancient *RISHIS*—embracing all people, all creeds, all thoughts. Gandhi was a devout Hindu. His autobiography reveals that his heroes came from Hindu folk tales, and he derived inspiration from the Hindu scriptures. Gandhi's maxim, that **Truth is God** is the epitome of the *SATYANARAIN KATHA* (that God is Truth Personified) recited in every Hindu home!

Hindutva captures the secularism of India. After all, terminology aside, how one is to capture all what India has done and stood over the centuries in welcoming believers of all foreign religions—including Jews, Parsis, Muslims and Christians. Hindutva is the spirit behind it, and today BJP is the only national party that is not ambivalent about it. During the later phase of the freedom movement, there were leaders—like Vinoba Bhave, Acharya Narendra Dev and Bhagwan Das, who were passive forces of Hindutva in Congress.

Hinduism and Democratic Traditions: Let us have a look at Indian secularism from a new perspective by examining the political evolution of countries of South Asia. Afghanistan, a Muslim country; Nepal, a Hindu country and Thailand, a Buddhist country, were never colonized by any European power. In Pakistan, the democratic model envisioned by its founding leaders, hardly survived a couple of years before the army took over it. The story of Bangladesh is similar—the democratic Govt. of Mujabber Rahman was thrown by the army after a couple of years, and the unrest continues. In the Buddhist countries of Sri Lanka and Myanmar (Burma), the democratic rules have been touch and go.

In India alone, a democratic model has survived all constitutional crises, civil unrest, wars, but never an army takeover! The system is resilient and getting stronger. It is a pertinent question to pose, why in a vast country like India, democracy and the cliché of unity in diversity continue to be vibrant. It is due to Hindutva that pervades all walks of life.

Hindutva transcends all religions of India. The communist parties, while in power in Kerala and Bengal, did not create re-education camps for their political opponents. Jyoti Basu did not stop the Bengalis from worshipping goddess *KALI*. The temples were not shut down, as the churches were done in the Soviet Union. The spirit of Hindu religion is too powerful and pervasive. The real secularism lies in Hinduism and is embedded in Hindutva. It is time to understand and support it.

June 22, 1996/July, 2012

COMMENTS

Hello Satish, It is very impressive. A very good analysis, with facts to back it up too. **GoPaul**.

1. Bhai Sahib, It was pleasure to read your article about Hinduism and how it is that secularism is imbedded in it. This should be read and understood by more and more people in India and abroad. How political ambition of Congress is distorting this years old pure Hindu philosophy needs to be spread. Ranjana Kumar from Charlotte, NC.

2. Very well said. And besides, Hinduism is not one monolithic philosophy, thought or practice. **Ved Sharma**

3. Satish, I agree with you 100% that Hinduism is a great religion. I am proud to be a Hindu. (I always considered myself a Hindu though in a narrow sense I am a Jain. To me, Jainism is a branch of Hinduism.) . . . . You raised the issue that Hindutva is secular. I am confused by this statement in practical terms. Are Hindus secular from within in a broader sense? **Sohan Jain**

ON THE MEANINGS IN SCRIPTURES

For the last couple of years, the IP (India Post, owned by a Hindu publisher) has been encouraging its readers to express their views on Islam and its practices. For this position, the IP has been threatened by the zealots on both sides to continue or discontinue the public debates. But the freedom of expression guaranteed by the US has not wavered the IP. The IP needs to be applauded for it. Having read all the letters and articles, I have come to a point of some saturation on the topic of Islam. However, I would like to make two general observations in this regard.

One, if one wants to understand any major religion by reading its scriptures alone, then it is full of pitfalls. No scripture is written in phrases that can be correctly understood; whether it is Quran, Old or New Testament, or the Vedas. I have personally gone through all of them and missed their meanings by miles on some points. The language is generally terse, metaphorical, and full of regional allegories. One must study any religious scripture with deep faith and deeper scholarship.

Having been raised in Arya Samaj culture, discourses on the Vedas always impressed me. In 1975, I bought a centennial edition of all the four Vedas— first time translated into Hindi. I wanted to taste the Vedas directly! Over the years, with my efforts alone, I have not found them more than the songs of the shepherds, as characterized by orientalists like Macaulay!

At the same time, the Vedic discourses (videotaped) of Pandurang Shastri, the 1997 winner of the ***Templeton Award for Religious Understanding***, have transported me into the states of intellectual ecstasies. It equally applies to other religious scriptures. To put it differently, any ten-year old kid can read any mathematics textbook written, say, in English. However, does it mean that mathematics behind English is understood? NO!!

It is time to limit this ongoing "debate" on Islam—particularly, when the Quran is directly quoted. That brings me to the point number two. If one wants to understand Islam, then it is better to deal with people of that faith around you and visit Islamic societies. Islam is practiced differently from Morocco to Indonesia.

One sees all kinds of contradictions and variations reflecting the history and culture that prevailed in that region before the advent of Islam in those regions. I just spent seven months in Malaysia and a week in Kashmir—they are two different Islamic worlds! President Jefferson, in a private letter, had said that one's personal conduct is the real index of the religion that one professes.

Dec 04, 1998/July, 2012

VATICAN AND YOGA

Yoga is a flagship of Indian heritage. It is India's best export. By any estimate, yoga is a worldwide billion-dollar industry. The Hindus do not have monopoly on the yoga anymore. Many foreigners have mastered its fundamentals. During mid 1960s, yoga got some international notoriety, when the Beatles boosted Transcendental Meditation (TM) propounded by Maharishi Mahesh Yogi.

During the very first phone conversation, Anand, a young itinerant yogi from India claimed that his yoga techniques can make a person look 15 years younger. Having practiced yoga *aasans* (physical postures) since boyhood, I could sense his 'sales' pitch. Anyway, I organized his eight yoga workshops on UNLV campus. Despite posting flyers at prominent places, only 4-5 white Americans came for it. Americans don't like anything free! In Las Vegas, there are at least five yoga centers charging $10-15 per hour for instruction. Most companies hold regular yoga workshops for their employees. The techniques and instruction in yoga are secular.

One day, on noticing a building custodian working around the area, I invited him to join Anand's workshop. He said, **"You can't recruit me!"** The tone of his response struck a strange cord in my mind. Nearly twenty years ago, the Vatican had issued a caveat against yoga. The Vatican believes that yoga gradually leads one into other aspects of Hinduism. This injunction against yoga puzzled me for a long time. But this simple remark of the custodian suddenly unraveled its mystery.

For the nation builders, a fundamental question is what type of society is needed. During the last 1000 years, the Hindus, despite making at least 80% of India's population, have been the weakest people in the world—run over by everyone. The poverty of India of the last 100 years has taken her soul out. The present India is only a shell of its glorious past.

The yoga *aasans* lead to surreal concepts—like *MOKSHA* and *SAMADHI*. What image of an individual doing yoga is conjured up? A person sitting in a lotus posture for hours with eyes closed. What inner changes are wrought by such a practice? Certainly such persons are incapable of physical adventures on land, sea and space. They don't explore the frozen tundra of the poles, burning plains of the Sahara desert, or the dark bottoms of the seas. The yoga would not produce he-men for WWF or players for the NFL and NBA.

Above all, the yoga does not inculcate any team spirit and togetherness. In ultimate analysis, **its impact is generally conceived otherworldly**. From my personal experience and observations of yoga practitioners, it is good for non-competitive and non-aggressive lifestyles. A misconception about meditation is that one gets enlightenment of all knowledge. Granting some knowledge, it can never be of modern science, arts and literature.

Therefore, the Vatican is not wrong in discouraging yoga—as, its acceptance may lead to the acceptance of other aspects of Hindu life that are not at all enviable. In general, the values of Western lifestyle are very different from that of historic Hindu life.

Personally, my quest has been to rediscover yoga as spiritual science of harnessing the mental powers through meditation. **Energy may then be harvested and stored in the body that is readied through specific yoga *aasans*.** Finally, the energy is released and distributed for the welfare of the society at large. This project is ongoing!

Yoga may help an individual to optimize his/her potential. But it is at the cost of the collective role in a family or society. **No two yogis are known to have pooled their energy in any one direction**. A vibrant society cannot let its men and women sit still for hours. I have no qualms with the Vatican's decree against the practice of Yoga. The key lies in moderation.

Apr 06, 2003/July, 2012

HEAVEN IS RIGHT HERE!

Sometimes, there is such a strong premonition of an event to come that I continue to wonder even after its materialization. Either it is the manifestation of my 'energy' focused on it for some days, or just some law of probability. My brother-in-law often arranges tickets for UNLVino, a wine tasting event in Las Vegas. It is a gala event held in a hotel and casino. Nearly 10,000 people converge to sample over 2500 different wines. This year he regretted his inability to get the tickets.

The show was set from 3-7 PM on Saturday of May 1. **It was during a short nap that my daughter called exactly at 3 PM about two spare tickets**! My new son-in-law had bought the tickets to oblige his clients, but they could not come. My niece-in-law and her husband are visiting Las Vegas, so we both men went to the Show.

Back home, my wife and niece being teetotalers, they wistfully inquired, "How was it?" "Heavenly," was my response. While returning home in a tipsy mood, I engaged the young man in a conversation on heaven and hell. Specifically, I asked, "What is the Hindu vision of a heaven?" We agreed on plenty of milk, honey, and nymphs floating around are the images of a Hindu heaven. About the Muslim heaven, there was little argument. The most voluptuous virgins wait for the Muslims in heaven, particularly those who die for Islam. **Heaven is a set of most dreamed and unfulfilled desires of men.**

The poverty and subjugation of Hindus of the last 1000 years do not let them think beyond measly milk and *rotti* (thin flat bread) The sexual suppression of the Hindus warps the mind. Muslims keep their women in *BURQUA* and prohibit exposure of any part of the body. Hence, their heaven projects females of their reverie. It was fun. We were still driving when I posed a question on the heaven of the Christians. Neither am I a Biblical reader, nor have heard of any good answer to this question.

However, I added that the Christians in the USA have actually created a heaven on earth! Las Vegas is an adult fantasy land, a heaven where every desire can become a reality. The heavens of the Hindus and Muslims are found all over in the USA. During the Wine Show, when plenty of wine has flowed in the system, the intoxication flows out. It creates an ambience that is a dream of the dreamers.

To enhance the mood, plenty of food is served and live music played on. Auction of rare wines and art pieces add another dimension. Men and women become carnivorous. Of course, a few hookers also land to entice tipsy men. There being no chairs and sofas, women sit, squat and sprawl on the carpeted floor against the wall with their bosoms, cleavages and thighs exposed for a visual feast. It is so tough on men in their 20s!

What is your heaven? You better have its vision!

May 04 2004/July, 2012

COMMENTS

Satish, It is interesting to see the alternate views of heaven and how they relate to what is "missing" or suppressed in this life. The Christian doctrine of heaven is different. It is not based on what we want but on what is best for us. (that may not be the fulfillment of ANY of our desires on this earth) The Christian doctrine of heaven is that it will be the same as here on earth now—only without sin and WITH the visual, real presence of God.

- we will have jobs to do
- we will not instantly know everything, it will be a time of constant discovery
- we will have no more tears or pain
- we will have no more chaos and disorder
- The rest of creation will join us in this renewal, animals and plants (but not weeds and thorns)

I think an equally interesting question is what happens when a person dies? Do they immediately go to heaven or is there some kind of purgatory? **Steve Wunderink/Pastor**

Enjoyed your write up "HEAVEN IS RIGHT HERE" I remember participating in such an even when I was at UNLV. I am looking forward to an opportunity of participating again along with you . . . . As for your query, MY HEAVEN IS HAPPINESS OF MY CHILDREN AND GRAND CHILDREN WHOM I ALWAYS SAY 'BE HAPPY AND RADIATE HAPPINESS' Sincerely, **RS Nigam**

Hi Uncle, I used to think of heaven as the place where all of your most intimate wants and needs were fulfilled. However, I have changed my mind about that. I tend to think that I am in heaven now. At present I have the ability to steer my life in any direction. I have choice (or at least the illusion of it, which is the same to me). I can raise children, find love, get married, travel the world, have great food/wine, experience and appreciate other cultures, meet interesting people, listen to fine music, drive fine cars, develop my community, and many other things that I hold dear. Yes, this comes with the ugly side of life; crime, lies, disasters, disease, and anything one can hate about life. But if heaven is only the good stuff, then I think I would not appreciate it as much without the bad.

Right now living my life is a challenge to succeed in it. The constant pursuit of success is my heaven. And if heaven is as described by certain religions as a universally and unique truth, then I choose to stay here. Yin without Yang? Good without Evil? Heaven by other's definitions sounds boring. Promiscuity can be had now, and has been had by many. Ask them what they want and I bet they will say a good woman to grow old with. Ask the dedicated husband, and he may say promiscuity. We always want what others have. Heaven should only be given out in doses, because no matter what, the idea of heaven changes. And if you can accept that, then I think am in heaven right now.
Tarak Patel

1. I can't tell if you were "drunk" or "sober" when you wrote this . . . it's the first time I've ever heard of a "sexual heaven" . . . . always thought it was a state of mind . . . or are you revealing yourself? Blessings and have a wonderful day! **Renee Riendeau**, Realtor

I wrote: Yes, I did write it right after the event. So I was between a state of "drunk" and "sober". What kind of a poet, artist and a writer is, if he/she does not bare himself/herself while he/she is baring down a truth?! Thanks.

OUR IMAGE OF HINDUISM

"I do not want to answer all kinds of questions," my wife said about not giving a copy my recent article on some salient aspects of Hindu religion to Pete a recent acquaintance. It stopped me for a moment and I wondered at Hinduism, our 'closet' religion. My wife has lived in USA for 35 years. She is educated, well read, and informed about religious beliefs and life styles. Pete is an 82-year-old writer, who shares his stories with us, as I do with mine.

In my recent writings on Hindu religion, I have been focusing on the public identity of Hindu individuals and Hindu religion. Publicly Hindus, whether young or old, do not want to have a discussion on their religious beliefs. They think Hindu religion is too personal. As a matter of fact, they often hide Hinduism behind the national origin, Indian. My nephew-in-law has told me several times as to how he feels defenseless at work when his co-workers ask questions on Hindu religion. Various gods in different non-human forms make him feel uneasy. Then, where and what is one Hindu scripture, and so on, and on?

In an effort to ease this tension and bring some information and education, my sister and brother-in-law recently formed a study group of individuals who seek out Hinduism. It meets every third Thursday from 7:30 to 9 PM. The idea is that first let us come to some consensus on some aspects of Hinduism amongst ourselves before confidently telling about it to the non-Hindus. The group is open to all who want to understand Hindu Dharma/religion.

What is your image of Hinduism that you are publicly proud of? Tell it all.

Aug 30, 2004

COMMENTS

1. . . . . Educated middle class Hindus are more westernized and take pleasure in ridiculing our culture and religion to show that they are (Pseudo) secularists. No other religion allows criticism of itself, and to critics they are always ready to response with do-or-die mantras with maximum scale of violence. Salman Rushide, Mahashay Rajpal, are some examples. For Hindu gods and goddesses, even non-Hindus take liberty in making naked photos as part of their artistic skills and commercialism (recently an Italian firm has started selling underwears : Kachchas with Hindu goddess printed on the lower part) and when Hindus object to such practices they are ridiculed by all (including their own brothers) as fascists, non-secularists. Can anyone dare to do the same with BIBI FATIMA OR MISS MARRY? Much can be written about the docile and negativism of the so called modern educated Hindus. We should make concerted efforts to educate our children on virtues of Hinduism for which all levels of books and literature are now available at nominal price. Thanks for your thoughts and reflections; **NIGAM**

2. Great idea . . . hope the curios show up!! **Renee** Riendeau

3. Very well written. Did you send me your latest article you mentioned? I am going to use your couple of articles on my website. Best wishes **Ted/ Sibia**

PERSONAL REMARKS

ARYA SAMAJ: CHAMPION OF WIDOWS

A question is raised as to how Arya Samaj has championed the cause of re-marriage of Hindu widows? Since the history of Arya Samaj, founded in 1875, is very short, one can go back to its source, the founder, Swami Dayanand Saraswati (1824-1883) He was absolutely a meteor, a visionary—100 years ahead of his time, and yet fully anchored in the social and political issues and events of his times.

Dayanand fully understood the British onslaughts on Hindu heritage, customs and institutions. The British did not want any repeat of the 1857 rebellion of Indians that was ruthlessly quelled. Soon after, several punitive bills were introduced in the name of social reforms. On the surface, not all social reforms undertaken—like the *SATI* and *THUGGERY*, were bad. The number of *SATI* instances was insignificant, but its evil side had gripped the Hindus of Bengal, in particular

Calcutta was then the capital of British India and Bengal was the first state to come under the British hegemony. Swami Dayanand witnessed the plight of Hindu widows during his visit to Bengal. He went there at the express invitation of Keshav Chandra (1838-1884), the leader of Brahmo Samaj, a contemporary Hindu renaissance movement started in Eastern India. The Arya Samaj movement started from western India.

Even after 100 years, the condition of the Bengali widows is pitiable. Most of them are forced to leave homes and beg or pushed to Mathura temples to sing *Bhajans* (devotional songs). Some are forced to live in **SONA GACHII** (land of gold), the brothel center of Calcutta. A celibate (**BALBRAHAMCHARI**) Dayanand alone could be moved by such sights. It was a time when many Hindu intellectuals like Raja Ram Mohan Roy had leaned towards Christianity. (Raja was his Muslim title—no Hindu royalty connection).

The greatness of Swami Dayanand lies in his five-star genius and scholarship. In reviving the Hindu intelligentsia, he led them to their very source, the Vedas. He preached for full equal rights for men and women, and when it came to remarriage, he unequivocally advocated equal rights to widowers and widows. He knew of undeniable glorification of *SATI*, as mentioned and sanctioned in Hindu folklore. One has to read Chapter Four of his magnum opus, **SATYARTHAPRAKASH** (Light of the meaning of truth) for his stand that Arya Samaj took upon in later years. In support of remarriage of the widows, he has given copious references to the *Vedas*, *Manusmriti* and other scriptures)

The other reason for his push for the widow cause was that he noticed that amongst the Muslims, widow problem is over-solved by polygamy. Amongst Christians, it is non-existent. It must have baffled Dayanand on seeing this scourge on the Hindu society that was limping due to one leg tied up. A question is: how far has the Hindu society come in gripping with this problem? Just look around your own families. Don't go too far!

Oct 28, 2004/July, 2012

PS. An example of worsening conditions of Hindu widows even after 100 years!

New Delhi, July 30 (Daily Tribune/Chandigarh)
Vrindavan widows in Uttar Pradesh are living in pathetic conditions as representatives of the NGOs running various welfare homes behave like jail wardens and exploit them, according to a seven-member panel appointed by the Supreme Court. Some of the NGOs were collecting funds ostensibly for the welfare of destitute women by showing the same set of women as residents of different homes, the panel said in an eight-page report placed before a Bench comprising Justices DK Jain and Madan Lokur today.

The welfare measures meant for the widows abandoned by their families were not reaching them, the panel headed by the chairman of the Mathura District Legal Services Authority said. The other members of the panel included representatives from the National Commission for Women, the Uttar Pradesh Government, the District Collector, the medical officer and the Mathura SSP. Whenever these widows get a considerable amount of money from someone, it is usually snatched away by NGO representatives, the report said.

"Only those who go to such places unannounced and without any official clout can see and realise the pathetic condition in which destitute women, known as Vrindavan widows, live there and the way they are exploited," the panel said.

ENCOUNTERS WITH ISLAMIC IDENTITY

"Do you know Urdu?" asked a fellow passenger on noticing me reading an Urdu magazine in topsy-turvy positions. It was in the Coimbatore Express Train that we both boarded from Mumbai. During a very long train journey— like the one taking 24 hours from Mumbai to Banglore, Indian passengers eventually loosen up socially for small talks and even exchange of snacks. After all, how much can one read/write and stare at the changing panorama of life out of the windows.

His curiosity was natural, as I was trying to figure out an Urdu calligraphy in a circle. I told him that I learnt Urdu from my grandfather nearly 60 years ago. The man, being in his 20s, had no idea of such bonds existed even in India two generations ago. Not feeling satisfied, right away he asked for my name. He was quiet afterwards on this topic, as he was convinced that Satish Chandra could not be the name of a Muslim.

Urban Hindus, by and large, do not display their religious identities. In contrast, a growing number of Muslim men of every age group are seen wearing skullcaps, long overalls and flowing beards with/out shaved moustaches. It was not that much noticeable in recent past years. Of course, adult Muslim women are seen in full burquas. I wear a French beard with moustache but shave the area above the chin and below the lip.

The conversation is associated with a general belief that only the Muslims study Urdu language that historically grew out of Hindi written in Arabic/ Persian script. Such a divisive thinking reminded me of a scene in a recent movie on the life of Mirza Ghalib. He was a great poet and far greater a liberal Muslim during the reign of Bahadur Shah Zafar, the last Mughal Emperor of Delhi. In the movie, Ghalib quipped to his Hindu and Muslim friends since when **Barfi** (sweet) became Hindu and **Jalebi** (sweet) Muslim? He ridiculed any religious classifications of sweets.

Within a week, a second identity encounter took place in a pearl jewelry showroom at Banglore airport. I was the lone customer browsing the showcases before my flight to Mumbai. Pearls always fascinate me. Most salesgirls are good at reading the personalities of their customers. My one niece, who worked at a pearl shop, used to tell stories about different clients. On inquiring about the origin of certain pearls, a small conversation ensued. Suddenly, a salesgirl praised my Urdu accent! That raised my alarm guards, as I was specifically examining a unique pearl set with a red corral rose and two green jade leaves around it in a necklace and ear tops. My wife loves anything that looks like a rose.

My mind was made up for buying it. The girl sensed it too, but was somehow convinced that I was a Muslim! Knowing the tremendous margin of profit in this business, I asked her discount before making an offer. On her telling it none, I countered it to buy the set at 25% discount. Immediately, she started fiddling with her calculator and finally agreed to sell at 20% for my being a Muslim. I told her that I was not a Muslim. She and her fellow salesgirl refused to believe my words. In a playful mood, I said how about giving me 25% discount, if I proved that I was not a Muslim? She then spurted that I got 20% in the first place for being a Muslim!

It was an amusing moment for me—not a dejavu. I had encountered this situation in Ambala Cantt 25 years ago. In order not to let down a beaming face of a stranger in a public function, I had said yes to him about my identity question, that I was a Muslim. My wife remembers it too. We had since several rounds of arguments on it.

However, here in a showroom, I pulled out my photo ID. The girls held it in their hands and kept gazing at it in disbelief! I could read the magic of ethnic identity from their faces. They still wanted my advice on good Islamic literature! I wrote on a piece paper about a monthly magazine the *Islamic Digest*. Nevertheless, I must have left a lifetime impression on them once they got hold of this magazine. Only six days earlier, I had bought a copy of the *Islamic Digest* from a railway bookstall to brush up on my Urdu. I myself had not heard of it before!

It is paramount to know one's identity and be proud of it. **Living up to its potential is nothing but self-realization.** But foisting symbols of ethnic identities is a different game. In the post 9/11 era, the symbols that unify one ethnic group, the same symbols can send signals of fear and intolerance to the other ethnic groups.

Jan 05, 2005/July, 2012

COMMENTS

1. Your memory remains so strong—Of course you're much younger than I am now at this age. Thanks for keeping me on your mailing list. I always get some important message from your writings. **Dutchie**

2. Dad, "It is paramount to know one's identity and be proud of it. Living up to its potential is nothing but self-realization. But foisting symbols of ethnic identities is a different game. In the post 9/11 era, the symbols that unify one ethnic group, the same symbols can send signals of fear and intolerance to the other ethnic groups". I have felt this way for quite some time now. Many people I encounter are taken by surprise that I am Mexican. I am proud of my identity, but have found that often living up to its potential takes on a different meaning depending upon who you are talking with. I also find on many instances that people's reaction to me changes when they find out my ethnicity.

While on a smaller scale, the same fear and intolerance is displayed towards many American-Mexicans. However, in this post 9/11 era, it is less a fear of violence and more of social disapproval. I might also add that one's identity is not always associated with one's ethnic culture but rather on one's social experience/present social conditions etc . . . In my case for example my identity has expanded to include the fascinating Indian culture. While I certainly do not consider myself Indian, I do feel a sense of belonging. I enjoy participating and learning. I feel a certain connection when I see or hear an Indian person. And the funny thing is that it doesn't matter whether they are Hindu/Muslim. To be honest, I haven't learned to distinguish yet. I guess ignorance is sometimes bliss!! I'm glad your back! I look forward to your next article. **Alex**

3. First of all your face and style suggests that you are a Muslim. So much so that way back I decided that you had been a Muslim in an earlier incarnation. However I understand that the girls thought about your identity as a Muslim after knowing that you could read Urdu. I did not know that you had knowledge of this language.

I have some more ideas on the incidents narrated by you. An average Muslim thinks that the Hindus are misguided because they believe in Gods with a tail or a trunk. No doubt it is also funny to believe in any human God without tail or trunk. So when Muslims find another Muslim they feel happy that he is not involved in Bull Shit (please do not mind my language)I have had similar experience. I also know Urdu

The other matter is that by face you look Cosmopolitan or confident. Majority of Hindus, in my view, look burdened by such irrational believes. Face betrays it. There is a kind of Suppression of mind. It is indeed a suppression to continue to consider some animal-man creatures as God. You can see this evident on face of devout Hindus. You don't see this type of expression on devout Christians, Muslims or Sikhs or even Arya Samajis. Muslims use a trick to find out whether you are a Muslim or not. They ask your name. Sometimes I tell my name as Iqbal (wrong name) which is sometimes used by Hindus

This tradition of giving concession is common in India. In Ambala Sikhs give concession to Sikhs and Sikhs try to do business with their Sikh **Bharas** (brothers). I agree that one ought to be proud of one's identity. But in India there are many problems for Hindus. If you are a scheduled Caste or lower caste person you try to hide your identity. There are some very funny examples. In Ambala City one Barber family has been claiming they are Brahmins and it has been found out with considerable setback to their image. I understand (partially) the logic given by believers in Hanuman, Ganesh and 31 Crore 99 lakhs 99 thousands 9 hundreds ninety-eight gods. But for me it is Bull Shit. Therefore I try to hide my identity or if I disclose it. I make it a point to explain to them that I don't believe in Bull Shit. Sincerely, **Subhash Sood**

4. Dear Friend, Thank you for remembering me and sending your reflections in two emails. No doubt I see the 'writer' in you and I suggest you should start collecting your reflections to make a full book and publish it . . . . I value and relish your friendship very much. Your affectionate friend, **P.V.N. Murthy**

MY RARE BOOK REVIEW

RAAMAAYANHA RAHASYA (Secrets of the Ramayan) by PVN Murthy, Vedsri Publications, 2004. ISBN 81-902001-0-0, pp 226; Rs 150.

For the last few years, I have been picking up books for reading pleasure, but seldom finish any one. Main reason: not much originality is seen that is worth my time. **Time is always precious, and it becomes more so after the age of 60**. However, I read this book from cover to cover. The main reason being that I know the author and we have communicated over the years. First time, I met Murthy was in 1999-Vedanta Conference in Hyderabad, and recently in a **WAVES** (World Association of Vedic Studies) Conference in Banglore in Dec, 2004.

The author does not come off a university or traditional line of scholarship. He retired as a system programmer with Air India. He is self-taught in Sanskrit and an independent researcher. Consequently, he tends to make claims that the traditional scholars won't make. About his book, Murthy claims, "*The Raamaayanaha Rahasya is an unbiased, dispassionate, analysis of Raama as a God, Raamaayanha as a myth, Raama as a mortal, Raamaayanha as history. Raama as a scientific phenomenon and Raamaayanha as a treatise in astronomy.*"

The book is based on the classical Valmiki's Ramayan. Murthy's innovation is also reflected in the English transliteration of Sanskrit and Tamilian words, though I continue to use the popular versions of some of those words. I do not want to detract the readers from the purpose of the book. I think a separate review is needed on the mathematical and scientific conclusions that Murthy has drawn from Valmiki's Sanskrit.

The book is written in the format of a roundtable mini conference between seven persons with diverse backgrounds. It reads like a play. In fact, there is one man, Murthy, who is speaking differing points of views through seven characters. Murthy is one of the rare exponents of Vedic scriptures having three meanings—religious, philosophic and scientific. I believe in it too, but find it hard to substantiate it through my researches. In the US, the land of topmost intellectual activities, there isn't even one three-star Sanskrit scholar who has in depth knowledge of three areas. In India, it is out of question.

Drawing a conclusion from a couple of observations is like making a composite picture by freely connecting a few dots. The greater the number of dots, better a picture is. The book has a blend of a travelogue, as Murthy and his wife visited all the sites in Sri Lanka associated with the legends of Ramayana. There is a lot of humor in his writing to balance seriousness and controversial passages of the book.

After 15 years of researches into the Vedas, he asserts that the Vedas originally were not composed in Sanskrit language at all. Furthermore, he points out that Sanskrit was only developed for technical and defense purposes by the elite of the society. This is in full agreement with my study of Sanskrit. It was never a lingua franca of India. Its purpose was to store and preserve the distilled knowledge of the scriptures, as writing was then rare, privileged and expensive. It was nothing close to modern printing.

The book is divided into three main parts; the second part has the heart of Ramayan. Yet, it has spots of diversionary nature. But Murthy, like a conductor of a symphony, is able to keep the matter connected in a bigger picture. With the exception of astronomical conclusions drawn from stray mathematical presence in the *Mantras*, the book is very stimulating for the readers irrespective of any leaning. Assertions like, that the ancient *rishis* were great scientists and also experts in martial arts require a new orientation of science and scientists in the present context.

The best part of the book is that Murthy does not dodge any issues. In fact, he constantly challenges and engages readers on topics like: Was Raam a Tamilian royalty? (Like the 19th century rulers of Gwalior being Marathas), Vedas codified in Tamil originally, Ravan belonging to an African race, Tamil and Sanskrit languages of the same region, the existence of Sinhalese. Also, there is a space for a debate on Aryan vs. Dravidian, Aryan invasion of India, meanings and perceptions of the terms Rakshas and Yakshas. He even dares the readers into alien and UFO connection with some characters of Ramayan. A few simple observations like similarities in the names of the mothers of Raam and Ravana viz. Kykeyi and Kykasi, irresistibly draw common readers into it.

It is asserted that nothing is achieved by simple chants of the *Mantras*, though Murthy's ancestors made their livelihood in priesthood, and astrology. Why is nearly all-ancient world literature in poetic form? Questions like: What is God? and Existence of God, are tackled along with an explanation of the

Hindu nomenclature. To put Raam and Ramayan in a perfect historic context, Murthy concludes that Raam was born on Jan 10, 4439 BC.

Whenever questions on historicity of a place and/or person are put forward, I often pose a counter question: **Write a few lines on the grandfather of your grandfather.** This exercise brings any finding, based on ancient history and archaeology, in focus. Often, we tend to rely or refute such claims very casually. Murthy raises a question that Sri Lanka, 6500 years ago, was not an island. Some earth movement has taken the land mass away from the Indian subcontinent towards Africa.

It may be noted that recent NASA pictures mapping the Indian Ocean have indicated the existence of a bridge between India and Sri Lanka. This has started archeological excavation in the coastal areas of Tamilnad. Hopefully, in the next 50 years, more light may be shed on the 'mythical' connecting bridge between India and Sri Lanka.

I hope in the next printing or edition of this book, some minor changes in the layout of some paragraphs, editing and clarification of a few concepts, are taken care. This will enhance the value of this book. The book is not yet available on amazon.com. However, it can be directly ordered from the publishers at this address: Vedsri Publications, 5/1, Titan Township, Hosur 635-110 (TN), India.

Mar 03, 2005/Aug, 2012

COMMENTS

1. Interesting hypothesis. **Rahul**

2. Respected Dr. Bhatnagar, Many thanks for all your writings which are very interesting. While working on the computer for most of the time, I find your literary, thought provoking and informative intrusions into the mailbox quite soothing. Could I get the address of Mr. Murthy (e-mail or physical)? With kind regards, **Raman**

3. It is an area which I dread to walk in. I believe in mathematical thinking. I do not feel happy with numerous interpretations of numerous things, mixing them and reinterpreting the mixture in a semi logical pseudo spiritual style and then gloating over it all.
   Some of these ideas are: Rome was founded by Rama. Maya civilization was Indian originally. Homoeopathy came out of Vedas. Every science is represented in Vedas. Sanskrit is the language of God. Amen of Bible is same as OM. Quran was derived from Vedas and in fact, it is translation of Vedas. Every language is derived from Sanskrit. These are few of them. I am short of time to go into the problem of proving these right or wrong. **Subhash**

4. Today's Indian media deplored everything which is associated with the irrelevantly called 'Hinduism' and ridiculing socio-religious structure and practices of Hindus and their beliefs . . . . I have seen your informative article in the latest issue of the ORGANISER. There is also a letter to editor making comments on your earlier print in the ORGANISER. I feel happy to get your reflections published in this periodical. **NIGAM**

HINDU CASTE MARRIAGES

This week, we received three matrimonial announcements. One is the wedding of a Punjabi Sharma boy (son of Sharma/Bhatnagar parents) with a Tamilian Krothapalli girl in San Francisco. The second is the engagement of a Bhatnagar girl with a Tamilian co-worker in Mumbai. Perhaps, her older sister had opened a door by marrying a Maharashtrian co-worker years ago—in Mumbai too. The third is the wedding of a Bhatnagar boy with a Sikh girl. This weekend, they flew from Washington DC to India.

My mind briefly surveyed the entire spectrum of marriages and Hindu caste system. It is debatable whether the grip of Hindu caste system is uniformly loosening up or not. The present Indian politics is deeply infested with caste considerations and has been getting worse. The sample space for this **Reflection** is my large extended family.

To give a personal perspective on changes in marital thinking over one generation, we, six out of seven Bhatnagar siblings married into Bhatnagar families. Only the youngest one married out with a Bihari Thakur. From my wife's side, again six out of seven Bhatnagar siblings married into Bhatnagars. The seventh one living in the US married with a Saxena.

There seems to be a quantum shift in matrimonial orbits from one generation to the next. My older daughter married a Nigam 18 years ago; the son with an Aggarwal and the younger daughter took a big leap by marrying with a Mexican American. My younger brother's son married a Singaporean Gujarati girl and his daughter a UK Gujarati boy. Both of my nephew and niece have lived in the US. The daughter of a younger brother in Bathinda married a Shrivastava. At the same time, the two kids of my brother-in-law, in the US, married with Bhatnagars in India. Furthermore, the two sons of a second brother-in-law in India married into Bhatnagars and Shrivastavas. A Bhatnagar nephew-in-law married a Trivedi girl he met in IIT Delhi. A very close cousin in India has four children; only the oldest one married into Bhatnagars, the rest into Sharmas, Shrivastavas and Gujarati Shahs.

The only conclusive argument is that as the life gets faster in big cities, matrimonial alliances are more likely to be made in close office circles. **A job defines a new caste**, like seen in the US. It reminds me of an interesting story. At the time of our son's marriage, my younger brother teasingly asked him, "Aggarwals are **banias**, and you know who the **banias** are?" My son

responded," Yes, the *banias* are the ones who wear *banians* (undershirts)!'"
There go Hindu castes out of any considerations.

By and large, our kids born and raised in the US have absolutely no clue of
the Hindu caste system. It is not a place to judge the gamut of caste dynamics.
However, for any idea, place or institution to survive a few millennia means
some inner strength in it. Survival with strength comes from adaptations to
changes—like a surfer does on a wave.

March 25, 2005/Aug, 2012

COMMENTS

1. As you know originally caste system was based on the occupation and now it is coming back full circle to the original thought. Any ways change is the way of life as no change means death. *Harkat ka naam zindgi hai.* **Rahul**

2. In my family the first non-Nigam marriage was that of my youngest brother with a Kulshreshta girl who was also a lecturer in a local college. All my children married (of course arranged by me, with reservations from my elders), in non-Nigams; Gupta/Mahajan, Bhatnagars and white American. I firmly believe that there should be socio-cultural compatibility between couples (of course, mostly among those working in the same organisation, same city/location, knowing each other fairly well) with gracious blessing of parents of both sides. In India of today most of the educated boys and girls do not have any regard to caste and families (except when teasing each other or having differences of minor type, then they resort to abusing each other's family members, especially parents). Their only consideration is compatibility and income supplementation to live a good life and ensure adequate funding for their children's education. HAPPY HOLI TO ALL. **NIGAMS.**

3. Happy Holi, Uncle—it was interesting to read your views. Do you know that in Karnataka, the festival is called "Kaamana Habba"? It is attributed to Kama, who was caught peeping when Shiva and his missus were going at it. I thought the sensuality is brought out appropriately, as Hindus had no inhibitions prior to the Victorian infested Brits came in. Regards— **Shankar.**

ON HINDU FAMILY VALUES

Today, around 11 AM, I got a call from the President of a local mosque for participating in the first anniversary of Muslim Family Day. A year ago, April 30, 2004 was declared as **Family Day** by the State Governor. Besides Metro Sheriff, as chief guest, the Head of Las Vegas FBI office, and two US House Representatives were represented by their staffers. I accepted to go there as President of the *American Hindu Association*, whose main mission is to project Hinduism in the context of post 9/11 life in the USA.

On arriving at 6 PM in the mosque, I was suddenly asked to speak on family values as an interfaith leader. Traditionally, the national interfaith organization includes Judaism, Christianity and Islam. The mosque President, being from India and known for over 30 years, invited me, perhaps, to enhance the diversity of the participants. It turned out that I was the only non-Muslim speaker in the forum.

The toastmasters' training in extemporaneous speeches proves very helpful on such occasions. The challenge before me was to identify the Hindu family values to the non-Hindu audience. In fact, I alone was a Hindu in a gathering of nearly 80 Muslims of various national origins.

My remarks were divided in three parts. On probing the meaning of the word 'family', I explained that family, based on the notion of 'blood is thicker than water', does not elevate human beings above other species. The familial bonds are also developed by common life styles—like, place, language, food and dress. Finally, the common religious belief systems generate a larger family of believers. **Smaller the set of common beliefs in a religion, greater is the number of its adherents!**

What are the sources of Hindu family values? The keynote speaker, following my short speech, quoted the *Quran* and *Hadith* for the Muslim family values. I pronounced that the source of Hindu family values is *Ramayana*, a great Hindu epic. All the lofty ideals of human bonds—whether of a husband, brother, father, mother and son, are drawn from it. That is why, since time immemorial, most Hindu names are taken from it.

Finally, I brought my remarks on family values to ground zero by telling specific instances on how father's younger brother, older brother, sister; and likewise, mother's brothers and sisters and so on, are addressed specifically. It highlights the importance of various levels of ties in a family. The respect for elders and love for children are unconditional. I related it with my experience of learning Urdu and English from my maternal grandfather much before learning them in schools. Some good habits—like, my love for long walks are imbibed from his passion for walking for 4 hours every day!

After I returned to my seat, a related question started churning my mind: In what respects the Hindu family values are unique? It is time to share your thoughts on it.

April 30, 2005/Aug, 2012

COMMENTS

1. Respected Bhai Sahib, Loved to read your article. It is great! **Pramod**

2. Hindu family values are essence of the entire humanity family values. Victorian values, as are popularly called in the English-speaking world, are in essence Hindu family values. In all societies, Hinduism included, every member of the society is entitled to respect; however, verbal differences are there due to environmental constraints/factors. Christianity, Judaism and Islam are religions springing from desert where not much of human needs and requirements grow from nature. As such dry lands population has to pursue somewhat different way of living, sustenance and even behavior pattern.

FAMILY relationship has been widely defined and positive code of conduct is given the highest place. Unfortunately, Hinduism is not well marketed way of living and religion; although it is the most accommodative one. Hindus have respect for founders/leaders of all religions and their holy books. Hindu religion books are fountains of eternal knowledge (even the most modern scientific inventions and thoughts). **NIGAM**

WHAT A BIG DEAL IN NAMING!

Yesterday, we were at an Indian family **khana** (eating binge). A conversation meandered around names of the Hindu children born in the US. These days, parents want to make sure that not only the non-Indians are able to pronounce names easily, but also, they are not distorted for fun making. This dilemma was not encountered when our daughter was born in Las Vegas 30 years ago. My wife wanted the name to begin with 'A'—like, the names of our two other kids. Born very tiny, we agreed on Anubha—meaning, the glory of an atom, the tiniest particle, yet packed with energy. She is living up to her name!

However, the latest trend amongst the Hindus is to choose Urdu names. I remember years ago when a friend named her daughter *Shabnam*. Recently, in our circle, the names like *Sahil*, *Armaan*, *Bulbul*, *Khushbu*, and *Mehak* have been given. Apart from scholarly aspects, every language is associated with a culture. Anubha has already chosen *Taj* as the name of her son to be born next month! If the choice is for its meaning, then the Hindi word *Mukut* is equally good.

For the last many years, I had discussions over the usage of Indian language. For instance, people generally deem Punjabi as a rustic language of village folks and unsophisticated urbanites. I have known some Punjabis who quit speaking it in favor of Hindi. Most of them migrated from Pakistan at the time of India's partition.

Having known a scion of Patiala princely house, I was surprised at their 'refined' Punjabi in the confines of the home, but British English outside. He told me the story how Patiala state accepted to Romanize Gurmukhi script, as Malaya, Singapore and Indonesia had done it. A large number of princely states opposed this British conspiracy of cultural denigration. However, the British succeeded in Romanizing commands in the army raised in India. As a sidebar, it was the army of Patiala State that joined the British in the defeat of the nationalist forces in the decisive battle of Kanpur, during the 1857 Revolt.

The Punjabi complex goes back to the reign of Maharaja Ranjit Singh. Even at the height of great Sikh empire, he did not adopt Gurmukhi as the royal script, though he fully submitted to the Sikh tenets. The language of his royal court and administration remained Persian. The masses always follow their king. **A language develops every fine aspect of linguist richness, flexion**

and nuance, when adopted by a victorious ruling class. For example, the English of the 15th century is nothing as compared with English of today!

My wife praises Urdu for its cultural overtones. It is because, until recently, Urdu had the royal patronage from the Muslim rulers. This is nailed down by a line, ***jiski zubaan Urdu ki trah*** (means, that her speech is as sweet as Urdu language) in a popular romantic song, *CHAYYAN CHAYYAN* of the 1999 Hindi movie, *DIL SE*. This song has generated an unprecedented mass popularity for Urdu. Lately, the names derived from Hindu deities, scriptures, history and culture have been relegated. This shift does bother me.

July 18, 2005/Aug, 2012

COMMENTS

1. Your daughter is welcome to use "Taj" but she should know that Taj was the name of wife of Shah Jahan. Language gains importance with the use by the public, government, and experts in various fields. The problem of choosing names for children born to Indians in America will remain till the generation which realises that they are FULLY in America and not in Bharat. Even in India people are using Muslim names. The other alternative is to let Hindi become more honourable or HONORABLE! **Subhash Sood**

2. Interesting article. To be honest, the fact Taj is an Urdu name didn't even cross my mind. I knew the meaning of it and I liked the strong, powerful feeling it evokes with three single letters. Taj illicits a sense of royalty and strength. Being raised here, I don't harbor the resentment or the disdain for Urdu names that your generation does. It's more important that the name he has will allow him to stand out from the rest.—**Annie**

3. Hi Satish: Greetings from across the Atlantic! Yes, I agree with your views on 'naming.' Evidently you have done research on the history to come up with a fine interpretive rendition. I like your views. **Moorty**

4. I'm curious why this *really* bothers you. Do these naming 'trends' represent to you a disintegration of Hindu culture . . . or is there some deeper reason? After all, anyone who has studied languages to any depth, knows that Hindi and Urdu derive from the same Sanskrit roots. The Mughals naturally downplayed this fact as they embraced Islam, and replaced the Devanagri character with Persian. While this diffusion gave rise to Urdu as a medium of poetry, art and music, the fact remains: linguistic distinctions between Hindi and Urdu are not only superficial; but more importantly, they are asserted by those who wish to divide the Indian culture along ethnic or religious lines. The British did so very successfully, and the modern-day Hindu and Muslim fundamentalist leaders continue pushing the same rhetoric. Meanwhile, the rest of the world (including Bollywood!) continue to recognize Urdu's lineage as a rich *Indian* language with such close ties to Hindi that they are used interchangeably. **Avnish**

I wrote: Sometimes one word fails to capture the whole background. So wait and watch for other Reflections.

Avnish: One word or one sentence, carefully crafted, *can* capture volumes of thought. That is the essence of fine writing. Besides, people's short-term memory these days is as limited as their free time. So don't assume readers can remember what they read even the day before!

PERSONAL REMARKS

HINDUISM AND ANTIQUITY

India, the land of the Hindus, also called Hindustan, defies any one description. One can find here any 'dead' or vibrant religion, any ancient mode of transportation and conveyance on the streets, any dress and food. It is a mosaic and a quilt of varied patches. **India is the best place in the world for antiques hunting; be it material, intellectual and spiritual**. Presently, Hinduism rejects nothing, but assimilates everything.

This morning, my younger brother, Dinesh and I walked up to meet a holy man, known as Baba in Bathinda. Dinesh spoke about his latent powers. He had known him for years, as his assistant in the railway service. Suddenly, Baba resigned his job in order to assume the ancestral spiritual seat (***GURUDOM or PEERDOM***). In India, it is still unthinkable to resign a prized government job.

Baba warmly greeted us. He lives with his three sons and their families. On inquiring the history of the ***GADDI*** (spiritual seat), he told of its dating back to nearly 1000 years! Googa, a Muslim Sufi (Peer), settled here when this region was under the Afghani invader, Muhammad Gori. Prithviraj Chauhan repulsed 16 attacks of Muhammad Gori, bur never chased Gori to finish him. In the 17th attempt Gori won. He slaughtered Prithviraj Chauhan and changed the landscape of India forever.

His dwelling covers an acre of land that has small shrines of various Hindu gods and mythology. During our meeting, a couple came over, reverentially touched his feet and sat down on a blanket spread out on the ground. Dinesh asked Baba to attend them first. He recited some syllables of different religions—both audible and inaudible. His one son, dipping a branch of a plant in mustard oil held in a brass pan, moved the stem in the clockwise direction, as Baba instructed. During this ritual, the pan was held on man's head, who had some health problem. The entire ritual took 5-7 minutes. The couple, feeling assured, placed a voluntary donation of Rs 50 on Baba's lap and left after his blessings.

Dinesh sought Baba's advice about a girl proposed for his son. From their names alone, Baba assured him of no hindrances. However, there was a bottleneck in negotiation. While listening to their conversation, suddenly a thought flashed my mind that I would be instrumental in it. Lo and behold, after a few minutes, Baba said, "Your brother (me) should approach the girl's party while keeping a special amulet (*TAAVEEZ*) in his pocket." It amazed me. Did I telepathically plant this thought in Baba's mind, or he read mine? Incidentally, Baba is functionally blind now.

At times, a person, ordinary in many walks of life, becomes extraordinary in a particular one. Also, an ordinary person becomes extraordinary, when he/she is called upon to meet a challenge. While walking back home, I felt amused at this experience.

Classical science demands identical results when an experiment is repeated under identical conditions. The **Hindu mystical experiences belong to a domain that asserts no one identity of two events or objects—that is the finding of modern quantum physics too**! Both scientific and non-scientific approaches are known to exist for millennia. A non-scientific experience may have to wait for decades for its scientific foundations.

Jan 02, 2006 (Bathinda)

COMMENTS

Dear Satish, Stories about India from you are more than interesting. One, because you are deeply involved in the culture and two, because you write so well. Thanks **Dutchie**

A MONK AS HOUSE GUEST

"There is something common between a child and a **SADHU** (Monk)," I told my wife about Anand Yogi, an itinerant Hindu preacher. "The more attention you give them, the more you **think,** they are requiring it." For the last ten days, I have been witnessing a unique drama of life. Due to her full-time job, our daughter brings her six-month-old son to our place—five days a week. At the same time, Anand Yogi, has been our houseguest.

Anand Yogi, being our guest three years ago too, I enthusiastically welcomed him when he called us from California. My wife was initially reticent, and in fact upset at my attitude. She tells me all the burden of guest obligations falls on her, as I take this whole thing normally without accepting a change in my routines.

For the last ten years, I have been letting my house be like an *ashram*. The guests are welcome to enjoy our home—help themselves in the kitchen and general house clean up. A few times friends visited, when my wife was out of town. The guests asked how come they were not told about her being out of town. And, my wife tells that I should have told them of her not being at home. Yet, the time we had on such occasions was good.

Also, my thinking is off the track. When I welcome someone in my home, then it is beyond conditioned guest etiquettes. For example, I do not take guest as a **DEVATA** (a little godly), as it stirs in my mind the historic blunders of Hindu kings towards the foreigners of different faiths. A host should not get so burnout out with guest caring that after two days the guest is mentally thrown out of the house! I can't endure even one moment of guest tension. We are now in our mid sixties, and hospitality varies with age.

The moment I hear our daughter's car stopping in the driveway, I run up to bring our grandson in while babbling with him in Punjabi. He smiles and keeps looking at me. My wife carries him all the time. I remind her that it is neither good for his back, nor hers! She won't go out of his sight even for bathroom calls—forget taking showers. Pampering spoils a baby—its physical and mental well-being.

My attitude is different towards the *SADHUS.* Generally, they are torchbearers of ancient heritage. That is exactly how I addressed Anand Yogi in the baggage claim area in the airport, "Salutations to you, as a symbol and preacher of Hindu religion!" They bring at least a small group of the Hindus together at one place. The unity amongst the Hindus has been the call of the ages. Adi Shankaracharya was the first to start the institutions of four Shankaracharyas of four *MOTHS* in four different corners of India.

Anand Yogi—like, an infant, asks nothing in the name of comforts. But when people insist, he speaks up to please them. When I told him about my comparison of a *SADHU* with a baby, he had a big smile. He tells how his hosts miss him when he is gone after living for a month some times.

Feb. 20, 2006

COMMENTS

Do you do the same when you visit people i.e. clean and help in the kitchen? I do not know if any Hindu believes their guest to be **devata** (god type) in this age and time I wonder where this is coming from. The other debatable issue is if the Sadhus/Sanyasis are torch bearer of Indian Heritage and are uniters. **Rahul**

WE CAN GET TOGETHER

"Where have you been?", "Not seen for a long time!", "Where have you been living?", "You never meet!" At the weekend parties, such remarks are commonly heard from friends and acquaintances. They are generic, filler questions, not much thought behind them. I often smile them away, yet some psychoanalysis is triggered. The more I observe, the more surprised I am. It is primarily a problem of the Hindus in USA. They are socially the most isolated ethnic community without any political clout.

For the last one year, my compelling response has been, "Christians meet in a church on a Sunday service. A new Sikh in town is likely to meet the community in a gurdwara on a Sunday. *LANGAR* (free kitchen) is an added attraction. Of course, the Muslims meet in mosques for the mandatory Friday Prayer." A typical dialog with Hindu strangers during their first run-ins runs as follows: "I have been in this town for 10 years." "And, I for 30 years!"

For the Hindus, there is no social or religious prescription. There are some historical reasons behind it too. The living environment in India—whether urban, rural or in-between, is such that never one is hit by social isolation and loneliness. Life in the US is very different. It is fast paced, white-race dominant, and based upon Judea-Christian belief system.

Generally, a Hindu socialization means weekend meeting at one home and go on eating and drinking binge. For health reasons and monotony, I am now turned off from these weekend dinners that I call feed centers to the consternation of my wife. The basic dilemma still remains, as to how to socially interact, exchange ideas and be viable partners in the US society? One solution lies in extending the premises of Hindu temples from religious rituals to social dialogues.

Now that our children are in the 30s and 40s, how their life has been impacted? Theirs is faster. It appears not only their houses and cars are mortgaged, but their entire lives are mortgaged. They are socially like colloidal particles in a fluid; neither floating on the top, nor sinking at the bottom. No matter how long they live in the US, they are going to be identified as the Hindus or Indians. They can grab leadership roles in Hindu community.

A society in which individuals get alienated becomes vulnerable, lose its freedom, and everything precious. This is a lesson of history! Last Sunday morning, a 23-year old unmarried new comer to Las Vegas called me up. I told him about the *Swadhayae* meetings held near his place. He was reluctant to go there, though a Gujarati. When I suggested him to go to the Hindu Temple by the noon *Aarti* time; he had a shopping priority! He still kept insisting on meeting people. Then, I explained him the **Chaudhary Formula of Socialization in the USA**. Look for Indian names in telephone directory and invite the first group of ten for dinner over a weekend. The following weekend, invite ten more and you will be the talk of the town. By the time, the third weekend rolls in, you will start getting dinner invitations that will never end!"

In India, new comers are invited first, but in the USA it may take ten years in waiting!

Sept 06, 2006/Aug, 2012

COMMENTS

1. Dear Satish, You have made some very important remarks. For years, I have been sort of unhappy with the superficiality of our "Indian' gatherings'. Though the intentions are above blame, and the labor put in by the host considerable, the interactions leave much to be desired. Up to this point in my remarks, most of everyone that I have talked to agree. But, as what is to be done to rectify the situation, is where there is no clear answer. In my younger years, where the official reason for the gatherings was the 'passing on our culture' to our children, the following was the order of events:

The men would get together and talk (a) latest politics USA or India (b) why India was great and the 'main' problem with India is . . . . (each person knew a different unique solution) (c) Have you already bought a house (d) What my company is doing . . . We make . . . etc In the meantime, the women in the kitchen are talking about recipes, children and their husband's quirks. The children are down in the basement or outside, chatting away in their "American accent' about TV shows and occasionally mentioning that their parents are doing some Hindu stuff upstairs . . . .

Announcement food is ready . . . children eat . . . . men, each say 'Aap Pailey' continue what they were chatting about, start eating right near the food table, obstructing traffic, lots of cross conversation, no one really paying much attention. Women now eat and again back to the kitchen (unless they were already eating in the kitchen). Men assemble again on the sofas to ramblingly discuss mystic happenings that defy scientific explanation, healing powers, divination etc, and in general the greatness that has been our culture.
The day comes to an end and the guests depart one by one, leaving the host doggone tired, needing sleep followed by a huge cleaning job !!

How much 'culture' did the children get out all this? I will mention to you an outstanding extreme example. It is at the temple. The adults are upstairs singing bhajans. Children running around downstairs. Someone distributed 'prasad' bananas to the children. The children did not eat the bananas. One 6-yr old child is chasing another 4-yr old, 'pointing' the banana at her and saying "bang, bang". The younger one kept on running for a while and then 'obediently' fell dead to the ground !!

Now a days in the few parties, that I sometimes am forced to attend, (old friends I have known for years), Children have grown up and gone, we talk of what ailments we have, what medications we are taking, medical expenses, malpractice, how to fix the medical system in the US. I try to exchange any useful medical information and someone rudely and abruptly says, "Change the topic, you are whipping the same topic". (This happened to me about 2 years ago and I still feel the hurt !!)

At any function, whether bhajan, swamiji visiting, drama, dance, fund raising banquet, lecture, musical concert; the conversation never stops. You can never hear the quiet. This grinding need for socialization of the superficial sort above! Any thoughts?
Shankar Raja

2. Dear Satish, Everything what you wrote is very true but that is the nature of Hindus. I don't think, anything can be done about it until there is some sort of small or big crisis upon us. **Rajendar Singal**

3. This is a really great article. I think you have nailed the problem all Indians—Hindus, Muslim, Sikh or Christian face in US. Our social structure in India is more family oriented and since that system has almost collapsed here in US, people have developed different ways to socialize. In another 20 years we will face a similar situation in India and I believe we will see an increase in social crimes as well. Though meeting in the temple is a good idea, for the most part that maybe just one of the ways to meet new people. I feel that meeting in a non—religious setting maybe more comfortable. I like the idea of inviting new people over for dinner, but I am sure that not many people will accept that invitation thinking that they would be subjected to some kind of sales pitch for the latest network marketing thing. There probably is a good way to meet new Indians, but it's not going to be easy to find. Let me know if you find anything that works and doesn't involve cold calling :-). Take care, **Ani**

4. Hindu temples need to become vibrant cultural centers where people could meet. New temples in USA offer some of these possibilities. However, temples in India are more for individual's needs of worship—there is not much of collective worship as Christians have mass and Muslims have Friday *namaz*. Another point is that Indians/Hindus need to go for a holistic approach towards life in the USA where all kinds of opportunities are available. A bias towards materialistic life is very

harmful. On this front, Americans are more open-minded and honest.
Harish Chandra

5. You are doing a lot for Hindus. We need people like you. Chaudhary Formula is very interesting. I may try it. Thanks for your beingness. **Subhash**

DANCE IN HINDU LIFE

Bharat Natyam Dance form is a pristine symbol of Hinduism. Islam has no such place for dances. 'Christian' dances seek the ultimate height in human arts and athleticism. **In the Hinduism alone, the dance takes the quantum leap from ground zero to divinity!** It can be measured by the transformation in the moods of the dancers, musicians and the audience. Sexuality turns into asexuality. These thoughts surfaced my mind while watching an *Arangetram* (Indian classical dance debut) of two girls last Saturday.

The girls were 15 and 16-year old, but in their costumes, make-up, and emotional expressions, they appeared beyond their ages. The next morning, that is what I exactly told one of them when she was in her jeans and t-shirt. We drove 300 miles to Phoenix for this performance. Bharat Natyam has been preserved for millennia in a region mainly comprising the present Indian states of Tamilnadu, Karnataka, and Andhra Pradesh.

There is nothing electronic in the musical ensemble. The entire orchestra has only 4-5 musicians; one for amazing vocal meters and others for the accompanying instruments; *veena*, flute, cymbals and *mridang*. Yet, mathematically they are able to generate infinitely many renderings— synchronizing them with dance choreography. **A professional dancer challenges the musicians, and conversely!** That creates an orgasmic moment in the performance.

During the nine dance routines, the girls changed their costumes four times. The costumes are isomorphic in stunning designs, but different in bright contrasting colors. They are not at all 'revealing'! The elaborate jewelry accentuates the visual impact. Each costume, costing at least $200, is ordered from India. The fabric is pure silk with gold and fine silver embroidery on the cuffs and brocade. They glow out with stage lighting. It is an ethereal sight with statues of deities and sacred fire burning in the lamps placed at the edges of the stage.

The girls achieved this milestone after 10-11 years of weekend dancing lessons and practice on the top of their high school work and club activities. Their teacher Asha Gopal is an institution by herself. Her strong beliefs in the preservation and transmission of this aspect of Hindu heritage prompted her to start *Aarthi School of India Dances* in Phoenix (1981). The school now has branches in Las Vegas/Nevada and Tucson/Arizona. Out of thousands of kids who must have taken lessons from her during the last 25 years, only 102 have completed the rigorous training of the basic course!

The dance education involves parents constantly motivating the kids, driving them around, and paying for the lessons etc. The father of one girl confided, "I really wanted my daughter to stay away from TV. It has paid off. Instead of nagging the kids to stop watching, we provided an alternative that also fitted into our family traditions."

Before the 1947 partition of India, dance form in public was completely absent amongst the Hindus in the North due to the Islamic influence. However, the sensual dancing and singing did flourish in houses of ill repute for the evening entertainment of the wealthy males. During the dance reception in the lobby in a gathering of 200 people, I spotted a Muslim wearing a long kurta and salwar. I went up to him and tried to engage him on the subject. But he diplomatically avoided it.

Ironically, though the Hindu kings of south India supported Bharat Natyam, its extreme emphasis on divinity was exploited. The dancers were forced to cater to the carnal desires of the powerful temple priests and social elite. Consequently, temple dancing was tinged with a shady reputation. Since India's independence, Bharat Natyam has been liberated from the temple monopolies, it has been reaching new heights in India and abroad.

The themes of the dances are generally related with Hindu mythology. Shiva is the lord of dance, also called *Natraj*. It means that life is a dance, a full body expression of freedom within to resonate with freedom without! Dance is a mode of self-realization, the ultimate purpose of an individual life! The Hindus lost this external freedom for a thousand years. Thus, dance also disappeared from their daily lives.

Dancing reminds me of a popular science book, *The Tao of Physics* (1975) by Fritjof Capra, a physicist. He has drawn dance parallels at scientific and yogic levels while describing the properties (dance!) of subatomic particles in physics with the Hindu Trinity—namely, creation, preservation and dissolution of the universe. Indian mystic Rajneesh, speaking on the importance of dancing in life, has said, "When it rains, then people should run out of homes and dance like peacocks, as seen in the hot plains of India." **In a fast-paced life, people are always hot and stressed inside!**

Oct 17, 2006/Aug, 2012

COMMENTS

1. Very well written and tied together. I never thought of dance so deeply before. **Aniruddha**

2. Hi Satish: A fine write-up! Giving a historical perspective and lacing it with modern revival, you have presented a larger overview. Actually on Sep. 30th I flew out of St. George to Los Angeles to attend Neela's dance performance for one and a half hours with live music. It was a treat! It was a joy par excellence! **Moorty**

3. Dear Brother, Your article on Bharata Natyam is superb! One of your bests penned! Indian dancing has many genres—Bharatha Natyam, Kathak Kali, Kuchipudi, Manipuri, etc. Two people stand out in bringing out this great art—Bharata Natyam-to the outside world and help to attain global recognition. 1) Dr. Rukmani Arundale of theosophical society, Chennai. 2) Anand Coomarasamy of Smithsonian, Washington D.C. Dr. R. A. was herself a great exponent of Bharat Natyam & she established a great school nearly 80 years back. Dr. AC (Ceylonese & Irish parentage) wrote a classic book, ***Dance of Siva*** wherein he presents the meaning & history of this great art. Thank you for presenting such a thoughtful reflection. **Soori**

4. I agree that life is a DANCE. I also admire ***Tao of Physics***. As far as Rajneesh: He was a rebel Jain regardless of what you think. AND I have never cared for rebels. If divinity is ignored in life the result will be a disaster. Basically I am a Buddhist, though for you Buddha made us eunuchs and non-believers in God. But I do not agree and I shall not discuss it. All religions deteriorate with time and Hinduism is no exception. Arya Samaj could not save Hinduism. **Subhash**

5. Dear Satish Uncle, It was an honor to have all of you this weekend. I really appreciated your company . . . . I really enjoyed your reflection. After I finished reading your discussion last night, I took time to understand the history, analogies, and Hindi words you had written. In the process, I was able to create my own reflection on this weekend. It is unfortunate how often we attend various events, celebrations, and occasions with a dark veil blinding our eyes. ***Reflection*** is a key to learning, growing, and it brings more significance to what we have just observed and experienced. I hope to read more of your ***reflections*** and I would appreciate your

feedback on what I have written. I have attached my reflection to this email.

Every day is a New Beginning While it is noted Bharat Nat yam Dance represents "poetry, drama, and color," the religious significance represented in the art is clearly distinguishable to other art forms. A Broadway show may encompass live music and drama, but it will rarely have religious connotation. American produced Broadway performances are so infatuated by sound effects, sound dynamics, and lighting that even the plot may become unclear. Astonishingly, the fact that there was a lack of a plot is not vivid to the viewer or audience member after the performance. Directors of American Broadway shows become so interested in the allure and mystery involved with stage effects; nevertheless, this is a topic we must be concerned with when discussing Bharat Natyam Dance.

Religious experience can take form in distinctive ways for each individual, and we can take this further to question if a mystical experience is present. Mystical experience related to religion can take effect in various manners, but is it fair to say that people from non-western backgrounds more commonly have a mystical experience. In addition, do art forms such as Bharat Natyam help one to have a mystical experience? Western art today has been surrounded by commercialized Broadway performances, and it is evident that no religious mystical experience can be gained from such composition.

Uncle, in your last two paragraphs you describe to us how one preaches to lord Shiva or Natraj, and how this resembles "a full body expression of freedom." Later, you continue with an analogy of how one should run outside when it rains, and this is compared to our fast-paced stressful life. Is the underlying message here that art forms such as Bharat Natyam allows us to escape daily hardships that occur in life? In the end, helping us and reminding us to feel like we are actually free. This is a really interesting comparison, but I am curious to what men did to feel free. **Sundeep Srivastava.**

PS: 08/28/2012

"Insurgents **beheaded 17 civilians** in a Taliban-controlled area of southern Afghanistan, apparently because **they attended a dance party that flouted the extreme brand of Islam embraced by the militants,** officials said Monday." AP News from Kabul/Afghanistan

WHEN 'UP' AND 'DOWN' ARE SAME

*"**YEH TO OOPER JANE KAA SAMYE HAI** (means: it is time to go **up**.)"*
I told Rana, a confidante of a spiritualist, Bhaisab, as popularly known
in Ambala Cantt. A couple of times a year, I get an urge to call him for a
'spiritual' kick. He never picks up the phone, as his time is prescriptive.
However, we do have a common thought domain. It was 25 years ago that I
met him. Any association that lasts so long, after age 60, has some merit.

This dialogue took place a week ago, when on asking to speak with Bhaisab,
Rana said, "Bhaisab has gone **down**." She meant that he went down to retire
on the ground floor, as the meeting place was on the upper floor. However,
a twist in my response was that the time was nearing to **check out** from the
Planet Earth. Generally, people timidly avoid talking about their deaths,
though they would loudly discuss immortality. A mythological perception of
life is that after death, the 'soul' goes **up** and body goes **down**!

Bhaisab has been literally under self-imposed 'house arrest' for the last 30
years. He never goes out for a walk, shopping, or socializing. His small circle
consists of his former students of the 1960s era, now retired, their children,
friends, or relatives. They believe in the divine love for **Baal** Krishna—from
his years of infancy to teen. I admire Krishna, as **Yogeshwar** who in his
60's (as I am these days!) orchestrated **Mahabharata,** the epic war for the
annihilation of evil whether embodied in close friends or relatives. To their
downfall, the present Hindus have forgotten this lesson.

Despite our divergent life styles and beliefs, we have continued to communicate
with mutual respect. Bhaisab earned master's in English and Political Science,
and taught in a local college. He resigned to run his own postgraduate college,
named **Sadashiv**. The college was closed in 1975, when he entered into his
own brand of ascetic order. They are identified with **Sadashiv** that may be
looked as a cult in the USA.

Recently, when they decided to change the name from **Sadashiv** (means:
eternally good) to **Gambhira** (means: place of seriousness), it jolted me.
While growing up in India, we were constantly reminded of being serious in
every walk of life. Giggling or showing teeth was considered insolence and
ill mannered. The name, **Gambhira** does reflect this congregation in a sense
that everyone appears withdrawn and un-sparkling.

Bhaisab is 'addicted' to silence and solitude. It creates a world of 'darkness' too. Lately, the most exotic creatures and geologic formations have been discovered in the dark depths of oceans. It became possible with new technologies and inventions. During the last 1000 years, Hindus sages have died without leaving any records of yogic science for the next generation. Most probably, they did not have much to leave, or it was a projection of the messed up minds. Science died in India, and the Hindus were run over by marauders. A bottom line of life is to give back to the society what one has accumulated while living in it.

Dec 13, 2006/Aug, 2012

COMMENTS

1. I do not agree with policy of withdrawal. I value your ideas far more. **Subhash**

2. *hum wahan hain, jahan se humko bhi kucch hamaari khabar nahin aati kaabaa kis muh se jaaoge 'Ghalib' sharm tumko magar nahin aati* **Rahul**

3. Your comments on and Up and Down confusion were nice. **SP Misra**

KAYASTHA; TO BE OR NOT TO BE

".... Was he *Kayastha* or *Atmastha*?" asked Dr Nemi Chand Jain from Dr Karunakar Trivedi during an interview a few days after the death of Vinoba Bhave (1895-1982). Vinoba had completely declined to take any food or water a week before his **LAST BREATH.** He had 'timed' his Departure with *Amavasya*, a sacred lunar day and Deepawali (Day of lights/enlightenment!) of November 15, 1982. It proves that during the last days he had transcended the ordinary bounds and functions of the body.

Kayastha means the one who lives for the body, with the body, and run by the body. **Atmastah** means a person fully rested and nested within one's soul; a detached state of body and mind. There are no precise coordinates to pin point soul/mind with respect to the physical body, as one has for various organs. Soul/mind may be understood as a 'field(s)' of an organ(s) like the magnetic field of a magnet. However, every culture has a reference and belief in soul and mind.

Dr Karunakar had attended Vinoba many a times over the previous several years. He along with a team of several physicians from Mumbai and Nagpur monitored all Vinoba's vital signs through regular examinations and tests during the last 15 days of his earthly sojourn. According to medical reports, Vinoba was in full consciousness, calm with clear vision when he passed into the alter state, *Nirvaan*. He defied all body pain and sufferings under the conditions, as generally predicted by modern medical sciences.

Last week, I read the detailed account of Vinoba's **Last Journey** in a special issue published by his *Ashram* in Paunar, India. I stopped right after reading a reference to *Kayastha* that I knew only when referred to as a broad Hindu caste—like, Brahmin and Kshatriya. According to its meaning, anyone who keeps the body in focus is a *Kayastha*. Surprisingly, I did not know, or think over its meaning ever before—hence, revealing.

My mind continued on Hindu caste track and thought of 12 divisions of the Kayasthas—Bhatnagar, Mathur, Nigam, Saxena, and Srivastava being some of them. Incidentally, the significance of *Kayasthas*, their deity, *Chitragupta*, or their sub-divisions have no meanings for our children and grandchildren brought up in the US, a 'casteless' society. They just don't understand Hindu caste meanings and interpretation in life. In that respect the scourge of **caste**

based on birth, still rampant amongst the Hindus in India, is nearly absent amongst the Hindus living overseas. Good or bad, is for another topic!

Of course, if one strictly takes the castes as profession based, then the Hindu caste system has an eternity and universality about it! A question remains: how good it has been for the national unity? Anyway, the thrilling moment for me was the very meaning of the word *Kayastha*—one embedded in the body, body needs, body pleasure and suffering in its actions and reactions. In ordinary parlance, the *Kayasthas* seek knowledge for making life enjoyable. A person with a renunciatory bent of mind is no longer a *Kayastha*!

Feb 19, 2007/Aug, 2012

A *VANPRASTHANI* IN OUR HOMES

In Hindu lexicon, **Vanprastha** is a phase of life where circle of dedication extends from one's immediate family to the society, at large. Usha Sharma's story of **Vanprastha** is as unconventional as is her scholarship. Her husband decided to initiate into **Vanprastha** without her knowledge! While he, at 80, serves the community from home, it is Usha who resigned her job and left India, when the Hindu leaders of Mauritius invited her.

Yesterday, Usha Sharma returned to Oakland after spending six days in Las Vegas (LV). Two months ago, when I told my wife of Usha's tentative program, she said, "Is there anything that we don't know that she would speak about Hinduism?" Other people were also cold. It is understandable as having a houseguest is unthinkable amongst typical Americans. Our typical white neighbor always wonders whenever we have a houseguest.

I consider supporting Hindu preachers in the US as an obligation, **rishi rinn** (debt towards sages of Vedic heritage), one of the four debts (**rinn**) starting from **matra rinn** (debt to mother who nurtures during infancy), **pitra rinn** (debt to father who cares through childhood) **guru rinn** (debt to teachers who build intellect). This support to preachers is all the more pressing in the US, where there is no Hindu identity even at regional level, particularly after the **9/11 Attack on America**. I am straight forward with visitors that they must contribute toward unity amongst the Hindus, when they address students or other groups. Any Hindu denominational baggage should be left behind. Usha was particularly impressed to see the idols of all deities in the Hindu Temple of LV. However, when on noticing the idol of Mahavir, she did wonder at the absence of Buddha's.

Our ties with Usha, being two pronged, her stay was relaxing. The discourses she gave in different groups, and the religious ceremonies she performed in private homes, were very much appreciated. Her forte lies in braiding her songs into speeches and ceremonies. Apart from being an erudite scholar, she is an accomplished musician and composer of 500 songs! For instance, three days ago, I was humming out my favorite line to her ". . . *kabhi tanhaion me hamaari yaad aayegi* . . ." (in moments of loneliness, we will be missed!). By the very next morning (She gets up at 3:30 AM), she had composed a very long and marvelous song on our family and sang it for us! Apart from its rhythm and melody, the words were rich and their meanings deeper.

The only place where I canceled her lecture was to the students and faculty of UNLV's Philosophy Department. In western academics, references to God, soul, heaven/hell etc. are not a part of scholarship in philosophy and psychology. They belong to the domain of theology and divinity which has no place, particularly, in state colleges and universities. In the US, people understand the distinction, but most scholars from India don't.

Mar 14, 2007/Aug, 2012

COMMENTS

1. Wonder if you knew the distinction between theology and philosophy, then why did you set a speaking arrangement there in first place? As for unity with in a religion I do not see it anywhere. Look at Shiias fighting Sunni with each other since last 1400 years. Whabi's declaring all other Muslim denomination infidel. Mormons are considered non-Christians by all other groups of Christian. Born again evangelicals think that they are the only group which will go to heaven as do Roman Catholics. Evangelicals are having problems with Hispanics who are mostly Roman Catholics coming to this country. I do not see any unity within one religion. **Rahul**

I wrote: I did not have the full idea of her scholarship until she came over and spoke to a few groups. Besides, her command over English was very rudimentary.

2. Thanks for your inspiring article. I did the same thing as you planned and invited and immigrated eight priests, Vedic Scholars, so called Acharyas and those who wanted to spread Vedic Dharma. But alas! None of them did or attempt to do anything once they got my hospitality and immigration. As soon as they were able to stand on their feet they showed their true color and disappeared as their selfishness could no longer be covered under the guise of being a preacher, priest / Acharya/ Guru Etc. This scenario repeated all over every time with more than eight people who claim to have studied in Gurukuls/other Arya Samaj schools and were insisting to dedicate their lives prior to coming to the USA. Therefore, I have lost faith in these cheaters of Vedic Religion and I learned my lesson that these are the very people that are responsible for the downfall of the Hindu Society. I hope you do not get the same feeling, therefore, I am writing this letter to you. Sincerely, **Deen B Chandora**

I wrote: You indeed have a management challenge since you have a grand Vedic Center to be run that I don't intend. I just provide hospitality to the itinerant preachers from 1-3 weeks. Overall, the memories are mutually good; some have come again. When I am alone, then I tell them that my house is like an Ashram, not the home of a *Grahsathi* (family person).

You are right, if India had true Vedic scholars, then India would not have been kicked around for a 1000 year. It is time to unburden ourselves from some weight of this 'glorious' heritage, if it does not connect us with the present realities of life. I believe persons like you can lead the Hindus in the USA to be modeled by the Hindus in India! It is always a pleasure to hear from you. Thanks.

A NEW BABA IN LAS VEGAS!

Yesterday came the newsletter of the Hindu Temple of Las Vegas. Amongst the announcements of the events was the first Saturday-of-the-month classes on **PRANAYAM** (*life force system* through breathing) to be held in the premises of the Temple by **Baba** Anal. The epithet Baba stopped me in the tracks for a while.

Anal, being married to my sister, Madhu, has been known to me for over 25 years. During late 1970s, both of them were very active in *yuv sangharsh vahini* (Youth Struggle Brigade) led by late Jay Prakash Narayan. Perhaps, due to Anal's leading role in the struggle, the name Baba got pinned on him. However, he 'earned' it when Madhu and Anal fought with UP state government in relocation of 1000 displaced poor in Agra due to 1982 floods. In Agra, he is only known as Baba!

The name Baba connotes all shades of perception in India. On one extreme, it is used for infants in affectionate manner, and at the other end, for the old and wise men. Of course, there are charlatans amongst the Babas too. India leads the world in 'spiritual' business 'run' by the Babas—like, Satya Sai Baba, Narayan Baba and Mehar Baba etc. Baba is used for father of the father. Webster dictionary gives many interesting meanings of **Baba** as a noun!

Anal is spiritual. He and Madhu are doing research on the 'lost science' of the **Power of the Mantras**. In 1999, I presented a paper on its rudimentary 'mechanics' during the 12th World Vedanta Conference in Hyderabad. Though Anal did not present any paper, he was engaged in dialogues with several delegates. Twelve years ago, an Agra youth, near 30, took '*Sanyas*' initiation from Anal! He is known as Swami Chakransh.

Anal does not belong to the category of 'spiritualists' with a past. He resigned from UP state judicial service and turned down political overtures. They ran schools in Agra, and Anal having a master's degree in law, practiced public issues in India's Supreme Court. In Las Vegas, he is well known for his name in paralegal practice. The **PRAYANAM** classes that he has been offering for the last two years in the Blue Sky Yoga Center are attended by mostly whites.

We often discuss the issues of Hindu identity in **Post 9/11 USA**. The basic concern is about projecting a 'unified' image of Hinduism despite its diversity.

American Hindu Association (AHA) is a newly registered body, and I am its founding President. The main credit goes to Anal for the work done in getting its non-profit and tax-exempt status.

Under the aegis of the AHA, Madhu and Anal have performed unique Vedic **Havans** for various occasions including marriages, new homes, before and after childbirth, anniversaries and Gayatri-thon etc. All the ceremonies are subjects of their researches. They are exploring as to how certain words and sounds gain tangible power; how some individuals generate and attain power; what are the steps from Number 1 to n for achieving it? We all know the ancient tales of curses and blessings in Hindu scriptures, but how this 'science' got lost? They want to provide a scientific foundation to it. The classes are likely to provide data for research reports in future.

April 04, 2007/Aug, 2012

COMMENTS

1. ***Badal kar faqiron ka hum bhes Ghalib***
   Tamashai-I-abl-I-karam dektan hai.
   What about Baba Satish? **Rahul**

2. Tauji Written Great about BABA . . . . It was December 2006. I have been to Agra for the PHILIPS Company conference. It was my 4 days tour as Bhua & Fufa Ji was also in Agra. After having tasty food, I was in mood to see the school and Bapu Nagar. Anal Fufaji, Bhua and I started the tour from their small school, to Bapu Nagar. When we entered I was little bit behind Bhua and fufaji as I want to see the impressions of poor people living there, whether they remember the Baba or not. It was a great thing about Bhua which I saw that she was not a little bit SHY or I can say in Hindi "heen bhavna" was not there. As, Bhua was hugging every single women living there and laughing in their own style saying ***Phir kabhi Chaya Peene AAUNGI.*** Fufaji going slowly answering my questions and People were around them saying it was b'coz of this BABA that we are residing here but Fufaji just smiling with both hands on chest in the response. Tauji It was a very good Trip. Yours" **MATAKDIN**" Ankit

PERSONAL REMARKS

INSPIRED BY *GURDWARA LANGAR*

Many social and religious customs of the Hindus stem out of their convoluted 1000-year of political subjugation, till 1947. It caused conditions of poverty unprecedented in human history. I wonder as to how various blobs would eventually wash out.

The Hindu community of Las Vegas has taken an 'historic' leap. The Hindus, who only met in private homes over the weekend *khanas* (heavy dinners), now run into each other in the temple too. The culture of temple visitation, people coming from different directions and walking away in other directions after hurried obeisance to the deities, is changing, though slowly. It is mainly due to their cultural isolation in fast-paced USA. There is a growing desire to mix spiritualism with socialization in temple premises. One offshoot is that for the last two years, small meals are voluntarily served after the noon *AARTI,* during weekends. It got so popular that there is a wait for months for sponsoring it.

I have wondered at the origination of *LANGAR* (food cooked and served in gurdwaras, the Sikh temples). There is no regular practice of food served after prayers amongst the Hindus, Muslims or Christians. Where did the *LANGAR* tradition come from? The great Gurus realized in 16th century that 95% Hindus were ruled by 1% Muslims, because untouchability, caste systems and excessive religious rites had divided the Hindus at every social level. The Gurus abolished all distinctions! During the *LANGAR*, rich and poor; high or low in public; men, women and kids—all sit together and eat.

The caste distinction remains a curse in India. The Hindus did bring it along in the US too, but it did not fly off in the American society. Once, my Tamilian friend told me how another Tamilian avoided him during a public function in the US, the moment he realized the caste difference. We had arrived in the US a week earlier. Though it happened 40 years ago, but it is etched in my memory! Now, the third generation of Hindus is growing up in the USA. Fortunately, they are free from the intricacies of the Hindu caste system. Nevertheless, they face a challenge to their cultural identity in the US that the first generation did not encounter. The weekend temple meals add an attraction for the families to visit the temple, otherwise considered a place for the elderlies only.

Yesterday, I called my brother-in-law for a special name to these meals served in temple premises. *Langar* is a trademark of the Sikhs. *Charnamrt* and *Prasad* are reserved for the micro quantities of solid or liquid food placed in the copped hands after offered to the deities. The weekend meals are served outside the temple sanctorum. The food, being vegetarian and non-alcoholic, preserves the traditional sanctity of temple environment.

The name, *Preetibhoj*, suggested by my wife, does not have spiritual ring. That gave me an idea of **Name Contest** for it. The winner(s) can win $100. **The final decision will be taken by the Board of the American Hindu Association**. So coin a new word for this temple tradition! The contest is global and open. The electronic submission deadline is May 31.

May 08, 2007

PS: The name should fit the food served after the Aarti in the temple premises or courtyards.
It may or may not be all cooked in the temple.
The cost of the food is born by individual families.
Above all, the name should be innovative and catchy in the US culture!

COMMENTS

1. Bhatnagar Sahib: You have come up with some interesting emails the last few weeks, such as San Francisco bike race, the mattress for the He-man, and three stages of life. On food served in the temple. We have been serving food after our Satsang in the MPLS Geeta Ashram for many years. We call it *Prasad* because it is served just after prayer meeting. We have never called it Langar. Langar has become associated with Gurudwara food. And Langar in Gurudwara is not served after prayers. It is served at food times some Gurdwaras, and all the time, 24/7, in others, for example Anandpur Sahib and Golden Temple, Langar is common term used for mass food servings in Punjab and Himachal. It is not dinner by invitation; it is food served to one and all, whosoever shows up. I have seen this practice in some smaller Hindu temples in Himachal Pradesh. Two years ago, I had some **Manni's** in a temple. It is about an inch thick sweetened roti cooked in very slow fire and does not spoil for days. **Ved Sharma**

2. Hi Satish, This is a grand idea. I have taken the liberty to forward this to many of my friends in US and around in the hope that a bigger pool of names would become available. I hope it meets with your approval. Love, **Gopal**

3. Langar is a Persian word. It literally means a resting place (remember that *Jhaz ne langar daal diya*) but is also used a word for free food served by Sufis'. Langar is also a name for anchor. Hindus like other religions have a long tradition of serving free food. I do not think it is invention of Sikhs. Guru Nanak borrowed both from Hinduism and Islam. It is true that now Langar has become a Sikh tradition. As for name at Barsana Dham, this free lunch is called Lunch/Dinner Prashad. **Dev Bhoj** is another name. **Rahul**

4. Dear Dr. Bhatnagar, Thank you very much for sharing inspirational writings and ideas with me. I often reminisce my last visit to Las Vegas and an enjoyable evening of conversation/dinner with you. Concerning the naming contest, two names come to mind: **BHAJAN-BHOJAN** or **PRABHUBHOJAN**. Sincerely, **Surendra Singh**

5. **'Langar' ke sthan par uchit hindi shabda**—Yajnya ke baad samoohik bhojan ke liye ek shabda prayog kiya jata hai—. **Yajnyashesh** arthat yajnya se shesh bacha hua. yahan yajnya ka artha keval havan hi nahin hai

balki iska artha vyapak hai jismein daan, agnihotra va sansaar ke samasta jad chetan ke hit ki bhavna hai. in sabhi kamon ko kar chukne ke baad jo apne paas bacha hai vahi yajnyashesh kahlaata hai.

Bolchal ki bhasha ke adhik nikat shabda ki drishti se ek doosra shabda aapke sub paimanon par sahi baithta hai. vah hai—**GORAS ya GORAS-PAK**. "GO " shabda ke teen artha hote hain. 1) DHARTI(land), 2) GAYA (cow), 3) Indriyan (sense organs—isi se 'Drishtigochar' shabda bhi bana hai.). Pak ka artha pake huve bhojan se hai. jaise 'Pak-shala ' arthat 'rasoi' Vaise Langar ke liye **GORAS shabda apne mein poorna hai,bina 'pak' jode bhi**. Dhanyavaad sahit.
Dr. Kavita Vachaknavee (HYDERABAD)

Following is the alphabetized names of all the entries received:

*1. Akshya-Patra 2. Alp-Bhojan 3. Annpoorana **4.** Bhagchar Bhoj* (Bhagwan ke charan ka bhog) *5. Bhandara/Bhnadaaraa 6. Bhajan-Bhojan 7. Bhaktibhaoj 8. Bhawprasad 9. Bhojan/Bhojana 10. Bhojanam 11. Brahma-Bhoj 12. Brahma-Sah-Bhoj 13. Devashish Bhoj/Prasad 14. Devbhoj 15 Devprasad 16. Eshwara Anna Thana* (godly food giveaway) *17. Goras* ("*GO " shabda ke teen artha hote hain. 1) DHARTI (land), 2) GAYA (cow), 3) Indriyan (sense organs— isise 'Drishtigochar' shabda bhi bana hai). Pak ka artha pake huve bhojan se hai. jaise 'Pak-shala ' arthat 'rasoi' Vaise Langar ke liye GORAS shabda apne mein poorna hai, bina 'pak' jode bhi.*)*18. Goras-Pak 19. Kalyani Bhoj/ Prasad 20. Kripabhoj* 21. *Krishna-Prasad 22. Mahaprasad 23. Maitri Bhoj/ Prasad 24. Mangal Bhoj/Prasad 25. Mann-Kut*.means *Mann Ka Milan 26. Manthir Anna Thana 27. Mitrabhoj 28. Narayni Bhoj/Prasad 29. Nivedh or Naivedya 30. Pavan Bhoj/Prasad 31. Petpooja 32. Prabhuprasad 33. Prasad/ Prashad 34. Prasadam/Prashadam 35. Prabhaubhojan 36. Prabhu-Sah-Bhoj 37. Prabhu-Kripa-Bhoj 38. Prasadanger 39. Preetibhoj 40. Prem Prasad 41. Rajbhog 42. Rasoi . . . . Rasoiprasad 43. Rasprasad . . . . Rasprasadam 44. Samajik Bhoj 45. Satvik bhoj 46. Shraddha Bhoj 47. Shraddha Bhojan 48. Shradha-Bhoj/Prasad 49. Surprasad 50. Yajnyashesh* (arthat yajnya se shesh bacha hua. yahan yajnya ka artha keval havan hi nahin hai balki iska artha vyapak hai jismein daan, agnihotra va sansaar ke samasta jad chetan ke hit ki bhavna hai. in sabhi kamon ko kar chukne ke baad jo apne paas bacha hai vahi yajnyashesh kahlaata hai.) **51. Sweekratamrat *52 Sehbhoj*

IT IS ALL IN THE NAME

At times, an idea explodes unknowingly like a nuclear fusion, yet its internalized experience is something else. It started a month ago while searching for an appropriate name for a new 'practice' of serving meals after the noon *Aarti* (concluding prayer), in the premises of the Hindu Temple of Las Vegas. The food is generally cooked in the homes, but brought and shared outside the temple sanctorum. The naming started with *Langar*, a historic tradition in Sikh gurdwaras. In fact, *Langar* means free board and lodging in the premises of gurdwaras, and it could for a couple of days. There is nothing close to *Langar* hospitality in any other religion.

Hinduism, having a long history, has gone through political phases of peaks and valleys. Presently, it is coming out of a long slumber. Due to deep-rooted practice of untouchability, caste system, social strata, complexes about public assemblies, and above all, a proverbial poverty of the masses, a question of Hindu strangers eating together does not arise particularly in India.

However, the corresponding story is different in the US. The Hindus here are very prosperous, but they live here in social and political isolation. The Hindu temples, being built since the 1970s, are bringing them together since the practices of caste system and untouchability have no functionality in the US! The temples are turning into places to meet and greet. Of course, they have miles to go in integrating spirituality with sociability when compared with the Christians, Jews, Muslims, and Sikhs. Like Neil Armstrong's first step on the moon, a luncheon tradition in Las Vegas Temple is a giant step in the direction of Hindu awakening! The new generations of the Hindus, born and raised in the US, will have no identity complex.

Four weeks ago, I abruptly sent out an e-mail with a $100 cash award for the best name suggestion(s). Such solicitations are very common practices in the US for naming any public activity—like, a new sports team, corporate logo etc. It was also an opportunity to generate awareness about 'unifying' Hindu practices, which is one of the missions of the American Hindu Association. It is pertinent since the ethnic landscape has changed worldwide after the **9/11** Attack on America. Despite Hindus being 2 millions in number, it is an invisible in the USA.

Today is the deadline for the entries in the contest. I can't believe that forty eight 'different' names have been received, and 12 more hours to go! I would not have thought of even five names. It is overwhelming and inspiring! While the number reflects the richness and diversity of Hinduism, it also underlines deeper unity amongst its believers.

Due to the power of the internet, the entries have come from every continent! A few years ago, a research survey had concluded that the Indians are the savviest users of internet, and 80 % of Indians are Hindus. My mailing list has 200 names. Obviously, it was forwarded to the second tiers in the networking.

What really awed me were the quality, and diversity of the suggesters. The numbers of males and females are even. A well-known scholar of Tamilian language suggested a name, and so did a Sanskrit scholar. Besides, there are physicians, PhDs, professors and various professionals. It was joyous to see entire families suggesting individual names. Yes, a few names are suggested by more than one contestant.

I sincerely thank all the participants on behalf of the AHA. My wife asked me, "Once a name is selected, then where do we go from there?" I said, "The Hindu traditions are not centrally 'legislated' like in other major religions". The key is to create awareness. Let the temple boards and congregations decide on the usage while keeping the bigger picture of Hindu unity in mind.

For me, it is really impossible to pick up one name. Well, here is the complete alphabetized list of all the 48 names, as they came. For obvious reasons of space, the proposers' explanations are included in a few cases:

1. AKSHAYA-PATRA 2. Alp-Bhojan 3. ANNAPOORNA **4. BHAGCHARANBHOG** (Bhagwan ke charan ka bhog) *5. Bhandara/ Bhnadaaraa 6. BHAJAN-BHOJAN 7. BHAKTIBHOJ*
8. Bhawprasad 9. Bhojan/Bhojana 10. Bhojanam 11. Brahma-Bhoj 12. Brahma-Sah-Bhoj

13. DEVASHEESH BHOJ/Prasad 14. Devbhoj 15. ESHWARA ANNA THANA (godly food giveaway) **16. GORAS** *("GO " shabda ke teen artha hote hain. 1) DHARTI (land), 2) GAYA (cow),3) Indriyan (sense organs—isise 'Drishtigochar' shabda bhi bana hai). Pak ka artha pake huve bhojan se hai. jaise 'Pak-shala' arthat 'rasoi' Vaise Langar ke liye GORAS* **shabda apne mein poorna hai, bina 'pak' jode bhi.)** *17. GORAS-PAK*

18. KALYANI BHOJ/Prasad 19. KRIPABHOJ 20. Krishna-Prasad *21. MAHAPRASAD 22. MAITRI BHOJ/Prasad 23. MANGAL BHOJ/Prasad 24. MANN-KUT.* (means *Mann Ka Milan 25. MANTHIR ANNA THANA 26. MITRABHOJ 27. NARAYANI BHOJ/Prasad 28. Nivedh or NAIVEDYA 29. PAVAN BHOJ/Prasad 30. Petpooja 31. Prasad/Prashad 32. Prasadam/ Prashadam 33. PRABHUBHOJAN 34. Prabhu-Sah-Bhoj 35. Prabhu-Kripa-Bhoj*

36. Prasadanger 37. Preetibhoj 38. Prem Prasad 39. Rajbhog 40. Rasoi . . . . Rasoiprasad 41. Rasprasad . . . . Rasprasadam *42. Samajik Bhoj 43. Satvik bhoj 44. Shraddha Bhoj 45. Shraddha Bhojan 46. SHRRADHA-BHOJ/Prasad 47. Surprasad* **48. Yajnyashesh** (arthat yajnya se shesh bacha hua. yahan yajnya ka artha keval havan hi nahin hai balki iska artha vyapak hai jismein daan, agnihotra va sansaar ke samasta jad chetan ke hit ki bhavna hai. in sabhi kamon ko kar chukne ke baad jo apne paas bacha hai vahi yajnyashesh kahlaata hai.)

Have fun too as you contemplate over the names other than yours. It is very educational and informative exercise. The official result should be out by the end of June. In the meanwhile, keep on thinking of our common heritage. Thanks again!!

May 31, 2007/Aug, 2012

COMMENTS

My dear Satish, I am your great admirer and avid reader of your 'Reflections'. You have done a great service to the Hindu society all over the world by asking for a suitable name for common eating among Hindus at religious functions. The list of names has been an education for me. The final selection of the name or names should be widely circulated among Hindus for adoption as may be found acceptable to Hindu Religious Congregations. I would do my bit. Kind regards, **S.R. Wadhwa**

SHRADDHA BHOJ DEFINES IT!

The partaking of food is the most engaging activity amongst humans and other creatures. With human beings, eating collectively, generally symbolizes unity and celebration of beliefs. Lately, among the Hindus, the social feasting has been limited to family and close friends. Also, some *mandirs* (Hindu temples), barring certain castes and non-Hindus, have traditionally discouraged communal eating in the mandir premises. The only food distributed in the mandir is *Prasad/Prasadam*, the food sanctified before the deities.

However, in the US, the Hindus are opening up in their mandir gatherings. Recently, a question cropped up as to what is the most appropriate name for the meals served in the premises of a mandir, but outside its main sanctorum. For the last couple of years, the devotees of the Hindu Temple of Las Vegas have been bringing food from homes and sharing it with friends and strangers alike after the Sunday noon *Aarti* (concluding prayer).

It is clear that this meal, always vegetarian, is unlike from the *Prasad/Prasadam*. The two are different in a sense that a meal has multiple food items and eaten outside the deity hall. On the other hand, *Parasad* is generally distributed in bite sizes of a sweet item inside the deity hall. Subsequently, a contest for selecting a suitable name of *mandir* meals generated worldwide interest. It is a testimony to the power of internet!

A total of 50 different entries were received before the deadline of May 31. People are emotional about their names of anything. For instance, my niece, even after spending a good part of her pregnancy period in selecting the names for her twins, was undecided after their birth! My sister loves to name the houses she has lived and the cars driven.

While charging the selection process to the Board of the American Hindu Association (AHA), I impressed upon them to set aside any regional prejudices and preferences on the nomenclature. Each name was given due consideration. Seven members are composed of four females and three males, all over 50 years in age, college graduates, widely traveled in India, and have lived in the US for 6-38 years. In order to remove any iota of bias, I stayed away from their deliberations, and provided no input.

.

Shraddha Bhoj is the unanimous choice of the Board! ***Shraddha*** means voluntary respect and devotion, and ***Bhoj,*** from ***Bhojan***, is for food. It has spiritual and ***sanskritic*** overtones. Also, it captures the mood of the ***mandir*** visitors and its environment. These words are common, and yet together, they have an uncommon zing about it.

Finally, this name was suggested by two persons: Amarnath Gupta (profession unknown) and Nisha Bhatnagar (retired Hindi teacher). Thus, the award of $100 is equally divided between them. I thank all the contestants on behalf of the AHA Board. Popularize this name, forward this e-mail, and post it on the ***mandir*** bulletin boards. It is easy to plant a tree, but without regular watering, fertilizing and caring, no tree reaches its height. I am sure, ***Shraddha Bhoj*** will make history in Hindu religious lexicon.

June 11, 2007/Aug. 2012

COMMENTS

1. Respected Bhai Sahib, Namaste. It was a matter of much happiness to learn that the name, "Shraddha Bhoj" suggested by Nisha has been finally approved. The very feeling of to be a winner of a competition, of whatsoever nature, carries a sense of pride to the winner. So, obviously Nisha felt much delighted over this development. Regarding prize issue, it's immaterial. What amount she is going to receive as it's the victory which counts. The decision to equally divide the prize money between the two winners is surely fair and warranted. **Vinod**

2. Dear Shri Bhatnagar Ji, Very good suggestion for the name. Here, at Hindu temple we call it 'Priti Bhoj'. I will forward your suggestion to the Board of Windsor Hindu Temple. In Sanskrit Shradha Bhoj makes perfect sense. Shradha, as you said means voluntary respect and devotion. However, when read aloud as written in English, it may be read and confused by some people with, 'Sharadh' which means offerings for deceased ancestors. Most of the time, in North America, Sanskrit and Hindi dialect is written using English alphabets and it does not take long before they are totally mispronounced. Please have some teenagers read it whose knowledge of Hindi is same as our knowledge of Sanskrit. Examples are many, Ganga has become Ganges, Ved has become Vedas and Hind has become India. (Hind came from the word Hindus valley, whose people were called Hindu by Persians and Babylonians; however, Hindus valley became Indus valley (at the time Alexander or Sikander) because Romans could not pronounce the word *'Hee'* or 'H' as in Hindu. That removed the 'H' from the now well known Indus valley. Indus gave our country the name of India. Great 'Bharat' is now divided 'India'. I will be glad to hear some stories you must have learned from the respected Swami Deekshanand Ji. Warmest Regards. **Arvind Arya**

3. Hi Satish, That is a great name and I like it better than any I saw. Thanks. Love, **Gopal**

HARISH CHANDRA IN LAS VEGAS

Harish Chandra is a Hindu preacher of his own kind! Yes, this is the profession entered in his Indian passport for getting visas. A year ago, I came to know him from an acquaintance's e-mail. His background aroused my curiosity. I spoke with him a couple of times during his annual trip to Canada, UK and USA, and welcomed him in our home during his 2007 itinerary.

Every religion has professional preachers of various cadre and categories. The US Christian evangelists have turned preaching into billion-dollar humongous corporate entities. The Mormons are simply incredible. The Islamic life, revolving around the mosques, has scholars and preachers often come and visit the mosques. The Friday prayers set the stage for the Muslim preachers. Amongst the Sikhs, Sunday gatherings in gurdwaras are usually climaxed by preachers touching upon issues affecting the community. The preachers of Hindu religion are generally free from any organizations. There are exceptions—like, the Shankaracharyas, Ramakrishna Mission, ISKCON and BAPS—all having ordained monks in their orders.

The make-up of Harish Chandra is an amalgam of classic Vedic Studies and scholarship in modern science and engineering. Vedic Studies means the knowledge of Sanskrit, its grammar and literature. As a student in IIT Kanpur, he leaned towards Hindu philosophy and Vedic foundations of Hindu religion. On coming to Princeton, a leading US university, he did PhD in Mechanical Engineering (1979). Despite the best training in engineering, he found the inner calls of his religion growing stronger. Finally, in 1996, he left lucrative positions fetching over $100,000/year in order to become a full time scholar and preacher of Hinduism. We often admire people who do what we fail to do, do what others only dream about, or simply excel us.

A couple of times, Harish Chandra met Swami Deekshanand (1919-2003), my MamaJi. His fame came from his persona of having an imposing physique, oratorical skills and Vedic knowledge in the context of social issues. He was the most sought preacher of Arya Samaj of his times, yet he did not nurture, or mentor any single preacher. However, many youths received his support for medical and engineering studies. He often pointed out that the son of a Hindu preacher was seldom a preacher—himself remained a lifelong celibate! During his last years on Planet Earth, I often pushed him to leave a piece of his legacy for the training of new preachers.

Irrespective of our experience with the *sadhus* and *sanyasis* (monks) in ochre or white garments, or preachers like Harish Chandra, unidentifiable by their dresses, the moot point is that we owe a debt to our heritage, particularly after the **9/11 Attack on America**. If some preachers bring its message, the least we can do is to welcome them and provide public forums.

Harish Chandra speaks in English, an impediment for most Hindu preachers coming from India. It is paradoxical that today's Indians in science, business and industry are even thinking in English, but the rest remain miles away from it. He is a prolific author of several books and brings out a monthly e-newsletter, the *Spirit Mag* of his **Center for Inner Sciences**. There is a lot of interesting information on his excellent website: **http://www.centerforinnersciences.org**.

Aug 26, 2007/Aug, 2012

STRUCTURED PRAYER AND RESEARCH

A week ago, as we were stepping out of a club in Malaysia, Said asked me to wait for him to finish his evening prayer in a few minutes. When he came out, I said, "Five prayers a day means that a Muslim doesn't have a block of more than 4 hours to immerse his body and mind into a long activity! Does it not handicap the devout Muslims to carry out such tasks?" I added that several times, my *Reflections* go over four hours. With one eye on the daily prayer schedule, you cannot effectively tackle deeper problems.

Said Abubakar, known since my first Malaysian assignment in 1992, is a retired airline executive. Now he finds more time for his neighborhood mosque, Quranic studies and pilgrimages to Mecca. Having studied in London, he developed an open and analytical mind. We kind of agreed that by and large, the prayer interruptions may not be consequential in mechanical chores. But when it comes to engaging the mind for doing the work like expected for winning Nobel Prizes, there is bound to be a negative impact. Actually, the number of Muslim Nobel Prize winners in sciences is relatively very small.

This is the first time I had posed this question to a Muslim friend, though it propped up in my mind a year ago while teaching a course on the history of mathematics. In the class, a correlation between mathematics and organized religions was investigated. A prayer in eastern religions, Hinduism in particular, is totally personal. Varied assembly prayers are only held during ceremonial functions. In western religions, Islam in particular, prayer, being one of its five pillars, is communal, highly ordained and structured ritual. A Muslim earns 23 times prayer merits when done in a group. That explains how years ago, while waiting for a train, I was invited to join a noon prayer at a Delhi railway platform.

Prayer is one word, but the images of its worshippers are infinite. An individual person in prayer may project an aura of harmony, peace, tranquility and contentment. However, the collective image of praying persons sends a message of discipline, order, strength and unity. It is linked with a reported finding that of all the ethnic groups in the US, the Muslims have the highest rate of completing the basic training courses of the Army.

A prayer is perceived as a conduit, a bridge for helping an individual make a connection with his/her Supreme. It may include rosaries, prayer beads, mantras, recitation of certain passages from the Holy Books. The great spiritual minds are known to take this highroad without any external aid. They transform any mundane activity into a prayer! That is the height of enlightenment and perfection.

I remain curious about the statistical connections between scientific laurels and religious affiliations. Certain areas of mathematics are very abstract and any seminal breakthrough requires days of mental tussle and labor. Specifically, it would be interesting to collect and analyze data on the impact of structured and unstructured prayers on the mathematical achievements of groups based on faith and/or national origin.

Jan 09, 2008/Sep, 2012

COMMENTS

1. *Yahi hai ibadat yahi dino iman,*
   ke kaam aaye duniya mein insan ke insan
   Asal-a-shahood-o-shahido mashhood ek hain
   haran hoon phir mushahida hai kis hisab mein.
   (You and He whom you are searching for are in fact the same.
   I wonder for what this search is going on?) **Rahul**

2. I think religion is mostly mythology, but we poor humans need to believe
   in something more than our own mortality. Otherwise, the existential
   anxiety is too much for us to bear. We have a brief moment of consciousness
   between two eternities! All religions have some things that are taken for
   granted. I was surprised to find that in Hinduism as well as Buddhism the
   existence of an immortal soul and reincarnation is built into the system
   and never questioned. I find Islam more sensible than Christianity in its
   basic precept, but Christ to be more likable than Mohammed. I feel prayer
   to be a private thing, which is probably the protestant in me. The trouble
   with all organized religions is that once they have the upper hand they are
   completely intolerant of other religions or soon become so. **Bob Gilbert**

HAVAN KUNDS FOR MODERN HOMES

Research, innovation and discoveries are privileges of affluent societies, not necessarily of rich individuals. Consequently, there is relatively no room for emotionalism in daily lives of individuals in a well-off society. It takes pride in cultivating a sense of history rather than riding on archaic traditions. It fascinates me to see this observation applied to any aspect of life. My life is so divided between India and US in every plane; be that physical, intellectual, and spiritual.

Havan is one of the most prominent symbols of Hindu rituals recognized all over the world. It has **two** major components; the **fire** in a special container, called ***Havan Kund*** and **chanting of** sacred ***Vedic Mantras*** chosen for a particular ceremony. Sacred fire, ignited in a ***Kund***, is created by a combination of ghee, ***Saamagri*** (a special mixture of herbs) and tiny wood splinters placed on fire, one or two at a time. It generates an unmistakingly Hindu environment for worship. To the best of my knowledge, no other major religion accords so much importance to fire per se.

Now here is a rub for most of us living in the US. The fire and smoke in ***Havan Kund*** sets off the smoke alarms in US houses that have no ventilators. Ventilators are disappearing in modern houses in India too. The rural or the old houses with 17'ceilings used to have at least one on each wall a few inches below the ceiling. The US walls, being 9' high, provides space only for windows. The windows of latest energy-saving houses are sealed that no panel can be opened.

Also, in the US, single-family homes, apartments and town homes are generally made of wood. A fire can reduce a 5000 square-foot home to ashes in 6-8 minutes during summer heat of Las Vegas. The fire engines arrive to save the adjoining houses. In most houses, the smoke alarms are wirelessly connected with security systems. The moment a smoke alarm sets off, security guard is at the door to investigate. States and insurance companies are tough on fire regulations.

Here is a challenge for the Hindu community worldwide! **Is it possible to perform Havan without tripping any alarm system?** Yes, *Havan* has to be performed inside. My sister and brother-in-law are invited to perform *Havan* almost every month. I have witnessed a total chaos when a fire alarm sets off.

The entire atmosphere for which *Havan* is performed is disrupted. Imagine water sprinklers in the ceiling showering to extinguish a small fire!

Last night, we were preparing for a *Havan* next weekend that I thought of posing this problem on-line before the Hindu community. Please send your solutions as to how you have modified the *Havan Kund* that can contain smoke and manage fire when placed in a room of 15'x15'. This challenge reminds me of Gandhi's dilemma when he was stuck with a technical problem in his modified *Charkha* (spinning wheel). For a long time, many minds worked to find a solution.

The American Hindu Association will award up to $500 in prizes for best tested solution(s)—not mere ideas! Please help us in spreading this word. The Hindus, young or old, enjoy *Havan* circles for socialization too. The deadline is Dewali/Deepawali of 2008. Send it by e-mail only at viabti1968@yahoo. com. We look forward to solution(s) of a problem, never tackled before!

Aug 23, 2008

COMMENTS

1. Second paragraph of your article: no major religion . . . When Parsis or Zoroastrians were forced out of Persia (Iran) by Islamic invaders, the Parsi left their mother land with holy fire (they were worshiping sun and its symbol fire as an idol of Ahurmazad. Incidentally Sun is a Major God or the Only God in many ancient and current faiths). They came to west coast of India at Sanjan and were given shelter by the king). Their holy fire is still burning in many of their Agiarys or Agni Gruha. Parsis are probably the noblest settlers in entire history of India. Indira Gandhi married to Parsi Firoz Gandhi but was not accepted as Parsi.

2ND reply to your problem of containing fire. In addition to wood, herbs, barley, til and ghee, one should keep an apple cut in 8 pieces. when placed in the havan kund all around, while fire is on, it controls fire and contains within the boundary of Havana Kaunda, in a mild way. I had performed hundreds of Havanas with this procedure without a single fire alarm waking up sleeping guests. It is also offered to Goddess Laxmi as phala ahuti. We were taught this in childhood with sugarcane as a substitute.

I wrote: You mean to place the apple pieces around the bottom of the kund before igniting the fire?

No. you light the fire with small wood chips. Let it stabilized with adding small amount of ghee and other dried herb wood called samidha. Now add apple cubes in fire, around the fire, in the havan tray or kunda. The fire is getting strength from ghee and other combustibles. At the same time it is heating apple chunks or sugarcane pieces and releases water or juice. This water absorbs latent heat of evaporation (about 540 calories per gram—a science no one worried about) and reduces heat. This is similar to adding controlled amount of water without extinguishing the fire. (It does not appear that you are trying to kill the fire). You offer this fruit or phala arpana with mantra from sreesookta (looks good !!!) well try at home without mantra and see what happens. Once Again, the Yajna or havan-fire is for attracting people, mantras add more beauty to it. Make some show as starting the fire with convex lens (soorya mani!!!) **Bhanu Joshi**

2. Sir, At the risk of being dubbed as an un—intelligent observation, I am narrating an experiment which we once did while performing Havan. The smoke generated by HAVAN SAMIGRI is nauseating and some kind of unrest is always created when there is smoke. To avoid the generation of

smoke while performing havan in a room which could accommodate only 15 to 20 persons we had put two exhaust fans on in the room and fixed an electronic chimney (this sucks in the smoke generated) right over the havan kund at a distance of 2 ft. Care was also taken to use dry woods and the ',Samigri' was prepared in home by the 'Pundit Ji' who gave us the list of ingredients which were to be mixed in it. This was mixed with a good quantity of pure Ghee and 'kapoor' (Camphor). It was also decided that one participating person will only pour 'Ahuties' of ghee from a spoon to keep the wood splinters and 'Samigri' sufficiently immersed in pure Ghee so as to provide good amount of inflammable material.

With this arrangement, very less amount of smoke was generated and was readily sucked by the electronic chimney. In this process the two exhaust fans strategically installed in the room also helped in uniform distribution of the aura generated by the Havan Samigri.
I am not aware, about the sensitivity levels of the 'Fire Alarm' systems and 'Water Sprinklers'

In our homes in India we do not generally install such gadgets and moreover our tolerance levels must be higher, given that we are habituated to such inconveniences. 'Havan kund' with sidewalls having small holes are also very common these days. These types of kunds also help in reducing the quantity of smoke generated. Thanks & Regards,
VS BHATNAGAR, Dwarka, New Delhi

As for your queries in regard to holes in the side walls of a havan kund, I am to inform you that the 'Havan Kund' which we are using has several holes in a circular pattern. The diameter of each hole do not exceed 0.3mm. With such tiny holes in the four walls, there is no chance of splinters or 'Samigri' falling apart.

3. Dear Shri Satish Ji, Saprem Namaste. That's a good move. Normally we do Havan with fire log available in Home Depot. We dip in Ghee and dip in Havan Samagri. We use only three stick for Samidadhan. We use lots of Ghee to prevent smoke. For smoke alarm we put a small piece of tape on the sensor. It works for us. If anyone can create a Havan Kund that will be great. Regards **Girish**

A SUMMARY OF SUGGESTIONS

1. Apple pieces in the Kund; **Bhanu Joshi**

2. Place an exhaust over Havan; **VP Sharma**

3. Exhaust fans and 'Havan kund' with sidewalls having small holes are also very common these days. These types of kunds also help in reducing the quantity of smoke generated. Thanks & Regards, **VS BHATNAGAR** Dwarka, New Delhi

4. The alternate, is to do Sandhya Hawan (Brahma Yagya) instead of Dev yagya. In which no fire, no kund, no samagri is required. Only Jal (Water) for achman is needed for that Hawan, All richaye (Slok/Mantra) are the same. So Sandhya Hawan is the best for U.S. Thanks **Lokesh,** Indore, India

5. Normally we do Havan with fire log available in Home Depot. We dip in Ghee and dip in Havan Samagri. We use only three stick for Samidadhan. We use lots of Ghee to prevent smoke. For smoke alarm we put a small piece of tape on the sensor. It works for us. If anyone creates such a Havan Kund then that will be great. Regards **Girish**

COMMENTATORS AND ANALYSTS EXTRAORDINAIRE

Ten years ago, I started writing *Reflections.* It is a reincarnation of my lifelong passion of writing letters. The big difference is that that my *Reflections* went public—from one to many—friends and relatives. And from there it went to their friends and relatives, and so on. Four years ago, a student of mine created a blog, but seldom have I posted anything. I don't have a website either. It is all emails in a bcc mode-electronically old-fashioned.

I have several mailing lists, though this is an inefficient mode of communication. I have Facebook and Twitter accounts too, but they too have remained unused. That is my approach to communication. Naturally some write back and give comments. However, at times, a small dialog takes place. It has added clarity to an issue or a topic, and sharpens my thoughts.

Not all the comments and commentators have been included—only those which are concise and strong—and non-repetitive. In reflective style of writings, inclusion of some comments adds a new flavor. Initially, I never saved readers' comments. Also, sometimes, no comments were received. That is why the space following some **Reflections** is blank.

It is not merely a time to thank them, but also share a piece of immortality that this book may bring! Who knows the future. When I look at the credentials of these persons I am myself awed and wowed. These comments have come out of their incredible rich backgrounds. I don't think this list can be easily matched. Here are the names in some order:

Raju **Abraham**: Known for six years. English professor—has taught in Baroda/India, Sana/Yemen, and presently in Oman with University of Nizwa, where I was a visiting professor for one semester, Spring 2009.

Avnish Bhatnagar: My son, age 44, works at Google. His comments are few, but deep.

Rahul Bhatnagar: Distantly related—physician by training in India. He has in interesting job of medical director of drug safety with a pharmaceutical company. Very astute commentator and analyst of nearly all my *Reflections*— and can refine an issue to a state undistinguishable from the one started with.

H S **Bhola**: Emeritus IU professor of education—known since 1971—remains witty and sharp at 80. He often tells me, how exceptional I am, as all math professors that he has known, can hardly write a sentence in English—far from being a literary writer. He continues to write papers and give invited talks.

Ved Bhushan: An 80-year old businessman in Ambala Cantt, India—known since 1980. He still enjoys the pleasures of the skin.

Gayathri: Knew her first as a student in Malaysia during 1998 visit.

Gopal Dass: Retired cardiologist, settled in Las Vegas—has interesting hobbies—known for six years.

Irma **Dutchie**: Our 82-year old neighbor, who lives life with and zing and zest—extremely generous. She is now a member of our extended Bhatnagar family.

S. C. **Gupta**: is a businessman and Arya Samaj leader in Mumbai, India—known for five years.

Alok Kumar: Physics professor in NY, PhD IIT, Kanpur—Known for 25 years.

Panju Prithviraj: Oncologist working out from Cleveland and Las Vegas

Prafulla Raval: Chemistry PhD, known for 40 years since IU days.

Ranjana Kumar: Director of an Adult Day Care Center in Charlotte, NC—know since 1977.

Satyam **Moorty**: Emeritus English professor, Southern Utah University—known since 1978.

Sandeep Shrivastav: Just finishing his MD, known for five years

Sham Narula: An octogenarian retired engineer—active in senior activities in Washington DC area.

Surendra Singh: Biology professor at Newman University; still engaged at 78.

R S **Nigam**: Retired Professor of Commerce and Director of Delhi School of Economics—known for 25 years.

Rene Riendero: Life explorer and realtor. Wrote a book on her experiences of visiting India. It encouraged her to become a writer.

Harpreet Singh: A rare combination of computer science, finance, active spirituality, and creative writing—always exploring and stretching his limits. He is 36 years old and known for 13 years through his parents first.

Subhash Sood: Physician by training in India, UK and USA. He never practiced for profit, though studied other systems of medicine too—eccentric to a certain degree. However, he was deeply drawn into by Scientology—established the first center in India, and translated several scientology books from English into Hindi. He died in 2007 at age 74-in a 100-year old, now dilapidated, mansion in which he was born, as the only son of a physician, in Ambala Cant. He was my most avid reader and friend for over 25 years.

E. **Sooriamurthy**: Retired physics professor Madurai University, India—known since 1968—our common days at IU. His son, Raja, computer science professor at Carnegie Mellon is an avid reader of my Reflections too.

Steve Wunderink: Got to know him as a toastmaster 14 years ago, and incidentally lives in the same development. He turned out an excellent speaker besides over 200 Lbs on 6'+ frame and booming voice. After working as a church planter for 20 years in different states, he and his wife are settled in Las Vegas. Steve with PhD in divinity is a pastor of his own church. His weekly e-mail columns—***Mind Your Spiritual Business*** urged me to start e-mailing my spontaneous ***Reflections***.

Tarak Patel: Born and raised in California. Loves wine, cooking besides other finer tastes of life—a rare combination of a contemplative mind and business entrepreneurship. He is around 40 and got on my mailing list for being married to my daughter's fast friend.

Ved P. Sharma: known for over 42 years—since our teaching in same Shimla College in India. Our wives and kids also know each other. Sharma, like me too, has spent all his life in college teaching—but his in economics. There is hardly a month when we have not communicated with each other—a blessed friendship!